Country Path Conversations

Studies in Continental Thought

Martin Heidegger

Country Path Conversations

Translated by
Bret W. Davis

Indiana University Press
Bloomington and Indianapolis

This book is a publication of

Indiana University Press
Office of Scholarly Publishing
Herman B Wells Library 350
1320 East 10th Street
Bloomington, Indiana 47405 USA

iupress.indiana.edu

First paperback edition 2016

Published in German as Martin Heidegger,
Gesamtausgabe, volume 77: *Feldweg-Gespräche (1944/45)*
© 1995 Geman edition by Vittorio Klostermann, Frankfurt am Main
Second edition 2007 by Vittorio Klostermann, Frankfurt am Main
© 2010 English edition by Indiana University Press

The paper used in this publication meets the minimum requirements of the
American National Standard for Information Sciences—Permanence of Paper for
Printed Library Materials, ANSI Z39.48-1992.

Manufactured in the United States of America

The Library of Congress has cataloged the original edition as follows:

Heidegger, Martin, 1889–1976.
[Feldweg-Gespräche (1944/45). English]
Country path conversations / Martin Heidegger ; translated by Bret W. Davis.
p. cm. — (Studies in Continental thought)
ISBN 978-0-253-35469-3 (cloth : alk. paper)
1. Philosophy. 2. Imaginary conversations. I. Title.
B3279.H48F4713 2010
193—dc22
2010004591

ISBN 978-0-253-02163-2 (pbk.)
ISBN 978-0-253-00439-0 (ebk.)

1 2 3 4 5   21 20 19 18 17 16

CONTENTS

Translators' Foreword

The present volume is based on a set of manuscripts which Heidegger wrote in 1944–1945, but which he did not publish during his lifetime apart from an excerpt from the first conversation (discussed below). Heidegger did make plans, however, for this trilogy of "conversations" to be published in his collected works—or rather, as his motto for the collection has it, in his "ways, not works" (*Wege, nicht Werke*)—and these intentions were fulfilled when *Feldweg-Gespräche (1944/45)* was first published, posthumously, as volume 77 of the Heidegger *Gesamtausgabe*.[1] *Country Path Conversations* is a translation of that volume.

On January 8, 1945, Heidegger wrote to his wife Elfride of feeling "increasingly clearly the need for simple saying; but this is difficult; for our language only applies to what has been up until now."[2] A month earlier, soon after having returned from a brief conscription into the *Volkssturm* to dig trenches in Alsace, Heidegger had left Freiburg on bicycle bound for his hometown Messkirch. Freiburg had been heavily bombed on the night of November 27, 1944, the old city almost completely destroyed. Once in Messkirch, Heidegger was preoccupied with safeguarding his manuscripts, which he eventually hid in a cave together with some manuscripts by Hölderlin, who, a century prior, had lived out his remaining years after his decent into madness in a tower in Tübingen. Heidegger reportedly "had the idea of having one of the towers of Messkirch Castle restored with a view to working there."[3] Work on restoring the Messkirch tower was, however, delayed and in the end never completed.[4] In the spring of 1945, Heidegger busied

1. Frankfurt am Main: Vittorio Klostermann, 1995; 2nd edition, 2007. For details on the manuscript remains and the editorial process behind volume 77 of the *Gesamtausgabe* (hereafter abbreviated as *GA*, followed by volume number), see the editor's afterword at the back of this volume.

2. Martin Heidegger, *Letters to His Wife: 1915–1970*, ed. Gertrud Heidegger, trans. R. D. V. Glasgow (Cambridge, UK: Polity, 2008), p. 182

3. *Letters to His Wife*, p. 179.

4. See *Letters to His Wife*, pp. 181, 186.

himself with attending to his manuscripts, teaching seminars to students who had retreated from besieged Freiburg to Wildenstein Castle in the vicinity of Messkirch, carrying on an affair with Princess Margot von Sachsen-Meiningen, and worrying about his two sons Jörg and Hermann, who were missing in action on the Russian front. It was no doubt difficult for him to find the rest and repose needed for thinking beyond the pressing needs of the day, and it seems that he fell into a bout of depression.

Yet on March 11, 1945, a reinvigorated Heidegger wrote Elfride to say: "I've got over the depression; I feel that my strength isn't at an end yet; perhaps the efforts of the last 7 years can resolve themselves into a quite simple saying."[5] One thinks of the often dense and halting prose of the many solitary manuscripts—starting with *Contributions to Philosophy (of the Event)* (1936–38) and ending with *Die Stege des Anfangs* (1944)—on which Heidegger had been hard at work for what was in fact the previous nine years, not to mention the many lecture courses, including his prolonged confrontation with Nietzsche and his close readings of Hölderlin and the Presocratics. Then, on March 23, 1945, Heidegger wrote again to Elfride:

> This Easter greeting is full of sorrow. And yet we mustn't yield to it. The fate of the fatherland is so mysterious in the midst of everything else that is happening that it must harbor within it something that towers far beyond our knowledge. From this painful secret comes wonderful strength. Even though my condition is still physically delicate, in the last few days I've gained such remarkable momentum that I'm almost completely oblivious to food & sleep. I suddenly found a form of saying I would never have dared use, if only because of the danger of outwardly imitating the Platonic dialogues. I'm working on a 'conversation'; in fact I have the 'inspiration'—I really have to call it this—for several at once. In this way, poetizing & thinking saying [*das dichtende und denkende Sagen*] have attained a primordial unity, & everything flows along easily & freely. Only from my own experience have I now understood Plato's mode of presentation, & in some form or other the Plato book intended for you must one day become reality after all.[6]

Heidegger's "Plato book" did become a reality, posthumously published as *Country Path Conversations*.

Of course, while Heidegger is taking up the form of Plato's Dialogues, he is hardly mimicking their content. Indeed his decision not to use the Greek term *Dialog*, preferring instead the German *Gespräch*

---

5. *Letters to His Wife*, p. 187.
6. *Letters to His Wife*, p. 187.

(p. 37), is perhaps indicative of his marking a certain distance and difference from Plato precisely as he is apparently appropriating his literary form. Heidegger later claims, in "The End of Philosophy and the Task of Thinking," that "throughout the history of philosophy, Plato's thinking remains decisive in its sundry forms. Metaphysics is Platonism."[7] Plato is only mentioned a couple of times in *Country Path Conversations* (pp. 58, 135; see also pp. 55–56), yet Heidegger's confrontation with Plato is clearly in the background, insofar as in these conversations as elsewhere he is attempting to think back before and out beyond metaphysics, that is, insofar as he is attempting to articulate and engage in a "non-metaphysical thinking" (p. 122).

Many of the basic contours of Heidegger's later non-metaphysical thought were first sketched out in the voluminous collections of private meditations that make up *Contributions to Philosophy* and its sequel volumes, which were composed during the years leading up to *Country Path Conversations*, that is, between 1936 and 1944.[8] These important texts are presently receiving the close scholarly attention they deserve. Yet because of the exceedingly *monological* character of those meditations, they are often notoriously difficult to decipher. To be sure, the unfamiliarity and difficulty of their thoughts must be understood at least in part as essential to the originary and enigmatic character of the matter itself. Heidegger indeed never writes for "public consumption," and in *Contributions* he even goes so far as to claim: "To make itself understandable is suicide for philosophy."[9] Common sense is all too quick to condemn as unintelligible what it cannot immediately understand on its own terms, and all too quick to neutralize and trivialize what it can. Nevertheless, while in those private manuscripts Heidegger also writes to be someday read and understood, at least by "the few and the rare," even the most careful reading of many of the esoteric meditations in those volumes can sometimes leave one with the sense of having eavesdropped on a solitary thinker's struggle to make sense of his own emerging and evolving thoughts, rather than

---

7. Martin Heidegger, *Zur Sache des Denkens*, 3rd edition (Tübingen: Max Niemeyer, 1988), p. 63; *Basic Writings*, 2nd edition, ed. David Farrell Krell (New York: Harper & Row, 1993), p. 433.

8. *Beiträge zur Philosophie (Vom Ereignis) (1936–38) (GA 65); Contributions to Philosophy (From the Event)*, trans. Richard Rojcewicz and Daniela Vallega-Neu (Bloomington and Indianapolis: Indiana University Press, 2012). Also see *Besinnung (1938/39) (GA 66)*, translated as *Mindfulness* by Parvis Emad and Thomas Kalary (London: Continuum, 2006); *Metaphysik und Nihilismus (GA 67); Die Geschichte des Seyns (GA 69); Über den Anfang (1941) (GA 70);* and the forthcoming volumes *Das Ereignis (1941/42) (GA 71)* and *Die Stege des Anfangs (1944) (GA 72)*.

9. *GA* 65, p. 435; *Contributions*, p. 344.

having been addressed by a writer endeavoring to invite others onto his path of thinking.

By contrast, *Country Path Conversations* was written precisely at a point when Heidegger had rounded the bend of the major turns in his thought-path, and it can be read as a fresh attempt to more openly convey—or rather, to more *dialogically* or *conversationally* unfold—the way of thinking he had found.[10] Heidegger in fact prefers the word *Gespräch* (conversation) to *Dialog* (dialogue), apparently because, while the latter might be (mis)understood as a subsequent speaking that takes place between two subjects about something predetermined, the former can be understood as an originary gathering (*Ge-*) of language (*Sprache*) which first determines who is speaking and what is spoken about (see pp. 36–37).[11] Insofar as it is especially through conversation that "what is spoken of may of itself bring itself to language for us and thus bring itself near" (p. 47), the literary form of *Country Path Conversations* would be vital to the furthering of Heidegger's path of thinking, and not simply a heuristic device used to communicate thoughts which had already been worked out privately.

In any case, while no less profound in content than his volumes of solitary meditations from the previous decade, and while at times as deeply enigmatic (indeed, abiding with what is essentially enigmatic is one of the volume's recurring themes: see for instance, pp. 19–21, 51–53, 78, 89, 138, and 141), *Country Path Conversations* is considerably more approachable and engaging; its dialogical or "conversational" character invites the reader to accompany Heidegger along his path of thinking. And with respect to this format—as *erdachte Gespräche*, imaginary or "thought-up" conversations—*Country Path Conversations* holds an almost unique place in Heidegger's writings.[12]

---

10. These "imaginary conversations" can also be contrasted with the significant interpretive works from this period, such as the lecture courses and essays on Heraclitus, Parmenides, Plato, Hölderlin, Schelling, Hegel, and Nietzsche. While such texts present Heidegger's dialogical confrontation with other thinkers and their thoughts, the freer format of *Country Path Conversations* allows him to develop and convey his thought both dialogically and yet in his own terms. While acknowledging the manner in which these terms are often critically retrieved from the tradition, the characters in *Conversations* are less bound to elucidation and interpretation, and freer to unfold their own path of thought.

11. All references to *Country Path Conversations*, whether given parenthetically in this foreword or in translator's notes, indicate page numbers in the present volume. The corresponding pagination of GA 77 can be found in the header of the text.

12. In the subsequent years of 1946–1948, Heidegger worked on, but did not finish, "Das abendländische Gespräch," which consists of an Older Man and a Younger Man discussing Hölderlin's poetry (GA 75: 57–196). The only other com-

The first and longest conversation is exemplary in this regard. It takes place between a Scientist, a Scholar, and a Guide, and it is precisely the interplay between these three distinct characters that moves their "triadic conversation" along.[13] While by the end of the conversation the three voices do frequently appear to be speaking in tandem and finishing one another's thoughts, this is far less the case in the beginning. In particular, the distance and disagreement between the Scientist and the Guide is marked in the earlier parts of the conversation. The Guide (*der Weise*) is clearly pointing (*weisen*) the way to proceed down the path,[14] while the Scientist[15] often finds it rather difficult to follow these indications insofar as this demands thinking beyond the horizon of established modern concepts. The Scientist's frank obstinacy and at times impatient eagerness for clarity contrast with—and complement—the Guide's radical yet guarded suggestions; and both are mediated by the contributions of the learned Scholar,

parable text is "A Dialogue on Language between a Japanese and an Inquirer," in *On the Way to Language,* trans. Peter D. Hertz (New York: Harper & Row, 1971), which was composed by Heidegger loosely on the basis of his conversations with Tezuka Tomio and other Japanese thinkers.

13. The title "A Triadic Conversation . . ." translates "Ein Gespräch selbstdritt . . ." The rare and obsolete expression *selbstdritt* combines the notion of "self" (implying "selfsame") with that of "three," indicating a relation of three-in-one. Indeed, the title could have been translated as "A Triune Conversation . . ." were it not for the almost exclusively Christian connotations of "triune," which would be misleading here. (It should be noted, however, that to my knowledge the only use of a variation of *selbstdritt* is in the case of paintings of "Anna Selbdritt," which portray St. Anne, the Virgin Mary, and the Infant Jesus.) Were it not for distracting contemporary connotations, the title could also have been translated as "A Threesome Conversation . . . ," especially given the etymological kinship between "some" and "same."

14. "Guide" translates here *der Weise.* Although this term would normally be translated as "wise man" or "sage," Heidegger makes clear that he means someone who is able to indicate (*weisen*) the way, rather than someone who possesses wisdom (*Weisheit*) (see p. 54). The word "guide" is in fact etymologically related to "wise" as well as to *weisen:* "the ancestor of guide was Germanic *wit-*'know,' the source of English wise, wit, and witness. . . . It eventually became Old French *guider,* and was borrowed by English. The semantic progression from 'knowing' to 'showing' is also displayed in the related German *weisen,* 'show, direct, indicate'" (John Ayto, *Dictionary of Word Origins* [New York: Arcade, 1990], p. 267).

15. "Scientist" translates here *der Forscher,* which more literally means "researcher." In German *Forschung* generally connotes "scientific research," and, even though we need to bear in mind that *Wissenschaft* has a somewhat wider semantic range than "science" (insofar as it includes the *Geisteswissenschaften* or humanities, as well as the natural sciences), *Forscher* is often best translated as "scientist," as in the present case where it refers to a physicist.

who seeks to cautiously follow up on the Guide's indications by relating them back to the history of philosophy. All three characters thus play indispensable roles in the conversational movement of the text. The Guide suggestively indicates the way, the Scholar provides erudite footing and cautions patience, and the Scientist repeatedly demands clarity and sometimes stubbornly drags his feet. But it is often precisely because the Scientist asserts familiar modern and "scientific" platitudes, and insists on clear explanations for unfamiliar (radically new as well as old and forgotten) ways of thinking, that we find ourselves drawn into and kept involved in the conversation. Indeed, let us confess that the Scientist often provocatively raises precisely the objections, or pointedly asks just the questions, that many of us—Heidegger scholars as well as first-time readers—at times find ourselves wanting a response to!

A significant excerpt from *Country Path Conversations* is already familiar to readers of the later Heidegger. In 1959, in a small volume entitled *Gelassenheit,* an abbreviated and slightly modified version of the climactic sections of the first conversation—approximately one-fourth of the entire conversation[16]—appeared under the title "Toward an Emplacing Discussion [*Erörterung*] of Releasement [*Gelassenheit*]: From a Country Path Conversation about Thinking."[17] An English translation of this text was published in 1966 as "Conversation on a Country Path about Thinking."[18] Although I have benefited from consulting this work, I have retranslated all the corresponding sections along with—and in light of—the original longer version of the conversation. In a few places where Heidegger modified these sections for the 1959 publication, I have inserted notes to alert the reader to what was altered.

Despite the fact that this excerpt from the first conversation was removed from its original context, it has nevertheless proven to be one of the most widely read and influential texts by the later Heidegger. One reason for this prominence is its explanation of a key term in Heidegger's later thought, *Gelassenheit.* I have followed the established consensus in translating this term as "releasement." However, it should be kept in mind that the traditional and still commonly used German

16. Although in her afterword to the present volume, the German editor refers to this excerpt as "roughly the last third," there are significant sections in the last third of the conversation that were not included in the 1959 publication.

17. "Zur Erörterung der Gelassenheit: Aus einem Feldweggespräch über das Denken," in *Gelassenheit,* 10th edition (Pfullingen: Neske, 1992), pp. 29–71 (reprinted in *GA* 13).

18. In *Discourse on Thinking,* trans. John M. Anderson and E. Hans Freund (New York: Harper & Row, 1966), pp. 58–90.

word conveys a sense of "calm composure," especially and originally that which accompanies an existential or religious experience of letting-go, being-let, and letting-be.

The word *Gelassenheit*—as the nominal form of the perfect participle of *lassen*, "to let"—has a long history in German thought. It was coined by Meister Eckhart in the thirteenth century and subsequently used by a number of other mystics, theologians, and philosophers.[19] In the context of Christianity, *Gelassenheit* is generally thought to entail both a releasement-from—a renunciation or abandonment (*Ablassen*) of—self-will, and a releasement-to—a deferral or leaving matters and one's own motivations up to (*Überlassen*)—the will of God. Heidegger certainly draws on this tradition. And yet, while he acknowledges that "many good things can be learned" from Eckhart, Heidegger explicitly seeks to distance his thought from any deferential obedience to a divine will. This traditional understanding of *Gelassenheit*, it is said, is "thought of still within the domain of the will." Heidegger does not want to simply reverse positions within this domain, namely from active assertion (willful projection) to passive deference (will-less reception). Rather, insofar as releasement as "non-willing" (*Nicht-Wollen*) would "not belong to the domain of the will" as such, he is attempting to twist free of this very dichotomy, and indeed to think "outside the [very] distinction between activity and passivity" (p. 70).

This attempt proves, however, to be extremely difficult. To begin with, this difficulty is due to the fact that "non-willing" can all too easily be (mis)understood to indicate a variety of comportments *within* the domain of the will, such as a willful refusal to will or a mere lack of strength to will. Each of these senses is shown to be a "variation" (*Abwandlung*) of, rather than a genuine alternative to, willing (see pp. 48ff.). Authentic non-willing must be thought of as radically beyond the domain of will, rather than as a mere shift of position or simplistic reversal within it. And yet, it is the very radicality of this difference that gives rise to the enigmatic character of the *transition* from willing to non-willing; after all, at least the instigation of such a transition would seem to require a "willing of non-willing." Much attention in the conversation is accordingly given to the Guide's intentionally paradoxical remark, "I will non-willing" (see pp. 33, 37–42, 68–69, and 92–93). In any case, the conversation-partners cannot simply and without further ado renounce the will and embrace the alternative of non-willing, but must "slow down their pace" and meditate on the

19. See *Historisches Wörterbuch der Philosophie*, ed. Joachim Ritter (Basel and Stuttgart: Schwabe, 2006), vol. 3, pp. 220–224. On *Gelassenheit* in Meister Eckhart's thought, see Bret W. Davis, *Heidegger and the Will: On the Way to Gelassenheit* (Evanston, Ill.: Northwestern University Press, 2007), chap. 5.

enigmatic transition out of the domain of the will and into the open-region of non-willing.

This crucial yet enigmatic transition from willing to non-willing is not just a central topic of the first text in *Country Path Conversations*. As I have sought to demonstrate in detail elsewhere, the meditations on *Gelassenheit* in terms of non-willing in this text play a pivotal role in a turn in Heidegger's thought-path itself, a turn which involves a transition from an ambiguous and often ambivalent philosophy of will to a radical and explicit critique of the (domain of) will, together with an endeavor to think non-willing(ly).[20] *Country Path Conversations* was written precisely as Heidegger was rounding the bend of this "second turn" in his thought-path. After this time, the will is seen as nothing less than the aberrant meaning of being—its revealing in extreme self-concealment, its withdrawal to the point of abandonment—in the modern epochs of the history of being, which culminate in Nietzsche's philosophy of the "will to power"[21] and finally in the contemporary epoch of the technological "will to will."[22]

While the first conversation treats a number of central topics of the later Heidegger's thought, including the question of technology, the transition from willing to non-willing could be said to reflect one of its two main themes. These two themes are, on the one hand, an explication of the open-region (*die Gegnet*), in other words, what Heidegger later calls a "topology of being";[23] and, on the other hand, a critique of

---

20. See my *Heidegger and the Will*. For an introduction to this topic, see my "Will and *Gelassenheit*," in Bret W. Davis, ed., *Martin Heidegger: Key Concepts* (Durham: Acumen, 2010).

21. See in particular the second volume of Heidegger's *Nietzsche*, 5th edition (Pfullingen: Neske, 1989), most of which was written in the five years leading up to *Country Path Conversations*. The English translations of these lectures and essays are contained in volumes three and four of Martin Heidegger, *Nietzsche*, ed. David Farrell Krell (New York: Harper & Row, 1987, 1982).

22. In an essay completed around this same time (1946), Heidegger writes: "The basic form of appearance in which the will to will arranges and calculates itself in the unhistorical element of the world of completed metaphysics can be stringently called 'technology'." Martin Heidegger, *Vorträge und Aufsätze*, 7th edition (Pfullingen: Neske, 1994), p. 76; "Overcoming Metaphysics," in *The End of Philosophy*, trans. Joan Stambaugh (New York: Harper & Row, 1973), p. 93.

23. "[The] thinking after *Being and Time* replaced the expression 'meaning of being' with 'truth of being.' And, in order to exclude its being understood as correctness, 'truth of being' was explained by 'location of being' [*Ortschaft*]—truth as locality [*Örtlichkeit*] of being. This already presupposes, however, an understanding of the place-being of place. Hence the expression *topology of be-ing* [Topologie des Seyns]" (*GA* 15, p. 335; *Four Seminars*, trans. Andrew Mitchell and François Raffoul [Bloomington: Indiana University Press, 2003], p. 41). In fact, from quite

the will—especially the willfulness of "transcendental-horizonal representation"—along with a search for a way of releasement from its grip and into an authentic, non-willing manner of thoughtfully dwelling within the open-region of being. Together, these two themes reflect Heidegger's abiding twofold concern with being and its relation to human being.[24] While he concludes elsewhere that "the deepest meaning of being is *letting* [Lassen],"[25] he proposes here that the most proper comportment of human being within the open-region of being is releasement (*Gelassenheit*). In *Gelassenheit*, human being properly corresponds to the *Seinlassen* of being itself.

This twofold concern with being and its relation to human being is in one way or another the fundamental question at issue throughout all three conversations. The guiding question of the first conversation, however, is the nature of "cognition" (*Erkennen*). Modern and scientific thinking is characterized as a willful representation, an objectification that transcends—climbs over—things to determine a transcendental horizon which delimits the forms through which things can only appear as objects to subjects (see pp. 55–56, 63, and 65). Heidegger traces this modern transcendental "thinking as willing" back to τέχνη (*techne‾*) as one of the Greek forms of knowledge, and forward to the "mathematical projection of nature" in the natural sciences, especially physics (see pp. 7ff.). It is even suggested that, in a sense, "physics is applied technology," and that "the thinking of physics and technology, which sets forth nature as object, shows itself as a human attack on nature" (p. 11). However, when nature is objectified, it is said to reveal a "mysterious defense against the attack of technology" which threatens to annihilate the essence of the human (pp. 11, 13). Hence the urgency and the stakes of the conversation's reflection on the essence of cognition and thinking.

This critique of willful representation (*Vorstellen*)—together with the other components of the essence of technology, production (*Herstellen*), ordering (*Bestellen*), and so on (see pp. 7, 117), which Hei-

---

early on Heidegger thought of the event of the truth of being as taking place in, or rather as, a clearing (*Lichtung*), in the metaphorical sense of a place in a forest where trees have been cleared so as to open up a space for meaningful habitation.

24. On the relation between these two themes and the place of *Country Path Conversations* in the development of Heidegger's thought, see my "Returning the World to Nature: Heidegger's Turn from a Transcendental-Horizonal Projection of World to a Releasement to the Open-Region," *Continental Philosophy Review* 47/3 (2014): 373–397.

25. *GA* 15, p. 363; *Four Seminars*, p. 59.

degger later names together as the *Ge-stell*[26]—gives way to a search for
an alternative, non-willing thinking. Whereas willful representation
projects transcendental subject-centered "horizons" of intelligibility, a
non-willing thinking would entail opening up to the "openregion"
(*Gegnet*) which surrounds all our horizons and lets them be in the first
place. In other words, the horizon is revealed to be only the side facing
us of this surrounding openness, a provisional anthropocentric delimitation of the open-region. Rather than insist that things be impos-
sibly set forth into unbounded unconcealment, non-willing thinking
would let itself engage (*Sicheinlassen*) in the play of revealing/conceal-
ing that allows things to show themselves within delimited and yet—
or rather, and *therefore*—meaningful horizons.[27] The open-region does
not replace so much as emplace or enfold our horizons of intelligibility. But now these horizons are recognized for what they are: always
finite delimitations of the open-region of being. The epochal events of
these temporally and spatially finite determinations make up the history of the open-region (see p. 91). The open-region is thus not just a
topological, but also a temporalogical name for being. Indeed, Heidegger speaks of the open-region not only as an "expanse" (*Weite*), but
also as an "abiding-while" (*Weile*) or, putting this temporal-topological
pair together, as an "abiding expanse" (*verweilende Weite*) (p. 74).

Much of the first conversation is concerned with how to rethink the
relations between open-region and human, open-region and thing,
and thing and human. The conversation attempts to think these relations in terms of a "selfsameness" (*Selbigkeit*) that essentially includes
difference, as well as a nearness and farness that mutually imply one
another. We might call to mind here Heidegger's later rethinking of
"identity" as a belonging-together, especially the belonging-together
of *Dasein* and *Sein* or of thinking and being,[28] as well as such claims as
"the essence of nearness appears to lie in bringing near that which is

26. See "The Question Concerning Technology," in Martin Heidegger, *Basic Writings*, rev. and exp. edition, ed. David Farrell Krell (New York: Harper & Row, 1993).

27. The Greek word *horizon* derives from *horizein*, meaning "to bound or limit," and from *horos*, meaning "boundary." Yet it should be borne in mind that for Hei-degger a "limit" is also what enables something to come to presence in a definite manner. He writes: "The boundary or limit [*Grenze*] in the Greek sense [of *peras*] does not block off; rather, being itself brought forth, it first brings to appearance what presences. The limit sets free into the unconcealed" (*GA* 5: 71; *Basic Writings*, p. 208, trans. modified).

28. See Martin Heidegger, *Identität und Differenz* (Stuttgart: Neske, 1957); *Identity and Difference*, trans. Joan Stambaugh (New York: Harper & Row, 1969).

near, in that it holds it at a distance."[29] The first country path conversation concludes with an interpretation of a one-word fragment from Heraclitus, Ἀγχιβασίη (*Anchibasie*), which suggests that proper knowing is neither a matter of maintaining an objective and disengaged distance, nor of abolishing distance with a technological attack that attempts to remove all that nature holds in reserve, but rather a "going-into-nearness" (*Indie-Nähe-gehen*), an approaching that cultivates a relation of respectful intimacy (pp. 101–102).

This going-into-nearness is at the same time a special kind of "waiting," another key term of *Country Path Conversations* with which Heidegger characterizes the non-willing essence of authentic thinking, and which he identifies with "releasement" and "surmising" (*Vermuten*) (see pp. 75–76, 78–81, 97–98, 140–143, and 146–153). All three conversations explain this authentic kind of waiting (*Warten*) in terms of an attentive and engaged openness to an arrival of something unexpected, in contrast to an awaiting (*Erwarten*) that would first actively project what it then expects to passively receive. A genuine non-willing waiting would be neither a merely passive reception of a fate nor an aggressively active projection of a plan, but rather an attentive and responsive "present-waiting-toward" (*Gegen-wart*) which allows what is far to come near, to be near in its farness and far in its nearness (pp. 146–150).

The intimate interplay between nearness and farness is also a concern of the second conversation, where the Tower Warden (*Türmer*) not only tells us, "He who lives in the height of a tower feels the trembling of the world sooner and in further-reaching oscillations," but also says that it is necessary to "catch sight of the tower from a distance" (pp. 105, 109). How to understand the figures of the Tower Warden and the tower is one of the topics this text invites us to ponder. In addition to the tower of Messkirch Castle that he was planning to have restored and work in, and the tower in Tübingen in which Hölderlin lived out his final years, perhaps Heidegger had in mind watchtowers on fortress hilltops, like the one in Zähringen near his home on the outskirts of Freiburg (see the photograph on the back jacket of this book)—or like the one in Staufen, a small town near Freiburg where Faust is said to have spent his last days. Indeed, having made reference to Goethe in the first conversation (see p. 22), in this second conversation Heidegger might even have had in mind the following lines spoken by a tower warden who appears near the end of *Faust* in a scene called "Deep Night" (part 2, act 5, scene 4):

---

29. Martin Heidegger, *Erläuterungen zu Hölderlins Dichtung*, 6th edition (Frankfurt am Main: Vittorio Klostermann, 1996), p. 24; *Elucidations of Hölderlin's Poetry*, trans. Keith Hoeller (New York: Humanity Books, 2000), p. 42.

LYNCEUS DER TÜRMER (*auf der Schloßwarte singend*):

Zum Sehen geboren,
Zum Schauen bestellt,
Dem Turme geschworen,
Gefällt mir die Welt.
Ich blick in die Ferne,
Ich seh in der Näh
Den Mond und die Sterne,
Den Wald und das Reh.
. . .
Nicht allein mich zu ergetzen,
Bin ich hier so hoch gestellt;
Welch ein greuliches Entsetzen
Droht mir aus der finstern Welt!
. . .
Sollt ihr Augen dies erkennen!
Muß ich so weitsichtig sein!
Das Kapellchen bricht zusammen
Von der Äste Sturz und Last.
Schlängelnd sind mit spitzen Flammen
Schon die Gipfel angefaßt.
Bis zur Wurzel glühn die hohlen
Stämme, purpurrot im Glühn.—
(*Lange Pause, Gesang.*)

Was sich sonst dem Blick empfohlen,
Mit Jahrhunderten ist hin.

FAUST:
Von oben Welch ein singend Wimmern?
Das Wort ist hier, der Ton zu spat.
Mein Türmer jammert; mich im Innern
Verdrießt die ungeduldge Tat.
Doch sei der Lindenwuchs vernichtet
Zu halbverkohlter Stämme Graun,
Ein Luginsland ist bald errichtet,
Um ins Unendliche zu schaun.

LYNCEUS THE TOWER Warden (*singing on the watchtower of the castle*):

To see I was born,
To look is my call,
To the tower sworn,
I delight in all.
I glance out far,
And see what is near,
The moon and the stars,
The wood and the deer.
. . .
But not for my joy alone
I am placed at such a height;
What a hideous threat has grown
Under me out of the night!
. . .
Eyes, must you behold this sight!
Must you see so very far!
Now the falling branches crash

Through the chapel, it falls down
As the flames, like serpents, dash

To embrace the lindens' crown.
To their roots the hollow trees
Have turned crimson.
(*Long pause. Song.*)

What for many centuries

Pleased all eyes—now is gone.

FAUST [*responds*]:
From up there, what a whining squeal?
It is too late to speak or plead.
My warden wails; at heart I feel

Annoyed at this impatient deed.
The lindens are part of the past,

Charred trunks are of no benefit—
Yet a good lookout is built fast
To gaze into the infinite.

Da seh ich auch die neue Wohnung,	The new estate I also see
Die jenes alte Paar umschließt,	Where the old couple has been sent:
Das im Gefühl großmütiger Schonung	Glad of my generosity
Der späten Tage froh genießt.	They'll spend their last years there, content.[30]

Of course, Heidegger's Tower Warden cannot be simply identified with Goethe's, but perhaps this passage from *Faust* can at least help us interpret the setting of, and that elusive character in, Heidegger's second conversation. Perhaps philosophers dwell in their "ivory towers" not only to wonder at the world, but also to serve as watchmen on the lookout for the looming dangers and promising new dawns on the horizons of their epoch of the history of being. The figure of the tower in the second conversation would thus not just be an ivory tower of useless speculation; or rather, given that speculation is defended in the first conversation (see pp. 5–6), as is the usefulness of the useless (or the necessity of the unnecessary) in the third conversation (see pp. 143, 152–153, 155– 156), the philosophy that takes place in such a tower would be a matter of what Heidegger calls elsewhere the "immediately useless, though sovereign, knowledge of the essence of things."[31] The seemingly lofty speculations of these conversations could be understood as immediately useless *though urgent* warnings to modern, Faustian humanity of a spreading devastation that goes unnoticed by those who cannot see it, see the spreading forest fire, on account of their immersion in the business and busyness of life among the trees, that is, on account of their "factual sense of reality which they claim lets the human first stand with both feet squarely on the ground" (p. 153). For Heidegger, who began his career by wedding a return to the concreteness of factical life with a retrieval of the seemingly most abstract question of being, it would be necessary to both dwell in the tower and, so to speak, to walk through the woods. Along with the way up and the way down, the overview from the tower and the underview from the path on the ground need to be interwoven in the selfsame task of thinking.

To help recover the essence of humanity, and to save it from this devastation, the second conversation further develops the temporal-topological understanding of the relation between being and human

30. *Goethe's Faust*, trans. Walter Kaufmann (New York: Doubleday, 1961), pp. 446–451.

31. *GA* 45, p. 3; *Basic Questions of Philosophy*, trans. Richard Rojcewicz and André Schuwer (Bloomington: Indiana University Press, 1994), p. 5.

being. What Heidegger elsewhere calls the existence of Dasein is referred to in this conversation as *Aufenthalt* (sojourn), a word which
can be understood in the dual sense of a temporal-spatial abiding, a
staying somewhere for a while, and a temporal-spatial abode, the time
during which and the place in which one stays. While Dasein's existence is thought as *Aufenthalt,* being (*Sein*) is topologically thought
here as the *Enthalt*. This peculiar neologism is clearly related to the
verb *enthalten,* presumably both in its sense of "to contain" (to hold
within oneself) and also in the sense of *sich enthalten,* "to withhold
oneself." (This ambiguity is enhanced by the fact that the prefix *ent-*
can signify either an intensification or a removal.) We can surmise
that both senses are intended by Heidegger here. I have attempted to
reiterate this intentional ambiguity in my translation of *der Enthalt* as
"the with-hold," in light of the fact that the "with-" too can be understood both in the sense of a withholding or withdrawing (*Entziehen*),
and in the sense of a holding within or nearby (*bei*) oneself. The apparent paradox of this ambiguity is perhaps resolved if we consider
that—as in the case of the open-region, which *both surrounds and ex-
ceeds* our limited horizons—one never has in full view that in which
one is contained. The whole both contains (holds within itself) and
withdraws (withholds itself) from the part.

   To be sure, human being is for Heidegger not just one among other
parts of an encompassing being; the human is that being which is
called on to take part in the appropriating event of being. Being requires (*braucht*) human Da-sein (being-there) as the locale for its presencing, for its arrival into truth as unconcealment (see pp. 95–96).
Da-sein—as being-in-the-world in the sense of an indwelling (*Instän-
digkeit*) or staying (*Sichaufhalten*) within the shelter of the clearing of
being—is thought of in the second conversation as "sojourn-in-the-
with-hold" (*Auf-ent- Halt*) (see pp. 118ff.). This sojourning in the with-
hold, that is, in the abiding expanse which both holds within and
withholds, is not simply described as a transhistorical given to be recognized, but rather spoken of as a historical task to be taken up.
Human beings must find their way (back) into this essential abode of
their most proper way of being: "we must continually turn back to
where we truly already are" (pp. 115, 117).

   In Heidegger's being-historical thinking, the question of "where we
are" must be understood both ontologically and historically. *Country
Path Conversations* was written at a crucial moment, not only in the
development of Heidegger's own thought, but also in world history.
All three conversations were composed on the eve of the end of the
Second World War. The third closes with the date 8 May 1945, and the
following remark: "On the day the world celebrated its victory, without yet recognizing that already for centuries it has been defeated by

its own rebellious uprising" (p. 157). The conversations attempt to explain why, in the realm of the essential, the end of the war "changes nothing," why Germany was not alone—even if in well-known respects exemplary—in the global insurgence of the technological civilization of the Occident. Here too, Heidegger maintains that an ontology of the essential events of history (*Geschichte*), or being-historical thinking (*seinsgeschichtliches Denken*), cannot be conflated with historiology (*Historie*) as a reckoning of ontic occurrences.

One of the reasons for the timeliness of a translation of *Country Path Conversations* certainly has to do with the hardly resolved (and perhaps never fully resolvable) "Heidegger affair," that is, with the controversy surrounding his official involvement with the Nazi regime in 1933–1934 and the political implications of his thought before and after this time. Although various external perspectives may still be called for in the critical debate surrounding Heidegger's political thought, as a growing number of *Gesamtausgabe* volumes become available, it is also time to return to Heidegger's own texts in order to hear what he has to say with regard to the relation of his thought to world-historical events. The three texts included in *Country Path Conversations*, especially the third, will be central to this endeavor. Although the characters in the conversations rarely speak directly of political events (their focus is meant to be on larger and deeper historical movements), the context is unambiguous. It is no coincidence, for example, that the third conversation takes place in a prisoner of war camp in Russia. Heidegger's own two sons were at the time missing in action on the Russian front. And Heidegger's exasperation with the malicious errancy of Nazism bursts to the surface in such lines from this conversation as the following: "And what is not all wounded and torn apart in us?—us, for whom a blinded leading-astray of our own people is too deplorable to permit wasting a complaint on, despite the devastation that covers our native soil and its helplessly perplexed humans" (p. 133).

Nevertheless, as we have seen, *Country Path Conversations* also offers much more than fuel to the fire of all sides in the controversy surrounding Heidegger's politics. All three of the conversations in this volume are exceptionally rich in philosophical content. They introduce or significantly illuminate a number of central ideas of the later Heidegger's thought, many of which do not find comparably extensive treatment elsewhere. Alongside the topics discussed above—including the problem of the will and the possibility of non-willing, the temporal-topological understanding of being as an abiding open-region that surrounds the temporally delimited horizons of human thought, the sense in which "physics is applied technology," the technological devastation of nature, the possible annihilation of the essence of the

human, and "the necessity of the unnecessary"—other key topics addressed in the three conversations include: listening and answering
rather than making statements and questioning (pp. 14–16, 47, 66, 78,
106–107, 146–148), a thing in contrast to an object (pp. 81–91, 127–
128), the two oldest occidental definitions of the human as the thinking being and the mortal (pp. 143–146), the as yet unrecognized essence of the German people as "those who wait" by means of poetizing
and thinking, an essence which has been covered over and distorted
by a tyrannical pseudo-essence of impatient and willful "nationalism"
(pp. 151–155), and the problem of evil (pp. 133–135, 139, 157–158).

The last of these topics deserves special comment since it receives
sparce treatment elsewhere in Heidegger's writings. In the third conversation it is suggested not only that "the will itself is what is evil" (p.
134), but even that "evil would dwell in the essence of being" (p. 139).
Thus, even though Heidegger suggests that the deepest meaning of
being is a letting beings be, and that the most proper human response
to this letting is a released involvement in this letting-be, he not only
acknowledges here that humans are prone to fall into a malicious
willfulness, but also intrepidly suggests that the potential for evil
haunts the very essence—or essential occurrence—of being itself.
And so, even though the third conversation speaks of the salutary
experience of a healing (*das Heilende*) in the midst of the devastation,
Heidegger would not be proffering here a theodicy—or an ontodicy—
that would seek to justify, much less have us close our eyes to, the
horrific and malefic possibilities and actualities of being-historical existence. The existentially decisive question then becomes this: How
are we, as the self-restraining-comporters (p. 119) who are required
by being (pp. 95–96), called upon to participate in "the strife of being
itself"[32] so as to aid in letting beings—including other human beings—
freely be, rather than so as to blindly assist in unleashing them into
the machinations of technological devastation?

It goes without saying that Heidegger is extremely difficult to translate. *Country Path Conversations* presents the translator with a number
of peculiar difficulties, starting with the fact that its language is at
once that of a conversation (albeit a rather formal one) and yet also
always terminologically precise, often poetically thoughtful, sometimes highly unusual, and on more than one occasion frankly enigmatic. I have commented above on the *relatively* accessible nature of
their conversational format (in comparison to the more "esoteric" volumes such as *Contributions to Philosophy*). But these conversations by no
means consist of small talk on strolls through a park. As "country path

32. See *GA* 9, p. 359; *Pathmarks*, ed. William McNeill (Cambridge: Cambridge
University Press, 1998), p. 272.

conversations," they veer off the pavement of our accustomed ways of speaking and at times venture into a thicket; their ponderous yet radical manner of speaking frequently transgresses the limits of our familiar horizons and goes several strides beyond our established "clearings" of intelligibility.

I have spared no effort in attempting to make the English *as* clear and accessible as Heidegger's German, but have generally not tried to make my translation any *more* smooth or transparent than its original. Where the German is intentionally ambiguous, dense, or out of the ordinary, so too, I felt, should be the English. Indeed, the occasionally awkward or cryptic manner of speaking is perhaps not only due to the fact that Heidegger (or one of his characters) is struggling to articulate an unfamiliar thought; it could also be seen as a signal that we are being asked to slow down the usual pace of our reading and thinking. The conversation partners are attempting to patiently follow the path of their meditations as it unfolds—and we are being asked to attentively join them in this endeavor.

Some of the highlights of the content of *Country Path Conversations* have been introduced above, in the process of explaining several crucial terms and their translations. Rather than comment here, out of context, on numerous other difficulties encountered and decisions made in the translation of particular words and phrases, I have inserted translator's notes at points where an explanation seemed necessary or potentially helpful. At other times I have merely inserted the German in square brackets to alert the reader to the word or phrase that is being translated. This was done especially when it was not possible to reproduce a set of cognate German words or phrases, and when Heidegger employs an unusual term or a usual term in an unusual manner. In the back of the book, the reader will find English–German and German–English glossaries that include many important terms and their translations.

I would like to express my appreciation for all the support and encouragement I have received while working on this translation. Let me begin by thanking John Sallis of Boston College and Dee Mortensen of Indiana University Press for their support of this project from the beginning, and for their patience till the end. While most of the work was carried out during a semester and two summers spent in Freiburg in 2007–2008, it was begun several years prior to that. I would like to thank the Center for Humanities at Loyola University Maryland for sponsoring a sabbatical leave, as well as the DAAD (German Academic Exchange Service) for a Visiting Faculty Scholarship to work on this project at the University of Freiburg in the fall of 2007.

I have Günter Figal to thank for officially hosting my research sojourns at the University of Freiburg, and for personally helping me with several crucial passages of the text. I am grateful to the participants in a compact seminar I gave on the first conversation at the University of Freiburg in the summer of 2008; our days of intense and cooperative discussion helped me to clarify my understanding of the text. I am especially grateful to Tobias Keiling, who generously met with me regularly during my stays in Freiburg to discuss the text and my translation. Not only did he direct my attention to the passage from *Faust* quoted above, as well as guide me on hikes to the tower in Zähringen, but he also helped me decipher the unusual German in numerous passages as we toured the cafés in Freiburg.

I would also like to thank my colleagues at Loyola, Paul Richard Blum, Timothy Stapleton, Richard Boothby, Catriona Hanley, John Betz, William Welton, Gary Backhaus, and Gregory Derry for fruitful discussions of a draft of the first conversation. Early on in my work on this project, Steffen Döll met with me during a stay in Munich to help me revise my translation of the second conversation. I am very grateful to Richard Polt and Daniela Vallega-Neu, who kindly agreed to go over a draft version of the translation in whole or in part, and who offered many helpful suggestions for improvement. I also have Richard to thank for sharing with me a useful draft version of the first fifteen pages of the text, prepared by him and Gregory Fried. An anonymous reader for Indiana University Press gave me a number of good ideas, and my meticulous copyeditor, David Dusenbury, made many insightful suggestions for final revisions to the text and notes. Needless to say, all remaining errors and insufficiencies in the translation are my own responsibility.

As always I am deeply grateful to my wife, Naomi, my son, Toshi, and my daughter, Koto, for making daily life and work—even in a two-room apartment in Freiburg—not only possible but also profoundly joyful and meaningful. Finally, I would like to dedicate this translation to the memory of my mother, Barbara S. Davis (1938–2009), whose nearness has always spanned the distance.

Country Path Conversations

Country Park Conversations

1. Ἀγχιβασίη:
A Triadic Conversation on a Country Path between a Scientist, a Scholar, and a Guide

SCHOLAR: This past autumn we met for the first time on this country path. That meeting was a splendid coincidence, for I owe a precious inspiration to it: an old Greek word occurred to me, which since then has seemed to me to be a very appropriate name for what we are seeking.

SCIENTIST: Our meeting was indeed splendid, but it was no coincidence. What we so name is always just the gap that still remains in our chain of explanations. So long as we have not ascertained the explanatory causes, we like to plug up the hole that remains with the name "coincidence." Yet the cause of our encounter, which has in the meantime been repeated so fruitfully, lies close at hand. Each of us wished to free himself from his daily work by means of a distraction.

SCHOLAR: The similarity of our occupations also quickly brought us to the thematic object of our conversation at that time. We spoke about cognition.

SCIENTIST: Our discussions did, however, get easily lost in generalities that were difficult to grasp. It often seemed to me as if we were just talking about mere words. All the same, the conversation offered a distraction, which diverted me from the laborious experiments that I had begun at the time with the aim of investigating cosmic radiation.

SCHOLAR: It is true that the definitions of cognition, which we talked through in connection with Kant's *Critique of Pure Reason*, were indeed grasped quite "generally." Is there anything that cannot be brought under the headings "intuition" [*Anschauung*] and "thinking" [*Denken*]—which, according to Kant, are what make up cognition?[1] Hence the physicist among us demanded—rightly so,

1. According to Kant, "there are two stems of human [cognition], namely, *sensibility* and *understanding*, which perhaps spring from a common, but to us unknown

1

from his standpoint—an experimental investigation [4] of the processes which accompany the human activities of intuition and thought. As for me, it was then that the previously mentioned inspiration came to me, which obviously pointed me in a different direction in accordance with my historiological occupation. On that autumn evening I also already felt the first breath of winter, that season which is to me always more favorable than the others for burying myself in the business of my work.

GUIDE: The coolness of the past autumn is still present to me.

SCIENTIST: Then, if you don't mind my saying so, you have evidently retained little from our conversation.

SCHOLAR: Indeed you barely took part in it; presumably because during the day you devote yourself all too ardently to the occupation of philosophy, and seek only a distraction by walking on this country path.

GUIDE: In the coolness of the autumn day, the fire of summer finishes in cheerful serenity.

SCIENTIST: This feeling for nature appears to be quite refreshing for you. You get enthusiastic and seek in such moods a counterweight to the abstractions of philosophy.

GUIDE: The cheerful serenity of the autumn coolness, which harbors the summer within itself, drifts about this country path every year with its gathering play.

SCIENTIST: Then on our walk, if I may say so, you allowed yourself rather to be gathered by the autumnal atmosphere of this path into a pensiveness which can be recommended only on occasion.

SCHOLAR: You were thus not distracted enough to follow our conversation.

GUIDE: Perhaps. [5]

SCHOLAR: By this do you want us to understand that in our conversation the *thematic object* [Gegenstand] of our discussion, the essence of cognition, was constantly slipping away from us?

SCIENTIST: That was hardly possible. We unwaveringly kept our eye trained on cognition with regard to *its* decisive fundamental trait. I mean that which fuels and rules our cognitive behavior.

---

root. Through the former, objects are given to us; through the latter, they are thought. . . . The capacity (receptivity) for receiving representations through the mode in which we are affected by objects, is entitled *sensibility*. Objects are *given* to us by means of sensibility, and it alone yields us *intuitions;* they are *thought* through the understanding, and from the understanding arise *concepts.*" Immanuel Kant, *Critique of Pure Reason,* trans. Norman Kemp Smith (New York: St. Martin's Press, 1965), pp. 61-62 (A 15/B 29), 65 (A 19).—*Tr.*

GUIDE: And that is?

SCIENTIST: Its character of work and achievement.

SCHOLAR: Accordingly, our inquiry also directed itself straightaway to thinking, as that component of cognition which, with Kant, we may speak of as the "active" component. In contrast to thinking, intuition is allotted only a preparatory role in the process of cognition.

SCIENTIST: This order of rank between intuition and thinking shows itself with optimal clarity in modern natural science. The intuitive element has here vanished except for a small remainder.

GUIDE: You are presumably saying here more than you think.

SCIENTIST: I always only say what I think; I mean namely that within modern physics, which is considered to be the model for all the natural sciences, theoretical physics lays the foundation of all research. It creates the mathematical projection of nature. Only then, within its purview, can experiments be thought up and constructed.

GUIDE: But what about the arrangement and construction of experiments, the putting in place of all the necessary apparatuses? Do you want to assign these matters of "experiment," which do *not* belong to theoretical physics, exclusively to the intuition side of cognition in physics? [6]

SCIENTIST: One could of course hardly do that. I would rather count the matters you introduced as belonging to the "technological" side of physics.

SCHOLAR: If we may speak of "sides" here, then a considerable quantum of thought-activity does indisputably lie in the "technological" aspect of experiments.

SCIENTIST: Indeed technology in general is a particular kind of thinking, namely, that thinking which is devoted to the practical application of theoretical natural science for the purpose of controlling and exploiting nature. Hence, we physicists also say that technology is nothing other than applied physics.

GUIDE: But what if physics, even as a pure investigation of nature, already uses technology in experiments? Just think for example of the machine that splits the atom!

SCHOLAR: Then would physics, and *with* it the *whole* of modern natural science, be nothing other than applied technology?

GUIDE: It is splendid that you yourself pronounced such a thing.

SCHOLAR: How so?

GUIDE: Said by me, it would have surely sounded like one of those at times unavoidable inversions of common views, inversions that are often received with suspicion.

SCIENTIST: And rightly so. For within the purview of rigorous research work—which everyone with sound common sense can follow in the main, that is, with regard to its fundamental bearing—it often seems as if the wisdom of thinkers were to consist in taking what sound common sense thinks and straightaway deliberately standing it on its head. [7]

SCHOLAR: This is how it seems to me as well. Moreover, this impression is confirmed by the testimony of thinkers themselves. After all Hegel says, if I remember correctly, that in order to be able to follow the thinking of metaphysics, one must attempt to stand on one's head and walk like that.[2]

SCIENTIST: And so whoever claims, in contrast to the usual characterization of technology as applied physics, that physics is applied technology is just playing with the tricky tactic of reversal.

GUIDE: To be sure. So it seems. Thus I hesitated to say this, for what appears to be a reversal is at bottom something other than a mere rearrangement of words.

SCIENTIST: I don't understand how this is supposed to be anything else.

GUIDE: I don't understand it either, but would nevertheless like to surmise that with your statement that physics is applied technology, once again more is said than was thought.

SCHOLAR: I thought only of that which stood under discussion, namely that the pure research of physics, insofar as it proceeds experimentally, applies technology.

GUIDE: You mean that, because machines as products of technology are used in the apparatus of experiments, therefore physics is applied technology.

SCHOLAR: This is exactly what I mean. Where machines are at work, there is technology.

SCIENTIST: Then the reversed statement, that physics is applied technology, is valid *only* for experimental physics. The reversal is not valid for theoretical physics, which remains, however, the foundation of "fundamental research" in all the natural [8] sciences. The reversal is therefore, rigorously thought through, invalid.

GUIDE: It is quite valid, and indeed precisely when we think rigorously about the matter.

SCHOLAR: By this you mean to say that you conceive of *theoretical* physics too as technology.

SCIENTIST: I must contradict this view; and everyone will agree with me that theoretical physics operates without any technological means, and that it cannot therefore be technology.

GUIDE: Certainly. And yet what is technological does not consist in the use of machines.

SCHOLAR: Rather, in the production of machines.

---

2. See *Hegel's Phenomenology of Spirit*, trans. A. V. Miller (Oxford and New York: Oxford University Press, 1977), p. 15 (par. 26).—*Tr.*

GUIDE: Or even in that on which the producibility of machines depends.

SCHOLAR: It depends on the laws of motion of natural processes.

SCIENTIST: The knowledge [*Kenntnis*] of which we owe exclusively to the cognitions [*Erkennen*] of physics. Physics first discovers in advance the laws of natural conditions and processes. The rules for building machines and for mechanical transformation, control, and storage of natural forces must conform to these laws.

SCHOLAR: And so technology is after all applied physics.

GUIDE: Contrary to this, I put matters the other way around: Physics must be technology, because theoretical physics is *the* proper, pure technology.

SCHOLAR: Then you are arbitrarily understanding something different by "technology." [9]

GUIDE: It is true that I am thinking of something different with the name "technology." Yet I do not do so arbitrarily, but rather so as to attempt to pay attention to what is theoretical in physics itself.

SCHOLAR: We can hardly then circumvent a meditation on the essence of theoretical physics. For as long as we *only* state that it does *not* operate experimentally and so does not use machines, this remains a negative determination. It is difficult, however, to say what physics is in that whereby its essence attains its basis.

SCIENTIST: Above all I fear that as soon as we take our inquiry in this direction, we lose ourselves in "speculations," whereby every clear way and sure foothold breaks off.

SCHOLAR: We cannot evade an inquiry into the essence of theoretical physics. I fear less the danger that we get lost in presumptuous speculations, than that we stray into the entirely different domain of technology, since what we are inquiring into, after all, is the essence of cognition with regard to modern physics.

GUIDE: Presumably we know so little of technology precisely because of our anxiety about speculation and its atmosphere. We think that knowledge about technology comes to us from descriptions of its procedures and reports of its achievements.

SCHOLAR: Then where does our anxiety about "speculation" come from?

SCIENTIST: From the obvious uselessness of speculation, in the face of which we fear that we will fall into vacuity with it. [10]

GUIDE: So everything useless is fearsome, insofar as we take the useful as that which *alone* is valid and pacifies us with its validity. But what is the useful useful for?

SCIENTIST: Such questions are strange. They always make me dizzy. In their vortex I lose every ground and all space.[3]

---

3. One might translate this sentence, *Ich verliere in ihrem Wirbel jeden Boden und allen Raum,* more freely as: "In their vortex I lose every footing and all orientation."

GUIDE: The human[4] only ever loses that which he does not yet properly *have*. Yet he "has" only that to which he belongs.

SCHOLAR: Now I too must confess that everything escapes me when I try to think what you just said. So I think it would be beneficial for me to bring our conversation back again to its path.

GUIDE: I am happy to entrust myself to your guidance, so long as you take into account that my interspersed remarks will sometimes slow down the course of our conversation.

SCIENTIST: Such delays don't harm anything, as long as they don't cause us to get off track.

SCHOLAR: This danger certainly exists. Today we have come back to our first country path conversation from last autumn. We were seeking the essence of cognition. We are now considering the fact that cognition is a thinking, and we are attempting to approach thinking in the form of research-work in physics. In this context arose the question of the relation between physics and technology. The essence of technology became puzzling to us, and speculation about it even more so. We are thus going to leave such speculation aside.

GUIDE: It seems to me that with precisely *this* intention we fall into the danger of being forced off track. What is called "speculation" is in fact also a thinking, if not indeed that thinking of those whom we call "thinkers."

Yet if we are afraid of speculation and [11] go out of the way to avoid it, how are we ever to get clear about the essence of thinking?

SCIENTIST: You mean we should speculate about speculation? Then under these circumstances I consider it to be safer and more fruitful to reflect on technology. You were telling us, if I understood correctly, that the technological essence of physics lies precisely in that it is theoretical physics.

The technological and the theoretical would then be the selfsame.

GUIDE: I surmise that it is so.

SCHOLAR: If you surmise such a thing, you must be able to give us some explanation of this.

But the final phrase is as unidiomatic in German as is "every ground and all space" in English. —*Tr.*

4. Here and throughout, *der Mensch* is translated as "the human," rather than as "man" or "human being," for the sake of a greater sense of gender inclusivity (even though, as in the German, the masculine pronoun is used), and in order to avoid an ambiguous use of "being" (and confusion with such expressions as *Menschsein* and *Menschenwesen*). Also note the distinction Heidegger maintains between the ontologically singular "the human" (*der Mensch*) and the ontical plurality of "humans" (*die Menschen*). —*Tr.*

GUIDE: Perhaps. And yet only in the manner of presaging. If you can make do with an approximate indication, then I would like to try to provide one. In the course of this conversation the mathematical projection of nature was mentioned. Thinking presents nature to itself [*stellt sich die Natur . . . zu,* more literally: sets nature toward itself] as the spatiotemporally ordered manifold of moving points of mass. With a view to this essence of nature, natural processes are re-presented [*vor-gestellt,* more literally: set-before]. In this fashion, nature is what is pro- (in the sense of toward the re-presenting human) pro-duced [*Her-gestellt,* more literally: set-forth]. As what is so pro-duced, nature is as that which stands over against the human [*das dem Menschen Entgegenstehende*]. As object [*Gegenstand*] of human representation, nature is set-toward human representation and is in this sense produced. Thought in this manner, producing is the basic trait of the objectification of nature. This producing does not first make nature in the sense of a manufacturing or creating. Producing sets to work a way in which nature turns itself toward [*sich zuwendet*] the human, and within this turning [*Wendung*] becomes deployable [*verwendbar*]. This producing turns, from the outset, everything natural into something objective for mathematical representation. In accordance with this turning, such representation is already the decisive deployment of nature into calculation. [12] But this representational setting-forth of nature into objectiveness remains a kind of making-manifest of nature. The basic trait of all objectification is the essence of technology.

SCIENTIST: Then the name "technology," strictly speaking, refers to a kind of representing, that is, a kind of cognition, and hence to a kind of theoretical comportment. The essence and the dominance of technology consist in the fact that, through it, nature has become an object. Nature is set up by the human, halted by him, so that it may be accountable to him and to his plans for it. Technology is the objectification of nature.

SCHOLAR: But then we are forcing a signification on the name "technology" which it does not have in the familiar sense and understanding of the word.

GUIDE: As if the domain of usual speech alone could find out what a word signifies [*bedeutet*]. As if the word itself, first of all and from itself, did not have to harbor the significance [*Deutung*] of the matter named by it.

SCIENTIST: What you mean to say is not clear to me. You distinguish between a customary linguistic usage, in which a word appears, and the word itself. And yet the word itself is only a word within a particular linguistic usage.

GUIDE: If you were to say that a word is always a word for a linguistic usage, then I could perhaps agree. In each case a word decrees [*ver-*

fügt] a linguistic usage, albeit such that this linguistic usage then for its part immediately, and in the sense of the usual language which takes up this usage, asserts its rule [*verfügt*] over the word and no longer turns itself back to the word's rightful decree [*Fug und Recht*].

SCHOLAR: The ruling [*fügende*] word in the name "technology" is the Greek τέχνη, which is usually translated as "art," whereby the word implies as much as skill. This [13] signification of the word τέχνη yields nothing for our understanding of the essence of "technology," granted that we may at all trust a word to show us into the essence—or even only to show us the direction of the essence—of what it names.

GUIDE: We hardly know what the word is capable of. But if it is supposed to indicate [*deuten*] to us that which is signified [*Bedeutete*] in it, then at least at first we have to attempt to pay attention to this indicating in the word. We neglect to do this, however, if we hastily run to the dictionary and, as in our case, thoughtlessly stick the word used to translate, namely "art" or "skill," in place of the word translated, namely τέχνη. We omit something essential if the word happens to be a fundamental word of the given language, and if special meditations have even been devoted to its signification and to the matter signified in it. Yet this is the case with the word τέχνη.

SCHOLAR: I take it from your explanation that the usual translation of τέχνη as "art" thinks past the proper signification, if it thinks at all.

GUIDE: Such is the case. Τέχνη belongs to the stem τεκ—"to bring forth." In the sense of the thinking to which the Greek language belongs, "to bring forth" means as much as this: to bring something to presence and to let it appear. Τέχνη indicates, however, not first of all the bringing-forth of an individual thing, but rather the setting-forth and setting-toward [*Her- und Zu-stellen*] of the sight and outward look[5] of a thing in accordance with which the thing is set-forth into what presences as a thing which looks like this or that. Τέχνη is the letting-see and bringing-into-view of that which a thing is according to its essence. "Technology" in the modern sense is a kind of τέχνη. Modern technology is that letting-see and set-

---

5. *Aussehen*, which will occasionally be translated simply as "look," is translated here and generally, below, more literally as "outward look" in the sense of "outer appearance." Elsewhere Heidegger uses it as a translation of the Greek *eidos*. (Compare below, p. 58; and see *Sein und Zeit*, 17th edition (Tübingen: Max Niemeyer, 1993), p. 61. Joan Stambaugh translates *Aussehen* as "outward appearance" in *Being and Time* (Albany: SUNY Press, 1996), p. 57.) A critical implication here is that when things are treated merely as objects of representation and technological production, their essence is reduced to the way they outwardly appear to human subjectivity (see below, pp. 55-56, 63, 82-83).—*Tr.*

ting-toward[6] in which nature comes to appear as a mathematical object. This technology is the deployment of nature into the [14] objectiveness of calculating representational setting-before [*Vorstellen*], where calculating is a quantitative measuring.

SCHOLAR: This explanation of course deviates considerably from the usual translation of the word τέχνη and from the accustomed conception of "technology." I just can't rid myself of the suspicion that you are interpreting the Greek word τέχνη in terms of your own dogmatically asserted definition of the essence of modern "technology."

SCIENTIST: If I have even roughly understood the remarks about the word and the linguistic usage, then we must conversely grasp the essence of "technology" on the basis of the word τέχνη—that is, insofar as we are going to accept for a moment the presumption that we can interpret a matter like modern technology on the basis of an individual word, in this case, the word τέχνη. Supposing that this audacious procedure has any orderly and secure basis at all, then first of all—and indeed without any sidelong glance at modern technology—evidence must be provided that with the word τέχνη the Greeks themselves named a kind of cognition.

GUIDE: This evidence has already been given by the Greeks themselves. According to Aristotle (*Nicomachean Ethics*, book VI),[7] τέχνη is a manner of ἀληθεύειν. This word means the letting-be-unconcealed [*das Unverborgenseinlassen*] of that which presences and shows itself as what is present. For this we could say in our language: revealing [*das Entbergen*].[8] Aristotle distinguishes various manners of revealing; alongside τέχνη he knew of ἐπιστήμη and θεωρία, manners of revealing which in certain respects correspond to what we call "science." Regardless of how Aristotle may have laid out the distinction between τέχνη and ἐπιστήμη, what is above all decisive is that τέχνη is grasped as a manner of revealing. The preconceptual Greek understanding of τέχνη is expressed in ἀληθεύειν as revealing. In their [15] customary linguistic usage, τέχνη is often equated with ἐπιστήμη, since like the latter it is a revealing.

SCHOLAR: Now the previous statement, "the technological essence of physics lies precisely in that it is theoretical physics," already sounds less perplexing. The mathematical projection sets nature forth in advance as object. As this setting-forth, the mathematical projection is the technology as which physics unfolds itself.

---

6. *Zu-stellen*, which may also imply "ob-structing," is later explained in terms of a representational setting-before that sets things toward us (see below, pp. 58, 63).—*Tr.*

7. See Aristotle, *Nicomachean Ethics* 1139b15–18.—*Tr.*

8. *Entbergen* is a neologism which more literally means "de-concealing."—*Tr.*

SCIENTIST: If this is what the statement, "physics is applied technology," signifies, then it is also not the reversal of the often heard statement, "technology is applied physics."

GUIDE: Certainly not. In each of the two statements, the words "physics," "technology," and "application" signify something different.

SCHOLAR: Then, as I now readily acknowledge, there are clearly peculiar circumstances involved in this reversing.

GUIDE: I agree. If you reverse the familiar statement, "technology is applied physics," and yet hold fast to the accustomed significations of the words, then by merely exchanging the names "physics" and "technology" you will never attain an understanding of the statement, "physics is applied technology." This statement could then at most only say that with its experiments physics makes use of technological apparatuses. But, rightly understood, the statement "physics is applied technology" is related first of all directly to theoretical physics. Because physics is applied technology in the sense of τέχνη, "technology" in the familiar sense can and must be applied physics.

SCIENTIST: I believe I have a rough idea of what you have in mind with these statements. [16]

GUIDE: As I earlier admitted, I too say what was indicated only in the manner of presaging. I only mean to point out that the essential provenance of "technology" stands in a concealed relation with ἀληθεύειν, letting-be-unconcealed. The noun that belongs to this verb is, as you know, Ἀλήθεια. One translates it as "truth." Looking back at what was said regarding τέχνη and technology, we could assert that the essence of technology is grounded in the essence of truth and is transformed along with it.

SCIENTIST: But one could now easily fall into the opinion that, according to your explanations, "technology" would have already arisen with the Greeks.

GUIDE: It would clearly be rash to jump to such a conclusion. Inquiry into the origin of something always falls easily into error when the essence of that which is to be explored in its origin, as well as what is meant by origin, remain in darkness. Does origin signify the cause of an actuality, or does origin bespeak the provenance of the essence, or neither the one nor the other? For example, how would we go about inquiring into the origin of language if we devote just as little thought to what language is as we do to what origin is? With this remark, however, I do not mean in any way to steer our conversation away from the question of the origin of technology, which we have just touched on. Nevertheless, it also seems to me that we would not be losing sight of this topic if we were to reflect on technology and the origin of language together.

SCIENTIST: So you think that technology is a kind of language, in which nature is interpreted?

GUIDE: And *you* think that language is a kind of "expression."

SCHOLAR: And I think that we are now well on the way to straying from our topic. [17]

SCIENTIST: I have already been asking myself for some time now where our conversation might be heading. We began by recalling our first conversation about cognition, and then we discussed thinking as the "active" component in cognition. In the meantime, we have ended up in the question of the essence of technology.

SCHOLAR: But is not the answer to this question at once a characterization of thinking? For in light of this characterization, the thinking of physics and technology, which sets forth nature as object, shows itself as a human attack on nature.

SCIENTIST: But surely you don't mean that nature is violated in physics? Nature and nature alone, in the manner that it shows itself to us, has the last word in physics. One of the overwhelming experiences of natural scientists is that nature often answers differently than might have been expected in the questions posed to it by the scientist. And this demonstrates that the human does not sit in judgment of nature, but rather directs himself according to it.

GUIDE: All the same we should reflect more often on whether nature in its objectiveness does not conceal itself more than it shows itself.

SCIENTIST: How are we supposed to assess this? After all, we know nature solely in the manner in which it shows itself to us. If this is the case, how are we ever supposed to check on what it is concealing from us? How can we even presume *that* nature conceals something from us at all?

SCHOLAR: That sounds convincing to me.

GUIDE: Perhaps, however, there lies precisely in that which nature gives of itself to be known, when human objectification affects it, a mysterious defense against the attack of technology. The discoveries of technology have unleashed [18] powers of nature that are already discharging themselves in a process of annihilation that encompasses the earth.

SCIENTIST: You are probably thinking that culture is now being widely destroyed by technologically steered nature.

SCHOLAR: It seems to me that the destruction affects rather the monuments of past cultures and not culture itself, from which and within which technology for its part arose.

GUIDE: But you might attend to the fact that I spoke of annihilation and not just of destruction. This was done deliberately.

SCIENTIST: Annihilation is the more encompassing destruction. In speaking of annihilation you are presumably also taking into account the destruction of countless human lives.

SCHOLAR: With the word "annihilation" you also want to indicate that the all-around destruction ascends to obliteration.

GUIDE: What is to be thought with the word "annihilation" I myself can only say with intimations, and even this only in the manner of pointing away from what is not meant. The annihilation to be thought here is in no way merely a higher or the highest grade of destruction. Annihilation is essentially other than destruction.

SCIENTIST: I believe the matter is becoming clearer to me. With destruction something is always left over—for example, with the destruction of a building the rubble is left, even if it is pulverized into the finest dust and blown away. So there is no "remainderless" destruction, any more than there is a round square. Even the most extreme destruction is but a change of condition, whereby something always remains preserved.

SCHOLAR: Then there is no annihilation at all, which [19] I cannot think otherwise than as that destruction whereby nothing more, or, better, only the nothing is left remaining. And this remainder is the nothing, which has consumed every "is" and itself.

GUIDE: But I stressed that annihilation is something essentially other than destruction.

SCIENTIST: And so it would probably not be permissible to say that annihilation is that destruction whereby. . . . In saying this we would place annihilation in advance into the essence of destruction. The transition from destruction, which always remains a change of condition, to annihilation would not be a gradual ascent, but rather a leap into another essence. This is probably what you want to make clear when you say that annihilation is something essentially other than destruction.

GUIDE: With this statement I indeed also want to say something else, namely this: In annihilation it is not just that nothing is "still" left remaining, as there is in destruction, but rather, in annihilation something of its own—and only its own—arises.

SCIENTIST: Who could understand this? An annihilation in which something arises is just as unthinkable as an unlimited that limits.

SCHOLAR: Moreover, in such use of the word "annihilation" there lies a misuse of language and an unjustifiable demand on linguistic usage.

GUIDE: If you both think this, then I can only ask for your patience, which you might have not only with me, but also with yourselves, in order to learn that the offence you now take to the word and the thought of "annihilation" arises elsewhere than in our arbitrary whim. [20]

SCHOLAR: Yet perhaps you will help us further understand if you tell us what the annihilation of which you speak relates to.

GUIDE: It affects the human.

SCIENTIST: Then you do in fact mean that through the technologically unleashed, technologically steered, and technologically aimed powers of nature an unusually large number of human lives will be obliterated. In this would consist what you call "nature's mysterious defense against the attack of technology." I can discover in this nothing "mysterious." Quite the contrary, I find a one-sidedness in your thought which I would have hardly thought you capable of. You overlook the fact that the technological releasing, transforming, and managing of natural forces brings the human just as many benefits and blessings for preservation and empowerment.

GUIDE: I do not fail to recognize this. I would like to go beyond this to point out that, with the calculation of the benefits and drawbacks of technology, nothing at all is said of its *essence*. Perhaps we still completely lack the horizon within which this question of the essence of technology can be posed. For the moment let it be expressly admitted that the previously mentioned thought of the defense of nature against the attack of technology—together with the thought of the annihilation of the human which prevails in such defense— is difficult to think. Perhaps it is, if a human may at all estimate here, precisely the most difficult thought for the contemporary human to think. In the face of it I am far less sure of matters than you, because I perhaps experience its difficulty a little more clearly, from the sense I have that we are altogether still far away from the essence of thinking. [21]

SCIENTIST: It does not help us proceed forwards when you say that what is called annihilation affects the human.

GUIDE: The indication indeed helps, albeit not forwards but rather backwards.

SCHOLAR: What do you mean by this?

GUIDE: I said that annihilation affects "the human" [*den Menschen*]; I did not say, "humans" [*die Menschen*]. As long as we advance from one case of an obliteration of human lives to the next, and imagine the greatest possible number of such cases, then we don't find "the human" whom the annihilation affects.

SCHOLAR: "The human is annihilated" says then: the essence of the human is annihilated. We must think back to the essence of the human.

GUIDE: Indeed.

SCIENTIST: You philosophers always think backwards. This is surely the basis for the often noted impression that philosophy and its history leave on every straight-thinking mind: that philosophy, in contrast to the progress of scientific research [*Forschung*], stays in the same place and never gets anywhere.

SCHOLAR: Philosophers always tread in place.

GUIDE: All of them even in the selfsame place.

SCIENTIST: This is how it in fact appears, and I am grateful to you for admitting this.

GUIDE: But, without myself being a philosopher, I have just admitted much more to you. Philosophers not only don't go forwards, they don't just tread in place either; rather, they go backwards. For there is what was referred to as the "selfsame place."

SCIENTIST: But where is "backwards," and what is in back? [22]

SCHOLAR: You say that annihilation affects the essence of the human. To what extent is this essence something "in back"?

GUIDE: The backwardness of the essence and what it is—in other words, the essentiality of the essence—appears to greatly unsettle you. That is good. But for the moment it may be better to first of all ask what the essence of the human consists in.

SCHOLAR: That has long ceased to be a question. We possess the answer in the definition of the human essence that has remained unchallenged for ages: the human is the rational animal. This phrase is so familiar to us that we do not even understand it as the answer to a question.

GUIDE: Perhaps it has never been an answer to a question.

SCHOLAR: By that do you mean to say that the question of the essence of the human has never been raised?

SCIENTIST: How then was the aforementioned statement about the essence of the human to have ever come about?

GUIDE: All statements of the aforementioned type, perhaps even every statement [*Aussage*] and story [*Sage*], is an answer. But not every answer is an answer to a question.

SCHOLAR: I can understand that not every statement is an answer to a question; but it is incomprehensible to me how an answer is supposed to not be an answer to a question.

SCIENTIST: The two belong together like mountain and valley.

GUIDE: But a question can surely remain without an answer.

SCHOLAR: It thus nevertheless remains related to an answer. The answer is that about which it asks. [23]

SCIENTIST: In any case, every answer is the answer to a question.

GUIDE: It is precisely this that I doubt.

SCHOLAR: That you can do only if, in your accustomed manner, you understand by "answer" something other than what sound common sense does.

GUIDE: "Answer," indeed, does also say something other. This other is not, however, something arbitrarily thought up by me, but rather the essence of answer, which includes the customarily meant "answer," the answer to a question.

SCIENTIST: In what, then, does the essence of answer consist?

GUIDE: The word "answer" itself answers your question. The answer [*Antwort*] is the counter-word [*Gegenwort*].

SCHOLAR: And counter to what is it the counter-word?

GUIDE: To what else can it be counter to other than to the word?

SCIENTIST: And yet what in the world is "the word"?

SCHOLAR: I'd also like to ask this.

GUIDE: For my part, I am still unclear whether we are able to ask this.

SCHOLAR: For what reason?

GUIDE: Precisely because not every answer is the answer to a question. Because the essential answers are perhaps "only" counter-words to the word.

SCIENTIST: Then would the proper way to essential answers not at all be questioning?

SCHOLAR: I have to say that everything is starting to get shaky for me. [24] Recently, in my dealings with ancient philosophy, I came across a passage in Aristotle's *Metaphysics* (Z 1, 1028 b 2 ff.),[9] which reads: χαὶ δὴ χαὶ τὸ πάλαι τε χαὶ νῦν χαὶ ἀεὶ ζητούμενον χαὶ ἀεὶ ἀπορούμενον, τί τὸ ὄν; "and so then, that which from ages past has been, and today is, and ever after will be the sought—but which is also never the found—is that which beings are."

τί τὸ ὄν: what are beings? [*Was ist das Seiende?*] What answer could be more essential than the answer to this question! And so the question of all questions is after all the way to the answer of all answers.

SCIENTIST: And in a contemporary book, I even found a question posed that goes further—beyond this question of the Greeks and of occidental metaphysics. This book does not just question what beings are, but rather what the truth of being [*die Wahrheit des Seins*] is.

SCHOLAR: Whoever so questions goes further back behind the usual fundamental question in philosophy.

GUIDE: There is probably something there of that going-backwards of which we spoke.

SCHOLAR: Thinking can hardly go further back than to being itself. There is not anything more essential that can be questioned.

GUIDE: But what if, as I have already said, questioning is not at all the way to essential answers? Then it seems to me that he who inquires into being, and devotes everything to working out the question of being, does not truly know to where he is under way.

SCHOLAR: I agree with you without reservation.

---

9. *Aristotelis Metaphysica.* Recognovit W. Christ. Lipsiae in aedibus B. G. Teubneri 1886.

GUIDE: If, however, this inquiring into beings and into being is the proper and sole concern of [25] thinking, yet questioning cannot be the proper way to the answer that is here sought, then proper thinking does not at all consist in questioning.

SCIENTIST: And it has never consisted in that, but rather in answering.

SCHOLAR: But answering was always an answering to a questioning, and so decisively so, that all efforts were aimed at gaining the right formulation of the question.

GUIDE: Originary answering is not an answering to a question. It is the answer as the counter-word to the word. The word must then first be heard. So what matters is hearing.

SCHOLAR: Yet is not all hearing a questioning?

GUIDE: Presumably not. But all questioning may well be a kind of hearing, and for the most part even a kind of willing-to-hear.

SCIENTIST: Permit me to disturb our conversation. It does indeed seem to me that it has brought us to many intelligent questions. But it is also certainly the case that we have almost entirely lost sight of our topic.

SCHOLAR: I share this worry with you.

SCIENTIST: Through my mathematical work, I am practiced at surveying long chains of inferences. From our conversation up to now only a loose thread of various items remains in my memory. Recalling our first conversation, we wanted to talk about cognition, and in particular about thinking, since thinking, we maintained, is the active component in cognition, in distinction from the more passive, because receptive, intuition. The activity of thinking shows itself today especially in the modern [26] investigation of nature. Hence we discussed the thinking in physics and thereby came to speak of technology and its relation to physics. On this occasion—I still don't know exactly through what connection—a remark was made about nature and its defense against technology. An annihilation of the human is supposedly at stake here. This annihilation, you said, affects the essence of the human. Comprehending the essence is said to be a matter of going back. In general going backwards is said to characterize the course of philosophizing. The question of the essential determination of the human then arose. This determination is supposed to be a statement, but not an answer to a question. Finally, this led to the discussion about answer and question. And yet we don't want to deal with this, and also not with technology; we want rather to gain a precisely defined idea of thinking as the active component of cognition.

SCHOLAR: Instead we let ourselves be diverted into all possible side-tracks. Although these do indeed offer interesting vistas, the fact that they only divert our progression was confirmed by the overview you just gave.

SCIENTIST: I miss altogether a strict order of thought-progression.

GUIDE: I almost suspect that above all you miss having clear, grasp-able results from our conversation.

SCIENTIST: In fact I do. To me the only sure approach is that of the deliberations that take place in the research of physics. This ap-proach alone promises an insight into the essence of the modern investigation of nature and therewith an insight into the contem-porary conception of the world. This conception embodies our ac-tual thinking, so called because it grasps what is actual. We are, after all, inquiring into the essence of actual thinking. But it is also clear to me that we have long strayed from thinking. [27]

SCHOLAR: By that you surely don't want to say that we have given up thinking. You just want to once again stress that we have distanced ourselves far away from thinking as the thematic object of our conversation.

SCIENTIST: I only meant this, of course.

GUIDE: But perhaps we are nearer to thinking than we know at the moment.

SCHOLAR: Despite my best will and intention [*beim besten Willen*], I cannot now find this to be the case.

SCIENTIST: It is exactly the same for me. Whether I am near to or at a distance from an object can, in fact, only be assessed if I have the object clearly before me. Yet the presence of the thematic object of our conversation is precisely what is now missing.

GUIDE: And how does it stand with the nearness and farness that you want to assess?

SCHOLAR: Without being a mathematician, I would like to say that what nearness to and farness from an object are, is self-explanatory.

GUIDE: And they are?

SCHOLAR: Simply said: the varying distance between an object and an observer.

SCIENTIST: We are simply taking here the self-apparent linear dis-tance between two points on a line and transferring it to the rela-tion between a human and his or her object at a given time.

GUIDE: But what if the thinking of which we want to speak were not an object?

SCIENTIST: Excuse me, but we have been speaking constantly about it. [28]

GUIDE: I thought that, according to your own explanation, we have gotten completely away from it. How is it supposed to be standing there before us?

SCIENTIST: Thinking is clearly not a thing.

GUIDE: How do you know that? Do we know what a thing is?

SCIENTIST: Thinking is a process.

SCHOLAR: It is our own activity.

SCIENTIST: We get involved in this activity when we go about our research-work, when you go about your scholarly business, when you go about your speculative trains of thought.

GUIDE: But then it seems to me that if thinking is our activity—if we are active in it and are ourselves the thinkers—then we don't have any possibility of distancing ourselves from thinking.

SCHOLAR: We are also in fact, strictly speaking, not near to it; for nearness is in each case a less great farness.

SCIENTIST: Then the talk a moment ago of nearness and farness to thinking has in fact no sense at all.

SCHOLAR: But you yourself were the one who pointed out to us that we had supposedly gotten far away from thinking. There must then be a distancing here after all.

SCIENTIST: Now I hardly know anymore where I am.

GUIDE: I don't know this at all anymore. Thinking is to us neither near nor far. It is also not an object.

SCHOLAR: All the same, we are talking constantly about it and making every effort to come nearer to it. You yourself just said that we are nearer to thinking than we know at the moment. [29]

SCIENTIST: And so I would like now for once to take him, who would assert such a thing, at his word.

GUIDE: I have long waited for this.

SCIENTIST: In our conversation about thinking you surmised that there is a nearness to thinking, and at the same time stressed that thinking is not an object. To think something, which is not an object, as nearer or farther away is a trick that I can't seem to pull off.

GUIDE: You are successfully thinking, without it needing to be a trick.

SCIENTIST: I don't see this.

GUIDE: But you are after all standing by what you already stressed several times, that our conversation has gotten away from thinking.

SCIENTIST: I do indeed stand by this view.

GUIDE: Well then if we, as you say, have gotten away from thinking as the topic of our discussion, then it could also be that thinking has withdrawn from us, and not that we have withdrawn from thinking.

SCHOLAR: But you yourself, in fact, asserted that we are nearer to thinking than we know.

GUIDE: I do not want to remain fixed on this statement. I am happy to concede to you that in this conversation we have distanced ourselves from thinking. What matters now is solely this: if we want now to be near to or far from thinking, at stake in this *is* a nearness and farness to something that we deny has the character of an object.

SCHOLAR: And since our thinking is in fact always our activity, there is for us a nearness and farness to something that we ourselves are. [30]

SCIENTIST: All this sounds to me almost as if nearness and farness were more essential than that which at any given time is near or far.

GUIDE: As if nearness neared [*näherte die Nähe*] and farness furthered [*fernte die Ferne*].

SCHOLAR: While in fact any given nearness and any given farness are obviously brought about by the given amount of distancing [*Entfernung*] and approaching [*Annäherung*].

SCIENTIST: I can indeed imagine—and we all do this constantly—that space, wherein nearness and farness belong, is in a certain sense independent of that which occurs in space. But this is not the case with nearness and farness, which first result from the manner in which something that has its place in space occurs. But if you were to say that nearness nears and farness furthers, and if this statement could be based on something tenable, then we would have to assume that nearness and farness are something which, as it were, prevails of its own accord and is independent like space, which first grants the lodging for all present-at-hand objects and objective relations.

GUIDE: Perhaps even space and everything spatial for their part first find a reception and a shelter in the nearing nearness and in the furthering farness, which are themselves not two, but rather a one, for which we lack the name.

SCHOLAR: To think this remains something awfully demanding [*eine arge Zumutung*].

GUIDE: A demand which, however, would come to us from the essence of nearness and farness, and which in no way would be rooted in my surmise [*Vermutung*].

SCIENTIST: Nearness and farness are then something enigmatic.

GUIDE: How beautiful it is for you to say this. [31]

SCIENTIST: I find the enigmatic oppressive, not beautiful.

SCHOLAR: The beautiful has rather something freeing to it.

SCIENTIST: I experience the same thing when I come across a problem in my science. This inspires the scientist even when it at first appears to be unsolvable, because, for the scientist faced with a problem, there are always certain possibilities for preparing and carrying out pertinent investigations. There is always some direction in which research can knuckle down and go toward an object, and thus awaken the feeling of domination that fuels scientific work.

SCHOLAR: By contrast, before the enigma [*Rätsel*] of nearness and farness we stand helplessly perplexed [*ratlos*].[10]

---

10. The noun *Rat* means "advice," "suggestion," or "counsel," while the verb *raten* means "to advise" or "to counsel." On the other hand, to be *ratlos* means "to be at a loss" or, more informally, but also more literally, *"clueless* as to what to do" in a situation. In this sense, to be *ratlos* is to be "perplexed" or even "disoriented."

SCIENTIST: Most of all we stand idle [*tatenlos*].

GUIDE: And we do not ever attend to the fact that presumably [*vermut-lich*] this perplexity is demanded [*zugemutet*] of us by the enigma itself.

SCHOLAR: You could almost be right. It seems to me as though something paralyzing were holding us up from making fresh progress in our conversation.

SCIENTIST: I would also like to point out that we have remained standing at the same place on this country path for some time now.

GUIDE: Almost as though we shy away from following its bend, which leads to the forest.

SCIENTIST: I was of course not thinking of this.

SCHOLAR: But by pointing out that we were standing still, you wanted to let us know that it is time to go further. [32]

SCIENTIST: That is exactly what I wanted to say.

SCHOLAR: Going further, however, means that we turn back to our topic.

GUIDE: I am also in favor of a return.

SCIENTIST: Then you are also in agreement with us that we should let the enigma of nearness and farness rest and leave it on its own.[11]

GUIDE: We probably must treat every genuine enigma in this manner.

SCIENTIST: But then I don't understand why you made it a topic of conversation at all.

GUIDE: Because we can only let something rest and leave it on its own if we have first of all thought about it.

SCHOLAR: Is the enigma then supposed to solve itself with time, or must we after all one day interject and push it to a solution?

SCIENTIST: Or are there still other possibilities of comportment toward an enigma?

GUIDE: That is a question of nearness and farness to the enigma.

SCHOLAR: Where nearness and farness are themselves the enigma.

SCIENTIST: Others might find a way out of this tangle of an enigma. I am hardly able to suppress the suspicion that this talk of nearness to the enigma and of the enigma of nearness comes from a word game, which is supposed to be clever, while it is perhaps just lacking in thought.

Etymologically, *Rätsel* is related to *Rat*, words which are in turn related to the English words "riddle" and "read." A *Rat* can thus be understood as a "read" on, that is to say, an orienting interpretation of a puzzling situation.—*Tr.*

11. The phrase translated as "let . . . rest and leave it on its own" here is *auf sich beruhen lassen*. This phrase usually means "to let some matter rest," as in to leave it alone and no longer pursue it or concern oneself with it; but understood literally, it means "to let something rest on itself" in the sense of "to let it be based on itself."—*Tr.*

GUIDE: Let this suspicion freely run its course. For after all there remains in the matter the persistent necessity to deliberate on what it means to let an enigma rest and leave it on its own. Does this mean: to let an enigma lie and thus also [33] to just pass over it? Or does it mean: to go into perplexity [*Ratlosigkeit*] in the face of the enigma [*Rätsel*] and to abide before it?

SCHOLAR: Those are certainly considerable questions; but now they obstruct us from going further on our path, which you yourself just spoke in favor of.

SCIENTIST: So that we now actually do go further, and so that we avoid the constant creeping in of delays, I'll take up our question of the essence of thinking in the form that seems to me to be the only fruitful one. We are inquiring into the essence of thinking in physics, which is not only the foundation of all investigation of nature, but also the foundation of all exact thinking about the world.

SCHOLAR: In this field I am, to be sure, hardly well-versed. Yet from our preceding discussions I see that here too a multitude of approaches and viewpoints offer themselves for our questioning. For the scientist what matters is to experience more precisely the inner structure and lawfulness of thinking in physics. By contrast, what arouses the interest of the scholar is the question—which was admittedly only touched on—of how, through being attacked by technology, a mysterious defense is set off in nature which aims at an annihilation of the human essence [*eine Vernichtung des Menschenwesens*].[12]

SCIENTIST: I too am keenly interested in this question, since the scientific investigation into nature is of course also an essential manifestation of modern culture.

SCHOLAR: With regard to intellectual history, however, the special significance of this question is that it casts light on the contemporary situation of the human and, moreover, helps to further illuminate the not yet conclusive relationship of the modern human to technology. [34]

SCIENTIST: Nevertheless, I consider it to be more logical if we first clarify what the alleged attack of the natural sciences on nature consists in; but that means first of all clarifying the kind of thinking that takes place in the natural sciences.

SCHOLAR: So, to express this in a scholarly manner, you give priority to the question of the inner logic in the method of the natural sciences,

12. The German word *Wesen* can mean both "essence" and "entity," and, although here the sense of "human essence" is at issue, elsewhere both senses are implied in Heidegger's use of the term *Menschenwesen*—for example, when he contrasts human being with animals or "living beings" (*Lebewesen*). Since the word "being" can also be understood in a manner that shares this ambiguity, I have sometimes translated *Menschenwesen* as "human-being."—*Tr.*

in short, to the methodological question over the historiological [*historischen*]¹³ question. The latter inquires into the position of the modern natural sciences within the history of human thinking, in which the relationship of the human to the world is also expressed.

SCIENTIST: I regard your distinction between the methodological and the historiological sides of our problem to be very useful. Yet I give the methodological question priority, not just because it happens to relate to my own field, but rather because only with a discussion of it do we first attain the prerequisite for treating the historiological question.

GUIDE: Assuming that this is such a question.

SCHOLAR: How would it not be? Historiology investigates, after all, the particular relationship of the contemporary human to nature, a relationship which is its own kind of historical fact and which differs from the relationship the human had to nature in the Middle Ages. By contrast, the methodological examination delineates the timeless relationship of the human in general to nature in general, a relationship which actualizes itself differently in different time periods.

GUIDE: One is indeed in the habit of seeing the matter in this manner. If we follow the matter, however, then we easily recognize that we have gotten stuck half way down the road.

SCHOLAR: How so? [35]

GUIDE: Well, the relationship of the human to what we call "nature" is after all only an extract from the relationship of the human to the world overall.

SCIENTIST: You are probably referring to the relationship that philosophy thinks as the relation between subject and object.

SCHOLAR: That is the identical [*das Gleiche*], which Goethe treats in terms of the relationship of the inner and outer; and I am convinced that he has conclusively determined this relationship. We all know of course his words:

> Nothing is inside, nothing outside,
> For what is inner, that is outer.¹⁴

GUIDE: What Goethe thinks is in fact not the identical, but on the contrary, the selfsame [*das Selbe*].

---

13. Here as elsewhere, Heidegger distinguishes the academic study of history or *Historie* (historiology or historiography) from the being-historical (*seinsgeschichtliche*) events of history (*Geschichte*).—*Tr.*

14. These lines are from Goethe's poem "Epirrhema." See also Heidegger's remark in *The Basic Problems of Phenomenology*, rev. edition, trans. Albert Hofstadter (Bloomington: Indiana University Press, 1982), p. 66 (*GA* 24: 93): "For the Dasein there is no outside, for which reason it is also absurd to talk about an inside."—*Tr.*

SCHOLAR: As far as I am concerned you can also express it like that. With the most general relations, among which what was just said indisputably belongs, it is no longer the precise linguistic expression that matters, since after all everyone understands what is meant.

SCIENTIST: I can only agree with this view. I would just like to immediately add that we should clarify this most general relationship with regard to its particular configurations, that is, with regard to its actual forms. In our case, this requires that we explain the relation between ego and object from the actual relationship thinking in physics has to nature.

SCHOLAR: In this way we avoid the abstract and remain in the concrete.

SCIENTIST: That's exactly right. Moreover, the fruitfulness of the approach that I called for with the methodological question is thereby confirmed. [36]

GUIDE: It seems to me, however, that you now advocate the approach of the historiological question.

SCIENTIST: Then I must not even know myself, if I changed my point of view so unawares.

GUIDE: It does not need to be a change of viewpoint. We can, after all, look out in various directions from the same viewpoint. And what initially and for a long time seems to us as two different viewing directions can basically be one and the same.

SCIENTIST: I don't understand what you just said. But surely I would at least notice a change of viewing-direction, especially since, in passing from the methodological manner of examination over to the historiological, I would have to set foot in what is to me a foreign field.

GUIDE: You mean, then, that the methodological manner of viewing is more familiar to you?

SCIENTIST: Of course; for it aims at working out the inner structure and lawfulness of thinking in physics. There I move about as if in my own house.

GUIDE: But not as a physicist.

SCHOLAR: As who else then?

GUIDE: Can you ever with your own methods—that is, with the methods of physics—investigate the essential structure of physics?

SCIENTIST: This could admittedly not be done. After all, it would entail having to make physics as a science into an object of a physics experiment, in order to gain well-founded physical[15] knowledge of the essence of thinking in physics. [37]

---

15. Here "physical" translates *physikalische* and should not be taken in the sense of "material" (*materielle*), but rather in the sense of what pertains to the science of physics. —*Tr.*

GUIDE: I have in fact never heard such an excellent formulation of the difficulty that prevails here.

SCIENTIST: I am extraordinarily pleased by your approval. Yet it does not help me get over a fear that has in the meantime arisen for me.

GUIDE: And that would be?

SCIENTIST: That I should be a stranger in my own house of physics.

GUIDE: It is not only the physicist that encounters this problem. Perhaps the human in general is not at home in his house.

SCHOLAR: That would mean that the human does not know his own habitat, so that he would be missing from his own premises—that is, be absent in his own presencing.[16]

GUIDE: And perhaps even the enigma of nearness and farness comes into play in this strange absence.

SCIENTIST: Faced with the unhomely [unheimischen] essence of the human, which is now dawning upon us, one could begin to feel uncanny [unheimlich].

GUIDE: That may well be. But this is not an occasion for fear.

SCIENTIST: It is rather an occasion for astonishment.

GUIDE: Fear clouds sight. Astonishment clears it.

SCHOLAR: I experience this now when I transfer that which was so compellingly said about the methodological view of physics over to historiological research. For with the help of historiological procedures the historian also cannot establish anything about the essence of historiology. However—and now I come to what I wanted to say—the historiological view, in contrast to that of physics and the other sciences, can after all [38] bring to awareness much that is noteworthy, not only about historiology but about all the sciences. The historiological investigation of the history of the sciences makes an important contribution to an insight into the essence of the sciences.

SCIENTIST: Then in fact the two modes of inquiry with regard to a science, the methodological and the historiological, do not at all lie so far apart from one another.

GUIDE: This is all I wanted to suggest when I said a little while ago that, with the call to investigate the concrete structure of the currently actual research of physics, you advocate the approach of the historiological question.

SCIENTIST: I admittedly cannot yet concede this even now. Just a moment ago the belonging together of the methodological question and the historiological question seemed to be clear to me. Now all

16. The phrase "be missing from his own premises—that is, be absent in his own presencing," translates: *im eigenen »Anwesen« abwesend*. Heidegger is playing here on the word *Anwesen*, which commonly means "estate," but which literally means "presencing."—*Tr.*

is once again murky. If I understand correctly, you are now asserting more than before. To express it pointedly, you want to say that
the methodological question is at once the historiological question.

GUIDE: That is in fact what I would like to say. But with this I assert
nothing more than what I previously suggested.

SCHOLAR: With regard to the essence and the essential history of a science, the methodological question and the historiological question
belong together; this has also become clear to me. Yet what belongs
together is not yet thereby the selfsame.

SCIENTIST: I too am stuck on the identical difficulty.

GUIDE: You mean on the selfsame difficulty.

SCIENTIST: You express it like this. But if you are so bent on the difference between the identical and the selfsame, [39] you must also tell
us what this difference consists in and what distinguishes the selfsame as the selfsame.

GUIDE: In one respect it was already said in my remarks on the relation between the methodological and the historiological question.

SCIENTIST: You mean the claim that what belongs together is the
selfsame.

SCHOLAR: Selfsameness would then be, if you'll permit the morphol-
ogy, belonging-togetherness?

GUIDE: Presumably.

SCIENTIST: And how about what is identical or what is similar [*das
Gleiche*]?[17] Do these not somehow belong together?

GUIDE: Strictly speaking, no.

SCHOLAR: But one in fact says: those who are similar associate well
with one another [*gleich und gleich gesellt sich gern*].[18]

GUIDE: Of course. They associate with one another only because prior to
that they are separate as what are similar. Similarity or identicalness
[*Gleichheit*] enables what are similar or identical to be—precisely as
such—by themselves and separate, and so to be without belonging
together.

SCIENTIST: Although from mathematics I surely know how to appreciate sharp conceptual distinctions, what you now propose is too abstract for me to be able to actually comprehend it.

17. In normal usage, *gleich* can mean either "similar" or "identical." These two
senses could perhaps be reconciled if we understand the similarity between two
things to be based on a shared characteristic. For example, two persons may be
"similar" in that they share a taste in music, such that they can speak of their taste
in music as "identical." The ambiguity or interplay between these two senses in
the text, here, could be understood in this sense.—*Tr.*

18. The idiom, *gleich und gleich gesellt sich gern*, is used in much the same sense
as "birds of a feather flock together."—*Tr.*

SCHOLAR: Perhaps we will succeed in this sooner if we illustrate with an example the essence of selfsameness and identicalness just touched on.

SCIENTIST: For this it is best that we choose the case which occasioned our abstract discussion, namely, the relationship between the methodological question and the historiological question. [40]

SCHOLAR: Now of course to begin with we have a rough idea—though I would rather not characterize it as a clear idea—of "what is methodological" and also of "what is historiological."

GUIDE: But perhaps these ideas will become clearer by bringing them into a relationship with the relations of selfsameness and identicalness.

SCIENTIST: A strange trick; that would be as if the concrete would become more concrete by means of the abstract.

GUIDE: Yes indeed. It would now be a matter of testing this case.

SCIENTIST: For me, though, what is more important is to find out something about the methodological in order to get to know what properly characterizes thinking in physics. After all, our entire conversation took off from there.

SCHOLAR: With the wider intention of bringing into view the essence of thinking in general.

SCIENTIST: And from this the essence of cognition, to which the intuitional element also belongs.

GUIDE: It is, however, still a long way to there.

SCHOLAR: I too have this impression.

SCIENTIST: Thus I am for going forward.

GUIDE: Of course we first have to settle our argument.

SCIENTIST: You claimed that the methodological view of physics and the historiological view are the selfsame.

GUIDE: In other words, the methodological view is a historiological view. [41]

SCIENTIST: I admit that the historiological view of physics supplements well the methodological analysis of its essential structure. But from this, it only follows that nothing historiological occurs in the methodological view.

SCHOLAR: We wanted, however, to pause in this discussion at an example.

SCIENTIST: We have one already on hand. While discussing the relationship of physics and technology it became apparent that theoretical physics, which lays the foundation for all physics, carries out a mathematical projection of nature.

GUIDE: Meanwhile, we have reflected no further on the mathematical, no more than on the experiment, which is an essential component of research in physics.

SCIENTIST: If we ascertain in such a manner that mathematical projection and experiment belong to physics, then we make no historiological statement, but rather pick out components that belong to the essence of physics. We think methodologically.

SCHOLAR: As far as I have been instructed, however, modern natural science places its pride precisely in that, by means of its mathematical-experimental conduct, it possesses a decisive superiority over all historically preceding investigations of nature—over the ancient as well as, above all, over the medieval—a superiority which is plainly enough confirmed in the enormous successes of technology in particular.

SCIENTIST: By this you want to say that in mathematical projection and in experiment the modern—and that means after all the historical—character of physics comes to light. [42]

SCHOLAR: Precisely that.

SCIENTIST: It is far from my intention to deny the temporally conditioned aspect of modern natural science [*Naturwissenschaft*], which, after all, it shares in common with all human creations. But with this nothing is decided about the inner essence of cognition in physics. When the natural scientist is immersed in his work—and it is precisely this stance that must be held in view in the methodological analysis of physics—he is entirely dedicated to the object. Everything that is temporally conditioned and personal drops away from the investigating physicist. In this stance there is nothing historiological to be found. Nature alone, which is after all sharply distinguished from history, speaks to the mathematically thinking and experimenting scientist. In the humanities [*Geisteswissenschaften*] the matter is different. Here, for example, in the interpretation of poems and paintings, everything depends on the personal experiential capacity of the researcher being brought into play. Here the subjectivity of the researcher is necessarily in play; and it is for this reason that the humanities also never attain to strictly objective, that is, to universally valid knowledge.

SCHOLAR: What the humanities leave behind in this respect they make up for with a harvest that issues forth from them in the form of spiritual edification and intellectual enrichment.

SCIENTIST: These treasures, however, are very often buried under mountains of scholarship and are at times rather meager and hardly distinguishable from what anyone moderately capable of experiencing can see in an artwork without the help of research. Be that as it may, I think that the natural sciences and the humanities can be accurately distinguished from one another according to the viewpoints we have touched on here—namely, those of objectivity and nearness-to-life.

GUIDE: Yet I would like to doubt whether what is essential can be clarified by means of this kind of calculating the degree of [43] objectivity and the amount of lived-experience content found in the different areas of science and the humanities.

SCIENTIST: Is there anything at all that you don't doubt?

GUIDE: Very much indeed.

SCHOLAR: And that would be?

GUIDE: The undoubtable.

SCIENTIST: But surely this answer should not seriously count as an answer.

GUIDE: This answer may not satisfy your question. But it is perhaps still an answer [*Antwort*].

SCHOLAR: Insofar as it gives us a word [*Wort*] for consideration.

GUIDE: This alone is what the reference to the undoubtable may provide.

SCIENTIST: We understand this word to indicate that about which a doubt is not possible.

SCHOLAR: When we doubt [*Zweifeln*] we always think of at least two [*zwei*] objects and objective determinations without agreeing, that is, without becoming one [*einig zu werden*] about the two and so thinking of one thing [*Eines*].[19]

SCIENTIST: But of course more than two objective determinations can be doubtful to us.

SCHOLAR: Certainly, the "two" stands here merely as a placeholder for a number, and expresses that what is two or more always remains divided and separated.

GUIDE: So wherever and whenever there are at least two, there is the possibility of doubt, regardless of whether and how the two can agree as one [*einig sein*]. [44]

SCIENTIST: The doubt [*Zweifel*], strictly speaking, has its eye on the numerical one [*die Eins*].

GUIDE: More precisely, on the One [*das Eine*], wherein this one and the other one—that is, the two—are as one.

SCHOLAR: The undoubtable [*Das Unbezweifelbare*] would therefore be present when all that is separated is unified and this unity is what everywhere provides the measure.

GUIDE: It seems to me that this is not yet the authentic undoubtable.

SCIENTIST: How is it not?

GUIDE: Because what is originally undoubtable is that which does not at all split up into two and into number.

---

19. Although, unlike *zweifeln*, the word "doubt" does not explicitly contain the stem "two," in English we do say that when we are in doubt about something we can be "of two minds" about it.—*Tr.*

SCHOLAR: So is there something like this?

SCIENTIST: It would have to be a manifold something in which all determinations in advance belong together.

GUIDE: That is entirely right.

SCHOLAR: But I still don't know whether there is something like this.

GUIDE: All the same, whether there is such a thing or not, if there is, it is what we have already considered and assigned the name, "the selfsame."

SCIENTIST: The selfsame, and what the selfsame is, is what is purely and simply undoubtable.

GUIDE: I surmise that it is so.

SCIENTIST: Can one then still surmise the undoubtable? After all, it is in itself certain and thus beyond all surmising.

GUIDE: To will to surmise the undoubtable and thereby to represent it as [45] the undoubtable would make as much sense as straining to see a sound.

SCIENTIST: But you yourself just said that you surmised that the selfsame, and what the selfsame is, is the undoubtable.

GUIDE: Certainly. But here I don't encounter the undoubtable as such with a surmise; rather, I surmise that the essence of the undoubtable is how we have said it is.

SCHOLAR: For us, then, the essence of the undoubtable can very well be doubtful.

GUIDE: That is the selfsame as when we are not at home in our habitat.

SCHOLAR: As I experience ever more clearly, this is also true of our conversation; within it we are constantly roaming away.

SCIENTIST: We are still standing after all at the identical place on the country path.

GUIDE: You probably mean: at the selfsame place. Perhaps this is a sign that we are straightaway, without roaming about, nearing the selfsame; I mean what is originally the selfsame and only the selfsame.

SCHOLAR: It seems to me more like we are roaming around without direction and have already once again lost our way.

GUIDE: Then permit me to try to usher the conversation once more along its way.

SCIENTIST: That would be most welcome, if you are able to do so. But I believe that you yourself must then finally give up the conversational tactics you have practiced thus far by involving yourself more in the course of the conversation and, if I may say so, by staying focused on its thematic object. [46]

GUIDE: Participating in a conversation is in fact difficult. It is even more difficult than leading a conversation. Since we met for the first time on this country path for a conversation, I have attempted to learn but one thing.

SCHOLAR: And what is that?

GUIDE: The art—or the forbearance, or whatever you would like to call it—of speaking together in conversation.[20]

SCIENTIST: That is easily attained if you just always deal with the matter at issue [*die Sache*].

SCHOLAR: One learns matter-of-factness [*Sachlichkeit*] best in the sciences.[21]

GUIDE: But now what if a conversation is only concerned with first of all finding the matter?

SCHOLAR: Then it is of course more difficult to remain within a matter-of-fact attitude [*sachlich*].

SCIENTIST: Especially for your kind of thinking. In the high-altitude flight of your speculative thoughts, you too easily lose sight of the object.

GUIDE: I would be grateful to you if you would more precisely instruct me with regard to this roaming away.

SCIENTIST: With pleasure, with the greatest pleasure even; for I believe that we will thereby at the same time finally come back to our path. To this end I might recall the point at which you last drove us once again onto a bypath.

SCHOLAR: Namely by doubting our characterization of the distinction between the natural sciences and the humanities.

SCIENTIST: We came to this distinction in view [47] of the natural scientist's exceptional dedication to the object.

SCHOLAR: Yet this in no way constitutes the proper topic of our conversation. And I must confess that, with the back and forth of objections, considerations, answers, and surmises, the coherence of the conversation has for me now completely disappeared.

SCIENTIST: I am afraid that you are making the gathering more difficult for yourself in that you want to hold on to all the accessory details. The topic lies clearly before our eyes. We are inquiring into the essence of thinking with the guiding thread of thinking in physics.

SCHOLAR: And so whatever else came to be spoken of belongs more to the ornamentation of the conversation.

SCIENTIST: Aptly said. If we finally want to pursue our matter in an orderly fashion and stringently analyze our topic, we must in the future abstain from ornamentations.

20. The word for "conversation" is *Gespräch*, which may be thought to imply a "gathering"(*Ge-*) of speaking (*Sprechen*) or language (*Sprache*).—*Tr.*

21. *Sachlichkeit* is commonly translated as "objectivity," a term which is reserved here for *Objektivität*. The word "sciences" here translates *Wissenschaften*, which includes the social sciences (*Sozialwissenschaften*) and humanities (*Geisteswissenschaften*) as well as the natural sciences (*Naturwissenschaften*).—*Tr.*

GUIDE: One can, however, think of ornament and adornment in a variety of manners. If the adornment [*Schmuck*], as the word says, adoringly nestles up against [*anschmiegt*] the matter, then through the adornment the matter can more beautifully shine forth; and it can do this without us especially noticing the adornment itself, which of course would not at all be its point.

SCHOLAR: Then, if I have understood correctly, only one who rightly knows an object could ornament and adorn it at all. Adorning would properly consist only in bringing the matter itself to light.

GUIDE: That is just what I mean.

SCIENTIST: That would then be identical to what I too strive for with an unadorned working out of the matter.

GUIDE: Not only identical, but even the selfsame.

SCIENTIST: Hence, what we just called ornamentation is after all needed for our conversation. [48]

GUIDE: I am pleased that we agree on this. Only I would not like to go so far as to claim that the embellishments which have come forth in our conversation are already genuine adornments.

SCIENTIST: Why not then?

GUIDE: Because I don't know whether we are already near to the matter that we mean; or indeed whether what we seek may be called a matter at all.

SCHOLAR: But if it were not a matter and therefore also not a possible object, then there would also not be anywhere for us to append an adornment.

GUIDE: Or it would have to be the case that here what is adorned first comes to appear by means of adorning with the adornment.

SCHOLAR: We would then be in search of something uniquely precious.

GUIDE: But for us everything would have to depend on that in which the precious rests.

SCHOLAR: Why should we not also take pleasure in the precious?

GUIDE: Because we would then all too easily concern ourselves only with relishing the precious [*das Kostbare auszukosten*] and clinging to the price that this costs [*kostet*] us.

SCHOLAR: We would not then properly belong to what the precious itself is, but rather wrap our own enjoyment with the appearance of appreciating the precious itself and solely for its own sake. Yet in what, if I may use your manner of expression, does the precious rest?

GUIDE: If you'd be content here with a surmise, I would like to say that the precious may very well rest in the beautiful. [49]

SCHOLAR: Yet what is the beautiful?

SCIENTIST: Unfortunately I must now interrupt your discussion, as violent as this may be taken to be. With the question of the beautiful you appear to have now merrily entered into aesthetics. And soon there will be no more science, which we touched on fleetingly enough in the course of our conversation—a course [*Gang*] that, to me, is threatening to become a real blind alley [*Irrgang*].

GUIDE: As long as we merely take all the things which our conversation has in the meantime addressed, and in the future will perhaps review, and assign them to the corresponding sciences, then the impression remains almost inevitable that we aimlessly touch upon everything that comes along in our path and yet don't grasp, much less hold on to, anything.

SCHOLAR: Then do you think that the orientation of our inquiry to the sciences is altogether mistaken?

GUIDE: Not mistaken, but misleading.

SCIENTIST: But we do want after all to determine the essence of cognition. Where in the world is cognition purer and richer and more impressively embodied than in the sciences?

SCHOLAR: And let us consider this: what would the history of occidental humanity be without science?

SCIENTIST: Even the most diverse worldviews, especially since the eighteenth century, are pressing to obtain a scientific foundation or to remain in harmony with science.

SCHOLAR: That is true even of Christianity in all periods of its history.

GUIDE: How could I presume to [50] contest in the least the points you both have just put forth regarding science and its historical significance.

SCIENTIST: Yet from your remark, namely that the course of our conversation, which follows the thematic thread of the sciences, is misleading, I have to infer that you speak from a suspicion of the sciences.

GUIDE: I am in no way suspicious of science. I merely surmise that it could be beneficial to our conversation if we would, where possible, keep what it brings to language for us away from the purview of the sciences.

SCIENTIST: Then our entire conversation—indeed, already our first conversation from last autumn—has gone off track [*auf dem Holzweg*].

GUIDE: Perhaps.

SCHOLAR: But how do you ever want to remove our topic, namely the essence of cognition and in particular of thinking, from the purview of science? Is it not the case that for us today, as a consequence of the intellectual development of the Occident, each and every object is in some manner scientifically grasped, even where we do not immediately recognize this?

GUIDE: We cannot consider carefully enough and often enough the matter you just bought forth.

SCHOLAR: Then I don't understand why you want to dismiss science or even just limit its role.

GUIDE: I don't want to take any action against science.

SCIENTIST: That would indeed be a vain undertaking. [51]

GUIDE: I don't want to go forth "against" anything at all. Whoever engages in opposition loses what is essential, regardless of whether he is victorious or defeated.

SCIENTIST: Then your stance is not at all so revolutionary as it appears.

GUIDE: Everything revolutionary remains caught up in opposition. Opposition, however, is servitude.

SCHOLAR: If then, after all that has been said, you are not opposed to science, then it would indeed be revealing and beneficial to the advancement of our conversation if you could say what it is that you really will to gain [*wollen*] from exerting yourself with us to illuminate the essence of cognition and especially thinking.

GUIDE: Since you so directly put me on the spot to say something, I must also directly, and therefore insufficiently, reply. What I really will [*will*] in our meditation on thinking is non-willing [*Nicht-Wollen*].[22]

SCIENTIST: Can one then will non-willing? With such willing, after all, willing is merely increased. And thus this willing works precisely and ever more decisively counter to that which it wills, namely, non-willing.

GUIDE: Against its will, by the willing of non-willing, willing entangles itself in itself and so loses precisely what it wills—namely, non-willing.

SCHOLAR: You yourself say this?

GUIDE: How should I not, since I was after all asked what I will.

SCIENTIST: So then was it in fact my insistent question about what you will that caused your disconcerting answer?

GUIDE: Not really caused, but [52] elicited the discourse of willing. You are thereby running the risk of shifting our conversation on thinking to the topic of willing, while it is you who are continually and at times violently struggling to keep the conversation on its topic. The topic, however, is thinking and not willing.

SCHOLAR: Yet it seems to me that willing belongs to thinking.

SCIENTIST: The two are of course often named together when one enumerates the main faculties of the soul: thinking, willing, and feeling.

---

22. The verb *wollen* can be translated as "to want" or "to will." While "to want" would in many cases be a more colloquial rendering, in this context *wollen* is translated as "to will" in order to indicate the problem of willing and the paradoxical tension of "willing non-willing" that is at issue. For example, even though "what do you *want* in our conversation" would be a more idiomatic and less awkward translation of "*was* wollen *Sie bei unserem Gespräch*" than is "what do you *will* in our conversation," the latter is more appropriate here since it is precisely the problem of "willing" (*das Wollen*) that is at issue.—*Tr.*

GUIDE: So we would after all be nearer to thinking than we realize if we speak of willing.

SCHOLAR: And hold in view the unified domain of the soul's faculties.

SCIENTIST: Evidently. And so I too am now inclined to let drop the thematic thread of our conversation, which has been tightly maintained up to this point.

SCHOLAR: Should that be taken to mean that you no longer orient the inquiry into the essence of thinking to an analysis of the essential structure of thinking in physics?

SCIENTIST: In no way do I want to give up this mode of inquiry which looks at the sciences. Indeed I cannot give this up, because it also takes my own science into consideration, and so can help me get clear on my own activity, such that I will become more at home in my own house. On the whole, however, connecting thinking with willing seems to me now to be more productive; for with this we come upon the original domain of thinking.

SCHOLAR: Even if this is only a [53] scholarly comment, perhaps I may mention that the philosophers, and finally in an exceptional manner Leibniz, have always been attentive to this connection between thinking and willing.

SCIENTIST: It is especially pleasing to me that you emphasize here in particular the name Leibniz. For we physicists believe that Leibniz still has something important to say for our science, even though physics, in the form of modern atomic physics, has progressed far beyond its state in Leibniz's time. I cannot assess the extent to which Leibniz can offer a clarification of our topic specifically, since I am not familiar enough with his writings.

SCHOLAR: I am thinking of his distinction of *perceptio* and *appetitus,* which one usually translates as "representing" and "striving." While all thinking is a representing, not all representing is already a thinking. While all willing is a striving, not all striving is already a willing.

SCIENTIST: With his distinction of *perceptio* and *appetitus,* Leibniz thus opens for us a view of the general domain in which willing and thinking are incorporated.

GUIDE: Moreover, what matters for Leibniz with his distinction is not just to duly hold representing and striving apart from one another. Above all the distinction serves the single purpose of bringing to light the belonging-togetherness of representing and striving.

SCHOLAR: All representing [*Vorstellen*] is directed toward that which it sets out before us and toward us [*was es vor uns hin und auf uns zu stellt*]. In that representing consists of this, it is a striving. Yet all striving is a striving after something, in which that after which it strives is somehow already [54] held before it. All striving is in itself a representing. The two belong together.

GUIDE: Thus thinking and willing also belong together.

SCIENTIST: Yet you said, however, that what belongs together is the selfsame.

GUIDE: That I did say.

SCIENTIST: Then are thinking and willing the selfsame?

GUIDE: This may well be the case.

SCIENTIST: Now, then, there is no doubt at all anymore that our conversation, which is concerned with thinking, has finally gotten a grasp on its topic with this view of willing.

SCHOLAR: One thing remains strange, which I pursued only in passing.

SCIENTIST: Namely?

SCHOLAR: The farther we roamed from the starting point of our conversation, the nearer we came to our topic.

GUIDE: Perhaps this is connected to the enigma of nearness and farness.

SCIENTIST: That I don't see. But I grasp now more easily why you are so averse to orienting our inquiry into the essence of thinking to scientific cognition.

GUIDE: In your opinion, what warranted this aversion?

SCIENTIST: Firstly, the path through an analysis of a science, especially physics, is demanding [55] and thus tedious. Yet if we examine thinking in its relation with willing, then right away we find it there where it actualizes itself directly and thus is also actual. Secondly, if we refrain from the previous orientation of the conversation, we escape the danger of holding thinking too one-sidedly in view, looking only at its epistemic side [*Wissensseite*] and thus overlooking its volitional side [*Willensseite*]. Besides its theoretical moment, thinking also has in itself a practical moment.

SCHOLAR: Also, already in our first conversation about cognition we unanimously stated that the achievement-character of the sciences has fortunately come ever more clearly to the fore, and that in our time it has earned its due recognition.

SCIENTIST: Scientific research is an essential form of work, which is testified to by its increasingly operational character. Contrary to this, Aristotle reportedly said that theoretical behavior is the highest form of leisure.[23]

SCHOLAR: Aristotle only gave expression to what the ancient Greek world always thought about the proper essence of thinking.

SCIENTIST: How far have we today then gone beyond the Greek world? If we now illuminate the connection of thinking with willing even further, the modern conception of science as a kind of work will at the same time gain its philosophical grounding.

23. See Aristotle's *Nicomachean Ethics* 1177b; see also his *Politics,* bk. VII.—*Tr.*

SCHOLAR: But it seems to me as though the Greeks too had already always been co-attentive to the practical side of cognition and thinking. I can easily provide evidence of this with a saying from Heraclitus that occurred to me already during our first conversation. But at the moment I don't want to hold up the [56] advancement of our conversation, which, by means of the perhaps somewhat intrusive question of what is really willed in this conversation, has taken such a favorable turn.

SCIENTIST: Yet what you find favorable is that, through my manner of questioning, willing was unexpectedly brought up for discussion.

SCHOLAR: After all, then, you also have the impression that we now suddenly, without a legitimate connection with what preceded, changed the topic?

SCIENTIST: It seems so at least; although I cannot deny that the reference to non-willing came forth entirely spontaneously as an answer to my question about what is willed in the conversation.

SCHOLAR: Then precisely the leaping quality of the transition—namely, from a discussion of thinking in physics to a meditation on willing and non-willing—was due to the manner of your question, which immediately occurred to you.

SCIENTIST: If you mean that the question I posed does not belong in the course of our conversation, then I cannot agree with you. What is more natural to a conversation than that in it something is willed? This belongs so originally to a conversation that I should have posed my question, what we really will in our conversation, right at the beginning.

GUIDE: Yet perhaps one could doubt whether a conversation is still a conversation at all if it wills something.

SCIENTIST: You mean, then, that we should leave a conversation to itself.

GUIDE: But what is the conversation itself, purely on [57] its own? You evidently don't consider just any mere speaking with one another to be a conversation. A speaking with one another can be found in every chat, discussion, debate, or negotiation; in a broader and vaguer sense these too are "conversations." Yet in the emphatic sense of this word we mean something else. Albeit what we mean is difficult to say. But it seems to me as though in a proper conversation an event takes place wherein something comes to language [zur Sprache kommt].

SCHOLAR: You understand this phrase, "to come to language" [zur Sprache kommen], quite literally.[24]

GUIDE: Indeed. I would like to say that the essence of an authentic conversation is determined from out of the essence of language. Perhaps, however, it is the other way around.

24. As an idiom, zur Sprache kommen means "to come up for discussion."—Tr.

SCIENTIST: But after all, a conversation [*Gespräch*] presupposes language [*Sprache*].

GUIDE: Presumably not language, though indeed the word.

SCHOLAR: Such that language arises from the word.

GUIDE: And authentic conversation first brings the word to language.

SCIENTIST: Although I don't understand much of what the two of you just said about word and conversation and language, could authentic conversation and what you understand by that be any different from what one customarily conceives of as "dialogue"? After all, it belongs to a conversation that it is a conversation about something and between speakers.

GUIDE: Yet a conversation first waits upon reaching that of which it speaks. And the speakers of a conversation can speak in its sense only if they are prepared for something to befall them in the conversation which transforms their own essence. [58]

SCIENTIST: Then in fact my question, what *we* will in the conversation, would be contrary to the essence of the conversation, since at best *it* wills something with *us*.

SCHOLAR: Assuming that it wills at all. Your question, what we will in the conversation, would at least be such that one could only answer it, as previously happened, by saying that one wills non-willing.

SCIENTIST: But then even with this answer, which indeed concerns the definition of any genuine conversation, nothing is yet resolved with regard to the topic of our conversation. Or is perhaps the non-willing named in the answer at the same time supposed to more narrowly delimit the topic of our conversation?

SCHOLAR: If, however, this delimitation was co-intended in the answer, then I cannot help but fear that we have come to this delimitation of the topic of our conversation at the expense of the necessary clarity of speaking, and at the expense of the necessary carefulness of hearing.

GUIDE: I agree. And I would like to hear if you have in mind the same difficulty that relentlessly burdens our conversation.

SCHOLAR: When asked what you really will in our meditation on thinking, you answered: non-willing.

SCIENTIST: And right away it became clear to us that *this*, what is in this case willed, is itself a kind of willing.

SCHOLAR: Certainly.

SCIENTIST: And thereby willing moved into our field of vision.

SCHOLAR: But we did not go any further into the answer that was given to us, which after all speaks of non-willing. [59]

SCIENTIST: It seems to me that we did this thoroughly enough, in that with a few steps of thinking we were able to show that the willing of non-willing contains a contradiction, and therefore also can never become what it wills to be, namely non-willing. The willing of non-willing [*Das Wollen des Nicht-Wollen*] indeed never gets around to willing non-willing [*das Nicht-Wollen zu wollen*].

GUIDE: From such an interpretation of my answer to your question, you would have had to infer that I willed something impossible.

SCIENTIST: And I did in fact infer this. However, I did not manage to expressly point this conclusion out to you, since right away the surprising connection of willing with thinking came into our view.

SCHOLAR: I myself am guilty of the overly hasty reference to this connection.

SCIENTIST: Why do you say "overly hasty" and "guilty of"?

SCHOLAR: Because this reference led us to leave alone the answer given to you.

SCIENTIST: I confess that this was in a certain sense my intent. I wanted to prevent our conversation from getting hung up once again in the thicket of dialectical discussions. Or is the back and forth talk about willing and non-willing, about the willing of non-willing and the non-willing of willing, something else?

GUIDE: The dialectical may come into play here. Yet we certainly must not simply suspect from the start that "dialectic" is devilish senselessness.

SCHOLAR: Even if it were the case that we had to do this, that would not legitimize skipping over the answer that stands in question as we did. [60]

GUIDE: Yet please don't fear that even for a moment I had the feeling that I was passed over in the conversation.

SCHOLAR: I do not in fact have this fear. But I am concerned that we neglected, not something personal, but perhaps something in the matter at issue.

GUIDE: As I said before, I certainly share this concern with you.

SCIENTIST: If this is how matters stand with our conversation, then you will also find me ready to retrieve what was neglected.

GUIDE: And this I never doubted, since I highly esteem the readiness to get down to the facts of the matter that lives in every genuine scientist. Indeed, even your constant urging to stay on the topic in our conversation today stems solely from this readiness.

SCIENTIST: In our conversation, then, what did in fact remain behind in essential unclarity? More precisely put: in what way was the content of your answer not adequately appreciated by us?

GUIDE: To your question, what I really will in our meditation on thinking, I answered, I will non-willing.

SCIENTIST: Yes. And I believe that I now see what remained unclear in our reply to your answer. But you must grant me the time to formulate it sharply and concisely.

SCHOLAR: I too am constantly searching for a formula that would get a grip on the clearly felt sense of having gone astray [*das Abwegige*] that adhered to the position we took in response to your answer.

SCIENTIST: I believe we will arrive more surely at the goal [61] if we simplify the matter on the basis of what we have already agreed upon.

GUIDE: How do you understand this?

SCIENTIST: The dialectical—not to mention the paradoxical—character of your answer still disturbs me even now.

SCHOLAR: You would like to eliminate this.

SCIENTIST: And it can be eliminated. Instead of "I will non-willing," I'll have you say: "I will willing."

GUIDE: You'll admit, though, that with this reformulation of my answer you impute to me precisely the opposite of what I will and say.

SCIENTIST: I admit that. I even claim that it makes no difference in the present case whether your answer is "I will non-willing" or "I will willing."

GUIDE: And what you mean by the present case is the task of illuminating what is unclear in the position you took toward my answer.

SCIENTIST: That is what I mean. I have thus come as far as to clearly say what is unclear.

SCHOLAR: Now, untie the knot at last.

SCIENTIST: If one says that with a meditation on thinking one wills willing or, what here amounts to the same, non-willing, then one does not even begin to engage in a delimitation of the conversation topic, but rather steps entirely out of the conversation about thinking.

GUIDE: It is true that with my answer I do not contribute anything directly to a determination of the conversation topic; but it is not the case that I set myself outside of the conversation.

SCHOLAR: If you had wanted to say what we [62] earlier imputed to your answer, then you would have expressed yourself roughly in this manner: "I will to steer our conversation toward non-willing as its proper topic."

GUIDE: Yet my answer deliberately stated: I will non-willing.

SCIENTIST: It is thus not important to you to gain knowledge of thinking by means of the conversation, nor to attain an insight into non-willing and willing. Your intention has nothing at all to do with gaining knowledge of something, but rather—well, how should I say it—with the actualization of a total human condition, namely that of complete inactivity.

SCHOLAR: That is, with a kind of denial of the will to live.

GUIDE: I find myself in a great predicament, since I can hardly respond to your comments without my statements right away giving rise to new obscurities.

SCIENTIST: But as soon as you resolve to plainly answer our questions without side-thoughts, everything will be cleared up.

GUIDE: There shall not be a lack of willingness on my part to answer your questions.

SCHOLAR: When you say: in our meditation on thinking I will non-willing, then it is evidently not your intention to orient the topic of our conversation to willing and the relation between willing and thinking.

GUIDE: No; the view toward this broadened topic arose through the manner in which you took up my answer.

SCHOLAR: Yet I also cannot accept that [63] with your answer you wanted to step out of our conversation and give up participating in it.

GUIDE: Least of all that.

SCHOLAR: With your perplexing answer you wanted rather to imply that your intention in our conversation reaches beyond its topic.

GUIDE: Not that either.

SCIENTIST: Yet our topic is after all the essence of thinking, and you are thinking of non-willing.

GUIDE: Indeed. But we are not endeavoring merely to construct a concept of thinking just to be in possession of this concept.

SCHOLAR: Certainly not. By means of the appropriate concept of thinking we would also like to attain to a carrying out of right thinking.

GUIDE: And this is, after all, a manner of human behavior.

SCIENTIST: And moreover a behavior that, as we recognized with reference to Leibniz, is most intimately connected with willing—indeed, even is a willing.

GUIDE: With our meditation on thinking, therefore, we in fact will a willing.

SCIENTIST: Certainly; and in no way a non-willing, as you will it.

GUIDE: That would remain to be considered.

SCHOLAR: What is left to be considered here?

GUIDE: So long as we, according to Leibniz's distinction, conceive of thinking as a representing, and of willing as a [64] striving, then the belonging-togetherness of thinking and willing is indeed evident.

SCIENTIST: Why should we not incorporate thinking and willing into this distinction of representing and striving?

GUIDE: Because we may not do this now.

SCIENTIST: Who forbids us to do this?

GUIDE: Our conversation. We are after all just getting under way in asking what thinking is. How is it that we can now unawares assert that thinking is a representing?

SCHOLAR: From long ago to this day it has been accepted as a universally recognized doctrine of philosophy that thinking is a kind of representing.

GUIDE: May this and other doctrines of the thinkers never lose what is venerable and mysteriously didactic, by means of which they surprise every new confrontation that lets itself into an engagement with their truth.

SCIENTIST: So then you attribute an authoritative character to the doctrines of thinkers?

GUIDE: In no way. Of course, when we still have so little understanding of the essence of thinking, we can now hardly conclude something reliable with regard to what the correct relationship would be toward thinkers and their doctrines.

SCIENTIST: Then you think that the doctrine which says, thinking is a representing, is false?

GUIDE: Not at all.

SCHOLAR: But you leave it still undecided whether thinking is already exhaustively determined by this characterization of its essence? [65]

GUIDE: It is more that I leave open whether the essence of thinking has at all been caught sight of originally. After all, it could be that the common characterization of thinking as a representing is indeed correct and yet nevertheless prevents us from experiencing the essential origin of thinking.

SCHOLAR: There is this possibility.

SCIENTIST: All the same, though, it should first be examined whether willing is a striving.

GUIDE: Presumably willing is also a striving; but it is not only this and this is not what is proper to it.

SCHOLAR: So the essence of thinking as well as the essence of willing remain questionable.

SCIENTIST: And together with these, the relation between the two.

SCHOLAR: Thus it could well be that thinking essentially has nothing to do with willing.

SCIENTIST: Which is why you also said, in our conversation about thinking, that you willed to go out toward non-willing.

GUIDE: I am thinking out toward something such as this.

SCHOLAR: And nevertheless do not stride beyond the legitimate parameters of our conversation topic.

SCIENTIST: But how are we supposed to thoughtfully pursue non-willing and its essence so long as we leave the essence of willing undetermined?

GUIDE: Perhaps we must also first experience the essence of thinking in order to recognize that thinking is not a willing.

SCHOLAR: Yet if we know already in advance the essence of thinking, we can spare ourselves the task of distinguishing it from willing. [66] In any case the look toward non-willing is without essential significance.

SCIENTIST: Of course, as long as you insist that we reflect on non-willing and its essence in order to come in contact with the essence of thinking, you are already presupposing a connection between thinking and willing.

SCHOLAR: Otherwise we could indeed with the same right proceed by way of distinguishing thinking from feeling.

GUIDE: Perhaps we could also do this.

SCIENTIST: Yet even if we are to leave this aside for now, there still must be a reason why you place thinking especially in relation—albeit a negating one—to willing.

GUIDE: This "reason," as you say, does indeed exist.

SCIENTIST: For the sake of furthering our understanding, I believe that it would be very helpful if you would divulge this reason to us now.

GUIDE: I cannot divulge anything here, because I do not have anything to keep secret. Indeed, you are clearly responsible for prompting the manner of my answer. You asked me: what do I really will in our meditation on thinking?

SCIENTIST: So did I myself then steer the conversation to willing?

GUIDE: Such is the case. In order to answer while keeping in line with your question, and yet at the same time in order to also name that which, in our thinking about thinking, seems to come to me as the essence of thinking, I could only say: I will non-willing. [67]

SCHOLAR: And so, not only the manner of the question directed to you, but also the essence of thinking itself provided you with the occasion to answer as you did.

GUIDE: Indeed. And thus everything also depends on whether we, in the right manner, let ourselves engage in[25] what is called non-willing.

SCHOLAR: Now do you mean that it depends on whether we engage in explaining the essence of this non-willing, or do you mean that it depends on whether we engage in non-willing itself?

GUIDE: I mean in a certain manner both.

SCIENTIST: But we can, after all, determine the essence of something without engaging in it.

GUIDE: For example?

25. This phrase, *sich einlassen auf*, commonly means "to engage in" or "to get involved in." Here and below, however, in order to draw attention to the "letting" at issue, it is sometimes translated more literally as "to let oneself engage in" or "to let oneself be involved in."—*Tr.*

SCIENTIST: We can define the essence of crime without ourselves having to be or become criminals.

GUIDE: That is the question.

SCHOLAR: But, in reverse, a person can surely be a criminal without knowing something of the essence of crime.

GUIDE: That too is a question.

SCHOLAR: Admittedly you may be right to have doubts where it is a matter of human behavior. However, what if we are determining the essence of plants?

SCIENTIST: After all, we define the essence of plants without ourselves being plants.

GUIDE: Even this I would like to doubt.

SCHOLAR: But a plant can surely live as a plant [68] without knowing or even thinking about the essence of plants.

GUIDE: Yet what does thinking mean here? What do we know of the essence of thinking?

SCIENTIST: But surely we can determine the essence of a jug or a bowl without ourselves being a jug or a bowl.

GUIDE: Even with regard to this question, I would not like to decide.

SCHOLAR: What is certain, however, is that the jug is a jug without itself thinking its essence; for indeed it cannot think at all.

GUIDE: We would do well to leave even this still open.

SCHOLAR: In order to let ourselves all the more freely engage in what you, in our meditation on thinking, think out toward.

GUIDE: Toward non-willing.

SCHOLAR: That is something which is presented to us through negation.

SCIENTIST: At the same time, through negation it withdraws from us.

GUIDE: But nonetheless, when we say "non-willing," something is given to us.

SCIENTIST: Negation also has that enigmatic quality, which has previously often unsettled us.

GUIDE: Because nearness and farness prevail in negation, insofar as it withdraws and yet brings forth.

SCHOLAR: Only I find that discussions about negating, the no, and the not or non [das Nicht] do not contribute anything to the determination of non-willing so long as we leave the essence of willing undetermined. [69]

SCIENTIST: Yet we have already spoken in detail about this; which is why I would also like to admit now that our earlier discussion, despite the sense of having gone astray that may have adhered to it, was not entirely futile.

GUIDE: Nothing is in vain in such conversations.

SCIENTIST: Although now and then they become tremendous tests of patience.

SCHOLAR: Which we will pass sooner if we let the conversation swing out freely on its own to a state of rest.

GUIDE: And in general let rest prevail in its essence.

SCIENTIST: I am more inclined to keep the conversation going. Movement is the positive. Rest is always only the null point of movement. The lack of activity constitutes the negative of work. It is work, however, that is the life-element of modern humanity.

SCHOLAR: As distinct from the ancients, for whom all work was only the interruption, and that means the negation, of leisure, the *neg-otium*.

GUIDE: Yet perhaps for them work was even considered to be, if I may say so, something still more negative.

SCHOLAR: Namely?

GUIDE: A failure in the face of rest.

SCHOLAR: A rest which, of course, they could never equate with a mere doing nothing.

SCIENTIST: Yet every doing is then necessarily once again a moving and thus a denial of rest.

SCHOLAR: And even if rest is something other than [70] a mere doing-nothing, also in rest the human must after all stay somewhere.

GUIDE: That in which the human stays in the resting state of his essence will even be essential for rest, if it is not indeed determined by the essence of rest.

SCIENTIST: Then everything pertaining to rest depends on that in the nearness of which the essence of the human rests.

GUIDE: You pronounce here yourself that about which I wanted to keep silent.

SCHOLAR: So what settles by bringing to rest [*das Beruhigende*], and rest itself, would come from nearness.

GUIDE: To which farness always remains related as a sibling.

SCIENTIST: According to everything you have just suggested, you take rest as the positive and movement as the negative. Of course, having been previously instructed in this matter, I would not want to straightaway assert that you merely reverse the customary view.

SCHOLAR: To which, in your opinion, we should in fact hold fast.

SCIENTIST: Not only the thinking of physics familiar to me, but above all the modern feeling of life we all bear, forbids seeing in work only a restlessness.

SCHOLAR: The *negotium* of the ancients can also be interpreted in another sense. The negation of *otium* can, after all, also mean the mastery and overcoming of inactivity.

SCIENTIST: This interpretation of *negotium* coincides with an idea that I stand for, according to which, as one often hears said, work as achievement ennobles the human. [71]

SCHOLAR: Certainly. But it remains to be considered whether the nobility [*Adel*] that stems from work is a nobility because it rests in what is noble [*im Edlen*].

GUIDE: And whether work and achievement are in general fitting measures for the essence of the human. Assuming, however, that they are not, then one day the whole of modern humanity, together with its much extolled "creative" achievements, will surely collapse in the emptiness of its rebellious self-oblivion.

SCHOLAR: Luckily it cannot come to that, because the growing appreciation of achievement and work is necessarily accompanied by increased work on securing the possibilities for and expansion of achievement.

SCIENTIST: Which is indeed also why the idea of a new world order, that is, the idea of a distribution of opportunities, means, and goals for work—just like the idea of a world security, that is, of a securing of the accomplishment of work and of its conditions—is attaining an increasingly clear configuration.

GUIDE: But presumably security [*Sicherheit*] does not at all come from efforts at securing [*Sicherungen*], which only drive their own prerequisite, namely insecurity, forth in increased degrees. Security rests [*beruht*] solely in restful repose [*Ruhe*], because through this it is reduced to an insignificant concern.

SCIENTIST: Yet I think that we should not lose ourselves in world-historical observations about work and achievement, order and security, *otium* and *negotium.* We will rather to let ourselves engage in non-willing.

GUIDE: It seems to me that we are near to this when we pursue such observations. After all, you yourself previously called non-willing a total human condition of complete inactivity. [72]

SCIENTIST: However, from what you just said about *otium* and *negotium,* it is becoming ever more doubtful to me that we may grasp non-willing in this negative sense.

SCHOLAR: Especially since the reference to non-willing is supposed to give us a preview of the positive essence of thinking. Still I must confess that, in the meantime, our path and the outlooks it has offered thus far have become more obscure than ever.

GUIDE: Before we realized it, the evening twilight has called forth the night.

SCIENTIST: We are also nearing the place where our accustomed path turns and heads into the forest.

SCHOLAR: And our steps will be doubly unsure on the forest path at night.

SCIENTIST: Which is why I would like to propose that we turn around and take the path home.

SCHOLAR: And also break off our conversation?

SCIENTIST: I think so; for our reflections have reached a place where the conversation can easily be taken up again another time.

SCHOLAR: And, as is often the case, after having talked about less urgent matters, the return path gives us the opportunity to also talk about daily necessities and current affairs. On the other hand, however, to break off our conversation so abruptly would seem unfortunate to me.

SCIENTIST: Why?

SCHOLAR: Because the manifold glimpses of light which, for all its opacity, the conversation granted us, are all too easily lost. [73]

SCIENTIST: This matter can easily be remedied. If you are both in agreement, we could of course also use the return path to summarize in a few main points what we have discussed thus far.

GUIDE: That would also be an opportunity to gather ourselves once more.

SCHOLAR: Not in the least do I shy away from this endeavor.

SCIENTIST: As far as my freshness and keenness for conversation goes, I could take part until deep in the night.

GUIDE: In order to properly gather what has been discussed so far, however, we would have to look ahead more clearly into what has not yet been discussed.

SCHOLAR: And so, after all, in a certain sense to continue onward with the conversation . . .

SCIENTIST: . . . and, as it were, make in advance the transition to what we will take up on the next occasion.

GUIDE: Yet to say it once more, we can gather what has been discussed and gather ourselves only if we make available that wherein what is to be gathered belongs.

SCHOLAR: But if I understand correctly, that is the essence of thinking which we are first seeking.

SCIENTIST: Then, strictly speaking, we would have to bring the conversation to its end in advance, in order to carry out the gathering.

GUIDE: At least we would have to bring it to that in which everything, in particular the sought-after essence of thinking, rests.

SCHOLAR: Then it would almost be more advisable to just carry on now with the conversation. [74]

SCIENTIST: Until by its own free swinging it comes to its own state of rest.

SCHOLAR: Only I am afraid that the return path will not suffice for this.

SCIENTIST: Then let us after all go further on the path through the forest!

SCHOLAR: And on this beautiful night not worry too much about path and time.

GUIDE: Clear evenings sometimes bring strangely bright nights.

SCIENTIST: Well then, let us go down the dark forest path!

SCHOLAR: And trust the sureness of our accustomed step.

GUIDE: As well as the near farness of the stars over the land . . .

SCIENTIST: For our conversation today a compass would in fact be quite useful.

SCHOLAR: We can easily fashion one for ourselves by more tightly organizing the task before which we have in the meantime been set.

SCIENTIST: So it seems that you already have in mind a plan for the continuation of the conversation.

SCHOLAR: It came to me of itself when we were previously considering whether we should summarize the conversation that had been cultivated up to that point.

GUIDE: A conversation that follows a plan is in our case probably an absurdity.

SCIENTIST: But a conversation without a plan is surely absurd.

SCHOLAR: Then let's choose something in the middle. [75]

GUIDE: Why then don't we let our conversation freely take its course?

SCHOLAR: Yet let us also be mindful that the conversation stays on its theme.[26]

GUIDE: Certainly. Of course, the more appropriately we are mindful of this, the more the theme disappears for us.

SCIENTIST: What do you mean by this?

GUIDE: I mean not only that we then lose the particular theme [*Thema*] of the conversation, but that in general we are freed from the ties to everything thematic [*Thematische*].

SCHOLAR: Why do you so mistrust what is thematic?

GUIDE: Because it is, as the name says, what is posited by us. In conversations of the kind ours is, on the other hand, what is spoken of may of itself bring itself to language[27] for us and thus bring itself near.

SCIENTIST: Then it would be precisely a matter of being mindful of what brings itself near yet also at times, or even very often, distances itself.

SCHOLAR: So that, in speaking, a "listening into" [*Hineinhören*] the conversation would almost be more essential than the "speaking out" of making statements [*Aussagen*]?

GUIDE: This alone is what I meant with my reservations against what follows a plan.

---

26. Up until this point, I have used the more idiomatic "topic" to translate *das Thema*. Here, however, the more literal "theme" is called for.—*Tr.*

27. The phrase translated literally here, *zur Sprache bringen,* is commonly used in the idiomatic sense of "bringing up a topic (for discussion)."—*Tr.*

SCHOLAR: Then you do not disapprove of meditating on the conversation during the conversation.

GUIDE: Quite to the contrary—assuming, of course, that meditating on and planning are fundamentally different matters.

SCIENTIST: But the two are not, after all, mutually exclusive.

GUIDE: In certain cases they challenge one another.

SCHOLAR: Above all when planning threatens to engulf all meditating. [76]

GUIDE: And meditating merely stands in service of planning.

SCHOLAR: Instead of planning serving meditating.

GUIDE: At times the latter is even sufficient unto itself.

SCIENTIST: Which, in your opinion, is the case with our conversation.

SCHOLAR: So let us meditate.

GUIDE: Where do we stand?

SCIENTIST: We are about to let ourselves engage in non-willing.

SCHOLAR: At the same time, if I understand correctly what was just said, we should think about it unthematically.

GUIDE: By thoughtfully pursuing non-willing.

SCHOLAR: And so then, after all, by thinking about what it is.

SCIENTIST: It would be difficult to pursue it otherwise.

GUIDE: But perhaps we come to know what non-willing is only once we have reached it.

SCHOLAR: And yet the question of what non-willing is stands at the beginning of our reflection.

GUIDE: At least in the sense that we reach an understanding among ourselves concerning what we properly mean with the expression, "non-willing."

SCIENTIST: It seems to me that attaining clarity about this is urgently needed, because various kinds of things can be so named.

SCHOLAR: We speak of non-willing when, for example, someone explains to someone else: "I do not will that [77] which you will of me." Non-willing here is a refusing.

SCIENTIST: Which can become an opposing.

SCHOLAR: That is, opposing a command found in the other's will.

GUIDE: Such that perhaps in general the essence of the will conceals itself in the command.

SCIENTIST: This seems to me to be indicated by another manner of non-willing, which appears when someone says: "I do not will that this happen."

SCHOLAR: In this case non-willing is a forbidding.

SCIENTIST: If we think of refusing, opposing, and forbidding as manners of non-willing, then it is quite apparent that they are at the same time really manners of a decided willing.

SCHOLAR: The non-willing meant in these cases is thus rather a willing that something not happen. This non-willing is not a negation of willing.

SCIENTIST: It is becoming increasingly doubtful to me whether there ever is such a negation of willing.

SCHOLAR: Yet how about when someone says: "I will no longer"?

GUIDE: Even the non-willing named here seems to me to be still ambiguous.

SCHOLAR: "I will no longer" can mean: "I have no desire or no strength any longer to will."

SCIENTIST: Or else: "I abhor willing."

GUIDE: Or even: "I forgo willing." [78]

SCHOLAR: Yet in abhorring, just as in forgoing and renouncing, does there not still live a will?

SCIENTIST: That is what I previously meant when I doubted the possibility of a nonwilling.

GUIDE: Thus, there is still will where we, as it were, suspend willing.

SCHOLAR: All non-willing of the said kind remains a variation of willing.

GUIDE: Even though the varying consists of a *negating* of willing, the variant is never a negation of the *will*, but rather each time an affirmation of it. And this is true of what is subject to the variation, that is, of what is varied, so long as we understand by this what lies at the base of the negation. But it is also true of what comes out of the varying in the sense of negation. The variations of willing in the form of its manifold negations are all carried out within the will.

SCIENTIST: You therefore distinguish between willing and will. I am, however, unable to conceive of what precisely is meant with this distinction. I am reluctant to expect of you the superficial view that the word "will" is merely meant to designate the faculty for willing.

GUIDE: With the word "will" I do not in fact mean a faculty of the soul, but rather that wherein the essence of the soul, mind, reason, love, and life is based, according to a unanimous yet hardly thought through doctrine of occidental thinkers. If we understand by "willing" the human carrying-out of this will, then there is concealed in the still completely obscure relation between will and willing a relationship; yet I lack the word to name it. [79]

SCIENTIST: I cannot at all conceive of what relationship you mean to suggest. Assuming, however, that the distinction between willing and will is a legitimate one, then the negation could also extend to the will.

GUIDE: Non-willing would thus imply non-will.

SCIENTIST: We would then need to keep separate that which is a non-willing and that which is not a willing, that is to say, not a will and thus nothing pertaining to will.

SCHOLAR: To what is not determined by the essence of the will belongs, among others things, thinking. I say, "among other things," because after all various kinds of things, not only thinking, lie outside the essential sphere of the will.

SCIENTIST: The answer to my question regarding what you really willed in our meditation on thinking, must therefore, precisely grasped, say "not a willing," and in no way as you said, "a non-willing." This expression seduced us into demanding a clarification of willing and its relation to thinking, while, in fact, with the question about the essence of thinking, what is a matter of will should not come into view at all.

GUIDE: Even though I do not presume to know something conclusive about the distinction between willing and will, you may still trust that I know what I say when I nevertheless use the expression "non-willing."

SCIENTIST: I do believe that you know this. But I cannot get over the impression that you used the expression "non-willing" intentionally in its ambiguity. [80]

GUIDE: That may be. And the intention was to lead ourselves into this ambiguity.

SCIENTIST: Yet what is problematic with your answer remains, namely that it has a negative character and does not extend any further than does the sentence: The stone is not a living being.

GUIDE: The answer is ambiguous and also negative, and yet this is a case where everything depends on the positive traits of the essential domain in which thinking belongs showing themselves to us unambiguously.

SCIENTIST: If you yourself so precisely realize the one thing that is necessary, then why did you answer in a manner that led us to wander about without a sense of direction in what is indeterminate?

GUIDE: Because I myself am only a seeker, and I would like to truly find the essence of thinking, not to establish it with the power of my own authority.

SCIENTIST: The joy of discovery, and of being the discoverer, is indeed a powerful incentive for scientific research.

GUIDE: Yet in the case of finding, it is a matter of what we are together seeking, not a matter of discovering.

SCHOLAR: Because our seeking is presumably not a scientific researching.

SCIENTIST: And the kind of finding is determined by the manner of seeking.

GUIDE: And the seeking?

SCHOLAR: By the kind of finding. But I see that with such statements we move in a circle and say nothing.

GUIDE: The kind of finding is probably determined by the essence of the possible find, that is, by the manner [81] in which what is to be found is concealed. Something can, for example, be so concealed that it is covered up.

SCIENTIST: With regard to what is covered up [*Verdeckte*] there is discovery [*Entdeckung*].

GUIDE: And only in regard to that.

SCIENTIST: But is not everything that is concealed something covered up?

SCHOLAR: So that the more covered up something is, the more concealed it remains.

GUIDE: That is an audacious statement.

SCIENTIST: And you are already on the verge of reversing it.

GUIDE: Indeed, if you are still thinking in terms of what we said about reversing.

SCIENTIST: So you mean that the less something is covered up, the more it is concealed?

GUIDE: The more it shows itself and, in so doing, veils itself.

SCHOLAR: What kind of concealment are you thinking of here?

GUIDE: We have already repeatedly encountered it.

SCIENTIST: Do you mean the enigma?

GUIDE: Yes, and indeed the enigma of nearness and farness, which is itself near and far. The more an enigma [*Rätsel*] divulges [*verrät*] — and yet in so doing covers over what removes [*löst*] the shrouding — the more it leaves us perplexed [*ratloser*]. The concealed in the enigma is properly what conceals. The concealed of the enigma is unconcealed when we find the solution [*Lösung*]: but never such that the enigma is discovered. Even where we first only come upon the enigma, this is not a discovery.

SCIENTIST: To many it may be tempting to keep on weaving this web of thoughts about seeking and finding, concealment and enigma. [82] However, we are dealing first of all not with the enigma of nearness and farness, but rather with the essence of thinking; and secondly, it would have to be shown that the concealment of this essence has the character of an enigma. I do, however, admit that this concealment must be of a peculiar kind, if I may conclude so from the trouble that it and its elimination are causing us.

GUIDE: I too merely attempted to indicate what is peculiar to our seeking in order to remain silent about finding from now on, since we have not yet found anything maintainable. But it remains the case that the answer I gave does not merely move our seeking into what

is indeterminate. It contains the positive indication of willing and
the domain of the will. Thinking can, after all, be a non-willing—
both in the sense of being a variation of willing, as well as in the
sense of not being a willing.

SCIENTIST: But rather?

GUIDE: The issue comes down to this "but rather."

SCHOLAR: What does that mean?

GUIDE: That we think about the essential domain in which even the
will and willing belong.

SCIENTIST: So we should already think out beyond the essence of willing and of thinking, without clearly knowing this essence.

SCHOLAR: In order to go into the domain which they inhabit.

GUIDE: Where the "not"/"non" [»*Nicht*«] and the "no" [»*Nein*«] prevail, which distinguish or even separate the two.

SCHOLAR: We have already made an initial run at thinking ahead into
this domain. [83]

SCIENTIST: In what sense?

SCHOLAR: Insofar as we said that in the meditation on the essence of
thinking we should let ourselves engage in non-willing, we spoke of
the actualization of a total human condition. I myself remarked more
in passing that non-willing is something like the negation of the will
to live.

SCIENTIST: Why do you now refer to these earlier remarks, which I
had in the meantime entirely forgotten?

SCHOLAR: Because the selfsame thing dawned on me already then,
which I see a bit more clearly now, and which I also meant when I
threw the name Leibniz into the conversation; this is also the selfsame thing that I had in mind a short while ago, when I wanted to
provide a plan for the advancement of our conversation.

GUIDE: It might be beneficial to our conversation for us to engage ourselves more closely with what unsettled you then. If I surmise correctly, it is the horizon in which all of our reflections are moving
more or less thoughtlessly and as if by themselves.

SCHOLAR: We must open up this horizon and, insofar as it is opened up
yet still murky, we must illuminate it. It seems to me that we humans
by nature move within such horizons. The human is—if I may put
this in a makeshift manner of speaking—a horizonal being.[28]

---

28. The German *horizontal*, commonly used as a synonym for *waagerecht* meaning "horizontal," can also be understood as the adjectival form of *Horizont* (horizon), and in this sense it is translated here and below as "horizonal." Likewise, *das
Horizontale* is generally translated as "horizonality," and sometimes as "the
horizonal."—*Tr.*

SCIENTIST: I think he is rather a vertical being, insofar as he is in a sense oriented upwards.

SCHOLAR: I understand [the German word] *horizontal,* not as "horizontal" in contrast to "vertical," but rather in the sense of "horizonal." That is to say, I understand horizonality to essentially entail an open circle-of-vision [*Gesichtskreis*] or a receding depth of vision [*Gesichtsflucht*] (*fuga*),[29] which surrounds it in all directions. What you mean by the vertical is possible only within the horizonal so understood. [84]

SCIENTIST: Could you further clarify what you mean by the horizon in terms of the context which has now led us to this notion?

SCHOLAR: I will try to do so, while admitting that I presage only a little of the essence of the horizon, and even this I can only intimate in a rough manner.

GUIDE: Surmises offer here a purer assurance than all presumptuous certainties, from which the enigma flees.

SCHOLAR: You give me courage to thoughtfully pursue what is barely presaged.

SCIENTIST: And it seems to me that we should learn that what is uncertain loses its truth if it is accommodated too immediately and altogether in certainties.

GUIDE: We learn the courage [*Mut*] to surmise [*Vermuten*] in the conversation from the conversation.

SCHOLAR: And all wisdom would consist then only in the higher thoughtfulness of surmising.

SCIENTIST: So it would be almost dangerous for a human to ever be called wise.

GUIDE: Presumably this would be his greatest danger, which he could never overcome, but could only at best withstand if he had something so enigmatic to surmise that there was never any time left for him to think of his name.

SCHOLAR: Then those who might help us with saying and naming could least of all concern themselves with names.

---

29. The uncommon term *Gesichtsflucht* presumably indicates here the perspectival depth-dimension of the horizonal circle-of-vision. A *Gesichtsflucht* might be understood in the sense of a *Fluchtlinie,* a perspectival "line of sight," such as a view of a row of houses down a street or of a row of rooms down a hallway. Like the English "flight," *Flucht* has two etymological sources. *Flucht* in the sense of a straight line or alignment is related to flight in the sense of "to fly," as in a row of flying geese. But Heidegger connects *Flucht* here rather with the Latin *fuga,* and thus with "flight" in the sense of "to flee," as in the case of an animal fleeing from a hunter. It is also noteworthy that Heidegger uses the term *Gesichtsflucht* in the singular, although it is said to surround in all directions.—*Tr.*

GUIDE: Because this is probably the case, there are presumably no wise ones, no sages [*Weisen*]. However, this does not preclude that one may be a *Weiser* in the sense of a guide,[30] where by this word I do not mean one who knows [*Wissenden*], [85] but rather one who is capable of pointing [*weisen*] into that wherefrom hints come to humans. Such a guide [*Weiser*] is also able to show [*weisen*] the manner [*Weise*], the way, in which these hints are to be followed.

SCHOLAR: Then wisdom [*Weisheit*] would be the capacity for such showing [*Weisen*].

GUIDE: Better yet, the privilege to attempt such showing.

SCIENTIST: These are strange things that we are touching on. And I would also like to no longer remain silent here about the following. In our conversations it always seems to me as if [one's] standing and name—indeed, even one's own accustomed daily being [*tägliche Wesen*]—were to vanish.

SCHOLAR: Would this not be due to the fact that during the conversations another horizon opens up?

GUIDE: Presumably it is connected with what we call "horizon," which we hardly yet know.

SCIENTIST: But which we are now attempting to clarify, in order to proceed more securely when we let ourselves engage in non-willing.

SCHOLAR: By "more securely" you probably mean that it will be more specifically determined for us wherein it is that what we mean by non-willing, and thus also thinking in its essence, belong.

SCIENTIST: That is what I mean. In fact I believe that much would already be gained if we even just had a name for the horizon into which non-willing directs us.

SCHOLAR: But prior to that we should have clarity about the horizon in general, so that we don't become fools of a mere name.

GUIDE: Though the fool is often nearer to the sage [*dem Weisen*] than are the [86] advocates of sound common sense. But anyway, you wanted to convey to us your surmises about the horizon.

SCHOLAR: What I have to say about that is hardly worth mentioning and has already frequently been thought by the thinkers.

GUIDE: But in frequent thoughts are perhaps concealed the *singular* true enigmas.

SCHOLAR: Everything among which we humans reside, whether it particularly concerns us or not, we know in a certain manner, for

30. The German name for "the Guide" in the conversation is *der Weise*. While this word usually means "sage" or "wise man," it is etymologically related not only to *wissen* (to know) and *Weisheit* (wisdom), but also to *weisen* (to show, to point) and to *Weise* (manner, way). While a *Weiser* is normally thought of as one who is wise, here a *Weiser* is understood rather as one who can indicate a way. On the translation of *der Weise* as "the Guide," see footnote 14 in the foreword to this volume.—*Tr.*

example the house, the mountain, the tree, the sky, the night, the goat, the jug. By "knowing" [»Kennen«] I mean that we are familiar [bekannt] with them.

SCIENTIST: We know our way around with regard to what each one of the objects is.

SCHOLAR: This knowing one's way around [Sichauskennen] with regard to what things are is what the Greeks named τέχνη.

GUIDE: About which we have already said a few things today. In τέχνη the outward look, into which individual things emerge, is brought into sight and is in *this* sense brought forward and produced [vor- und hervorgebracht].

SCHOLAR: By means of τέχνη a surrounding circle of the visible outward look of things, the circle-of-vision, is held open. When we, for example, stand before a tree and look at it—be it fleetingly or be it studiously—then we always catch sight of more than what we see in this tree. We catch sight of treeness [das Baumhafte].[31] We look—at the moment I cannot say this otherwise—out into treeness and so look over and away from what we see, and yet in such a manner that it is only through this looking out beyond what is to be seen and what has been seen, that we see the individual tree.

SCIENTIST: But treeness is not something that grows somewhere next to or above individual trees. I don't understand [87] why you then say of treeness that it, as it were, lies out beyond the individual tree. Treeness is after all simply the general representational idea that we make for ourselves of trees.

SCHOLAR: "Of trees," you say. From where do you get "trees" unless you have already looked out into the nature of trees [das Baumartige]?

SCIENTIST: To be frank, I am also perplexed here.

GUIDE: We are all perplexed here. And I almost think that we are never yet perplexed enough, and accordingly are never yet sufficiently watchful. When you say that the nature of trees, from out of which we first see a tree as a tree, is a representational idea [Vorstellung], this is accurate to the extent that what is tree-like is set out before us; but it is in no way made by us. The nature of trees is brought forth in τέχνη, as we said. But this does not mean that it is manufactured. Some-

31. The term "treeness" (das Baumhafte) is used here in the general sense of "what is characteristic of trees." A Platonist would of course understand "treeness" as the metaphysical Form or Idea of a tree (see below, p. 58); the Demiurge creates trees with an eye to the Form of treeness, analogous to the way in which a carpenter makes a table by looking beyond the wood-material to his idea of what the table should look like. Heidegger, however, is not only raising again the question of the nature of this treeness that lets a tree show itself as a tree, but also critically reflecting on the manner in which transcendental-horizonal thinking and the metaphysics of production have responded to this question.—Tr.

thing is brought to sight, which we—from where and how, I do not know—have received. Treeness, indeed the entire circle-of-vision for that among which we reside, is not our work. The horizon goes out beyond us and our capability. By looking out into the horizon, we look and we climb out beyond ourselves.

SCHOLAR: Insofar as treeness and everything of its kind never remain restricted to individual trees and individual things, what has the character of a horizon does not only go out beyond us humans, but also goes out beyond the corresponding objects. The talk of going out beyond and transcending, or literally climbing over [*Übersteigen*], is thus in various respects justified.

GUIDE: We would, however, still need to take into consideration the fact that we conceive of what we name—more awkwardly than knowingly—"the horizon," from us and from objects, and not from that which the [88] so-named is in itself and in its own relation to us and to objects.

SCHOLAR: If this were to be considered seriously and together with all its consequences, then indeed all that we have said about the horizon and the horizonal essence of the human would with a single blow be rendered untenable.

GUIDE: To begin with I would not like to go so far. In the representation of the human's horizonal going out beyond himself and of the horizonal transcending or climbing over objects, there presumably lies a particularly formed, but at the same time an initially necessary, interpretation of a relationship which could, however, in its time manifest itself otherwise and indeed in its originary truth.

SCIENTIST: In our comments just now on the horizonal essence of the human, what we are dealing with is after all, if I see this correctly, the traditional determination of the essence of *homo* as *animal rationale*, except that a few traits of his essential constitution have been more clearly drawn out.

SCHOLAR: Certainly. The reference to the horizonal essence of the human does not mean to introduce any innovations, but rather solely to appropriate the soundness of the old.

GUIDE: With this attitude, follow the thinkers to whom reckoning with the distinction of new and old is foreign; for the more clearly a thinker experiences that every thinker thinks the selfsame as every other, the more purely he attains to his calling.

SCIENTIST: You understand the selfsame here in the previously mentioned sense, and do not mean the monotonous homogeneity of the indistinct.

SCHOLAR: What is selfsame can only be what is different; indeed [89] the purest selfsame rests in the most different. I would almost like to assert the reverse: The different rests in the pure selfsame.

GUIDE: You are now thinking of what came to us regarding rest?

SCHOLAR: I am most decidedly thinking of this.

GUIDE: And also of what we noticed about nearness and farness?

SCHOLAR: Why this?

GUIDE: Perhaps one day we will have the good fortune to experience something of this, if we attend not just to the thinkers, but moreover to what addresses itself to them.

SCIENTIST: So you mean that what the thinkers say, for example, about the essence of the human, is not put forward and worked out by them?

GUIDE: The essential determination of the human is an event [Geschehnis] that the thinkers do not make, but rather only express.

SCHOLAR: Thus you also said that the relationship, which gives itself to be known in the horizonal essence of the human, could in its time manifest itself more originarily.

GUIDE: It is such as you say.

SCIENTIST: Yet such a manifestation would have to entail that first the established essence of the human would be, as it were, eliminated.

GUIDE: As I recall, we already spoke of something similar.

SCHOLAR: When we referred to the defense of nature against technology. [90]

SCIENTIST: The discussion at that time was in fact of an annihilation of the human. My feeling, however, was that this was an audacious and largely indeterminate assertion.

GUIDE: Presumably we are now on the way to removing the appearance of audacity and indeterminateness.

SCHOLAR: That is, if we first get sufficiently clear about what it is that is supposed to fall prey to the annihilation; and this is, after all, the essence of occidental humankind that has held sway up until now.

GUIDE: Hence, I also made an effort to prompt you to provide a sharper characterization of the essential definition of the human, which appears to be attainable with reference to horizonality.

SCHOLAR: I do not want to purport to achieve too much with an illumination of the horizonal essence of the human. I thus ventured only to touch on this, because I expected from this reference a greater clarity regarding the direction of our path. What mattered for me was only that we reach an understanding in advance regarding that out-toward-which we think when we, following your answer, let ourselves engage in non-willing. Now I am concerned that, by means of an all too eager discussion of the horizonal essence of the human, we are only conferring with one another about the direction of the path instead of bravely advancing down it.

GUIDE: It seems to me that this concern is groundless.

SCIENTIST: If you were right, then, while examining the horizon-essence of the human, we would have to already be advancing in the direction of the path indicated to us by your answer. I would in addition like to note the following, if for once too I may speak paradoxically: The horizonal essence of the human—by which is meant that, in looking into a horizon, the human transcends the objects and his own representing [91] of these objects—and this relationship between the human and the horizon, to which relationship the horizon belongs as a member, in sum, this entire relationship would itself be the horizon into which our conversation is now thinking.

SCHOLAR: I don't find your formulation to be so paradoxical at all, but rather, in spite of all its awkwardness, to be excellent.

GUIDE: It is so fitting that it enables the direction and object of our conversation to be more clearly delimited.

SCHOLAR: With regard to the essence of the human just explicated, we can say: The human is, as the *animal rationale,* the living being who thinks. However, insofar as horizonality—that is to say, the relation to the horizon—is what distinguishes the human, while thinking is the distinguishing characteristic of the human, thinking must, as it were, embody the essence of horizonality. Thinking is really nothing other than the representational setting-before [*Vor-stellen*] and setting-toward [*Zu-stellen*] of the horizon, that is, of the circle-of-vision, in which the outward look and the essence of objects—Plato named it the Idea of things—becomes[32] visible to us.

SCIENTIST: Our conversation's question about the essence of thinking is thus a question about the distinguishing characteristic of the living beings that we ourselves are.

SCHOLAR: Our conversation is then really concerned with the essence of the human.

SCIENTIST: To formulate and answer the question of the human is the task of philosophical anthropology, which today is repeatedly heralded by everyone to be the obvious foundation for all philosophy. [92]

SCHOLAR: It seems to me as though it has suddenly become quite bright over our path.

SCIENTIST: And I am almost shocked that we did not settle from the start on this simple and unambiguous horizon for our inquiry into the essence of thinking, and thereby spare ourselves the many detours.

SCHOLAR: If it had right away become clear to us that the question of the essence of thinking is an anthropological one, we could have

---

32. The singular "becomes" would seem to be a grammatical error in the text, since the subject—namely "the outward look and the essence of objects"—is plural. But presumably this is intentional, stressing that these are thought to be the same thing.—*Tr.*

also immediately turned to the doctrines and theories of contemporary anthropology, by means of which we could have enriched our conversation and brought it more quickly to actual results. It is just remarkable that we could have so clumsily overlooked a correct procedure which lies so near and is so simple.

GUIDE: There is something very peculiar about the simple. Perhaps nothing conceals itself so stubbornly and deceptively behind a mere appearance of simplicity as does the simple.

SCIENTIST: Such that what looks to be simple in the highest degree is in truth the most confusingly entangled.

SCHOLAR: And what presents itself as a jumbled knot which cannot be disentangled, is the simple itself.

SCIENTIST: Now, even with my best will and intention [*beim besten Willen*], I must admit that I cannot discover anything confusing or unclear in our present inquiry. To recount yet one more time what we have already ascertained, we are meditating on the essence of thinking. We will to let ourselves engage in non-willing, because supposedly the sought-for essence of thinking is to be found in this vicinity. We ask: into where is it that we are looking ahead in this procedure? We seek the horizon in which non-willing stands, and so attempt to determine the circle-of-vision in which the essence of thinking appears to us. [93] Insofar as the human is the living being that thinks, it becomes apparent that the single and unambiguous horizon into which we are inquiring is the essence of the human. Is there, so I ask, a simpler manner of posing a question than this? Answering this question may indeed involve greater difficulties. Yet, as one is accustomed to saying, with the right manner of posing the question one is well on the way to arriving at the answer.

GUIDE: The essence of the human is for us the horizon in our meditation on the essence of thinking. As we found, however, the essence of the human as the living being that thinks is itself distinguished precisely by its relation to the horizon, that is, by its horizonal character. What serves [*dient*] as the horizon for our meditation on the horizon, namely the essence of the human, already carries horizonality with itself. By looking out-toward the essence of the human, and with this essence, we make use [*bedienen uns*] of a horizon which is supposed to encompass the essence of horizonality and which at the same time is itself co-determined by horizonality.

SCIENTIST: Evidently.

GUIDE: And you call this a simple posing of a question? I find that the initial positing [*Ansetzung*] of a horizon for the question about the essence of horizonality is confusing. This apparently unavoidable approach [*Ansatz*] is perhaps the formula for an entanglement from which it is difficult to free ourselves.

SCHOLAR: In establishing a horizon for the determination of the essence of thinking, we are, in fact, initially positing the horizon for the horizon.

SCIENTIST: We are endeavoring to attain a horizon to the second power [*Horizont in der Potenz*], whereupon, it seems to me, this second power will itself in turn require a horizon.

SCHOLAR: Hence, with the unavoidable raising to the next power [*Potenzierung*][33] of the horizon, the question immediately arises: In [94] what power [*Potenz*] is the conclusive [*abschließende*] horizon— that is, indeed, the proper horizon—reached?

SCIENTIST: This question is here superfluous, since what ensues is an endless succession of horizons encased in one another.

SCHOLAR: Then there would be no final horizon. Since each horizon is referred on to a further horizon, the horizon as such would remain without limit. But then how is the horizon supposed to be what its own name says?[34] How is it supposed to be what delimits if it essentially lacks limits? A limitless horizon is like a crooked straight line [*ungerade Gerade*].

SCIENTIST: Something that annihilates itself before it can exist; a sheer impossibility.

GUIDE: And yet you said that accommodating the question of the essence of thinking in the horizon of the question of the essence of the human would be the simplest manner of posing the question for our conversation. Now this simplest matter, the question about the horizon of horizonality, has suddenly become a sheer impossibility.

SCIENTIST: The matter of the simple is, in fact, not at all simple.

GUIDE: With the simple itself matters are presumably simple, but not with our relationship to the simple.

SCIENTIST: Then we must avoid precisely the question about the horizon for the horizon and its essence.

SCHOLAR: And so attempt to determine the essence of the horizon and of horizonality—and this means to determine the representational relation to the horizon, and that means to determine the essence of thinking—without a horizon. [95]

SCIENTIST: That would amount to saying: the horizon is horizon.

SCHOLAR: It is itself and nothing other.

---

33. The term *potenzieren* is used in mathematics to mean "to raise to the power of." The image evoked here is that of a horizonal circle of, say, 2 meters diameter, which would be encompassed by a further horizonal circle of 2×2 meters diameter, which would in turn be encompassed by a horizonal circle of 2×2×2 meters diameter, and so on. In other words, what is at issue is the problem of "the horizon of the horizon of the horizon . . ."—*Tr.*

34. The Greek word *horizon* derives from *horizein*, meaning "to bound or limit," and from *horos*, meaning "boundary."—*Tr.*

SCIENTIST: Indeed, the horizon need not be anything further.

GUIDE: But then what in the world is the horizon?

SCHOLAR: To say, the horizon is horizon, surely remains what is most simple.

SCIENTIST: Then again the sentence also says nothing.

GUIDE: Or everything, if only one could rightly think it.

SCHOLAR: Yet what does "rightly" mean here?

GUIDE: I too ask this.

SCIENTIST: And what does "thinking" mean here?

GUIDE: We are all asking this, and together hanging helplessly over the abyss of the simple.

SCHOLAR: Why is that?

GUIDE: There cannot be, after all, a simpler task than to grasp the horizon just as horizon.

SCIENTIST: One would have to experience the horizon itself, to experience it as the selfsame with itself.

SCHOLAR: Instead of proceeding out beyond the horizon and on to something else.

GUIDE: But insofar as the tendency to such a going-out-beyond would subsist, indeed would even be firmly rooted in the human, then he would have to attempt to right away and constantly turn back to the horizon as the selfsame, rather than to go beyond and away from the horizon.

SCIENTIST: How should one and why does one need to first [96] turn back, if he does not at all go forward, but rather simply remains?

GUIDE: As if remaining were so simple.

SCHOLAR: It of course does not occur of itself by means of a mere not-going-away.

GUIDE: By what means does this occur, assuming that it does even occur?

SCHOLAR: Remaining consists in an abiding [*Verweilen*].

GUIDE: During which we release ourselves over to an abiding-while [*Weile*] which takes us up, such that this abiding-while is what, as it were, brings us to abide [*uns ver-weilt*].

SCHOLAR: And we would only have to be mindful that we release ourselves to it.

GUIDE: Mindfully turn ourselves toward it.[35]

SCHOLAR: Toward that which it has left behind for us of what holds in reserve.

GUIDE: Such that we turn back into the abiding-while, and so remaining would after all be a re-turn, a turning-back?

---

35. The phrase *sich an etwas kehren*, literally, "to turn oneself to something," idiomatically means "to mind" or "to care about something."—*Tr.*

SCIENTIST: Do I sense correctly, or is it only an idea that has coincidentally occurred to me [*zufälliger Einfall*], when I surmise that something similar prevails in remaining and in the selfsameness of the selfsame?

GUIDE: That is a magnificent idea that has occurred to you [*Einfall*]. Everything essential that we think is an idea that has come (in)to us [*uns ein-gefallen*], whereby we would only need to know into where it is that it comes, when it occurs to us [*wohinein es uns zu-fällt*].

SCHOLAR: And perhaps also, from where?

SCIENTIST: So the occurrence of a coincidence [*Zu-fall*] is something other than a gap in a series of causes.

GUIDE: Coincidence is interrelated with the essence of the selfsame and selfsameness. Whenever a coincidence comes forth [*Zu-fall*], something turns back. [97]

SCIENTIST: Yet we found that the selfsame is a matter of something belonging together with something. If something, for example the horizon, is itself supposed to be the selfsame with itself, then it must itself be, as it were, an other.

GUIDE: Not just as it were, but truly.

SCHOLAR: Therefore an other belongs to the horizon.

GUIDE: Or the horizon belongs to an other. This is why I repeatedly had the desire to push you to describe the essence of the horizon still more precisely.

SCHOLAR: Should I once again declare that I can only bring forward a few things, and what I do bring forward remain for the most part only historiological references? Of such a kind is also the precious inspiration that I mentioned at the beginning of our conversation, although even now is not yet the opportunity to bring it into the discussion.

SCIENTIST: But historiological references have often helped us along in our conversation; think of the revealing mention of the Greek word τέχνη in the discussion of the essence of technology; think of the reference to the Leibnizian distinction of *perceptio* and *appetitus* on the occasion of our discussion about the relation between thinking and willing.

SCHOLAR: This time—that is to say, for the explanation of horizonality that is now necessary—I refer back to Kant, even though the horizonal character of representing and thus of striving was first clearly seen and said by Leibniz in his doctrines of mirror-being, of the concentricity of world-being, and of the eye- and view-point of the monad.[36]

---

36. While it is not clear what specific terms Heidegger is referring to here, relevant passages can be found in Leibniz's *Monadology*, paragraphs 50–60.—*Tr.*

GUIDE: Nietzsche thought the selfsame, albeit with the difference that this entails, in his doctrine of the [98] perspectival constitution of the will to power. But you wanted to explain to us the essence of horizonality by way of Kant.

SCHOLAR: To the horizonal belongs the transcendental and vice versa. "Transcendental" [»*Transzendental*«] is the designation Kant used for what we already spoke of in terms of transcending or climbing over [*Übersteigens*] and going-out-beyond [*Hinausgehens*].[37] What treeness is in relation to a tree and individual trees, actual as well as possible ones, that is objectness in relation to objects. It contains the outward view [*Aussicht*] into the outward look [*Aussehen*] of what is objective and its particular field, for example into that of nature or of an art-work. This view surrounds as circle-of-vision the perceptual representation of individual objects. It is the horizon of these objects and of the perceiving that is directed at them, and is itself a construct of a representational setting-before [*Vor-stellens*]. Going-out-beyond individual objects, this representational setting-before in advance first pro-vides [*zu-stellt*] perceptions with an outward view into the possible outward look of objects. This pro-viding representation [*zu-stellende Vorstellen*] forms the horizon as an accessory to all representing. Kant named the climbing over objects and over the perceiving directed at them, which prevails in such horizon-forming representing: the transcendental. With this naming, however, Kant did not just introduce a Latin designation for something already known; rather, by means of this naming he first of all clearly brought the transcending or climbing-over character of horizon-forming representation into view.

SCIENTIST: According to your account, one could almost think that Kant's philosophical achievement consists in the introduction of the word "transcendental."

SCHOLAR: So it does in truth; it remains only to be noted that this word "transcendental" was already in use since [99] the Middle Ages, which is why Kant's achievement is to be further restricted to the fact that he merely assigned to this word an especially emphatic usage.

SCIENTIST: But surely you would agree that it would be an awful exaggeration if one were to claim that the achievement of the great thinkers consists in each case in the introduction of a new word or even just in the emphasis of a word already in use.

SCHOLAR: This exaggeration would not be so awful at all.

GUIDE: If it is even an exaggeration.

---

37. Kant writes: "I entitle *transcendental* all [cognition] which is occupied not so much with objects as with the mode of our [cognition] of objects in so far as this mode of [cognition] is to be possible *a priori*" (*Critique of Pure Reason*, p. 59 [A 11–12/B 25]).—*Tr.*

SCHOLAR: One could, for example, imagine the possibility that a thinker would be a thinker solely on account of the fact that he reintroduces into linguistic usage a single, long-familiar word—for example, the Greek word ἀλήθεια.

GUIDE: Such a thing seems to me to be quite possible.

SCIENTIST: But I could not really allow this to count as research work and as creative achievement, which are after all the predicates we want to use to distinguish all genuine philosophy.

GUIDE: Perhaps this tending to a single word would be neither work nor achievement.

SCHOLAR: What else would it be then?

GUIDE: Perhaps only a waiting upon the coming [*Einfall*] of the word.

SCHOLAR: Which suddenly comes in [*einfällt*] like the wind.

GUIDE: Into the tree towering in stillness.

SCIENTIST: Then would work not be what is highest?

GUIDE: Neither work nor discipline. [100]

SCIENTIST: But rather?

GUIDE: Thanking and attentiveness.

SCHOLAR: Whenever I have been able to be attentive, I have long heard the word "thanking" [»*Danken*«] in the word "thoughts" [»*Gedanken*«].

SCIENTIST: So would thinking be a thanking?

GUIDE: Presumably we could tell if we were to know what thinking is.

SCHOLAR: We are yet still on the way to this.

SCIENTIST: And in such a manner that even the byways always have something to offer.

SCHOLAR: What do you mean by this?

SCIENTIST: We just touched on the relationship of thinkers to linguistic usage. Assuming that within single words dwells the carrying capacity [*Tragkraft*] to gather within themselves the thinking of a thinker, then these words would also have to be understood in the fullness of their saying capacity [*Sagekraft*].

SCHOLAR: Which entails that a thinker says more with such words than we others think with the word.

GUIDE: The thinker even says more than he himself can know, such that he is surprised and above all surpassed by the inexhaustibility of his own word.

SCHOLAR: So the word "transcendental" carries the entirety of Kantian metaphysics.

SCIENTIST: And by the "transcendental" Kant always also means the horizonal.

SCHOLAR: Why do you make special note of this?

SCIENTIST: Because, according to my admittedly in no way [101] expert knowledge, Kant characterizes the horizonal neither as clearly nor certainly as specifically as he does the transcendental.

GUIDE: What might be the reason for this?

SCHOLAR: Presumably the reason is that, for Kant, what we call the horizon is the construct of transcendental representation.

SCIENTIST: And what does this mean for Kant?

SCHOLAR: The horizon is constructed as construct [*bildet sich als Gebild*] in the productivity of the transcendental imagination [*Einbildungskraft*]. As the being that transcendentally represents, the human is in a certain sense creative. But Kant avoids depicting the construct of creative imagination, namely the horizon, specifically on its own. All the same it is there for him, though not as an object.

GUIDE: Then out of caution would Kant prefer to remain silent about the horizon?

SCIENTIST: And not because he overlooked it.

SCHOLAR: The transcendental and the horizonal are inseparable.

SCIENTIST: And thus the selfsame. If we attempt to more precisely determine this selfsame, now in view of the transcendental, just as previously we did in view of the horizonal, then we run into the same difficulty as we did with the determination of the essence of the horizon, where we inquired as a matter of course into the horizon of the horizon. In order to be able to find out something about the transcendent [*sic!*],[38] we must representationally climb out beyond over-climbing representing, and so on *ad infinitum*.

SCHOLAR: Just as a limitless horizon makes no sense, so does a bridgeless transcendence collapse in on itself. [102] Thus, in order to grasp the essence of transcendence, we must refrain from climbing over it and remain with it itself.

SCIENTIST: But, as we now realize, this means that with regard to transcendence we must also attempt to experience the other of itself, which it itself is as the selfsame.

SCHOLAR: If now what was just said is the case for transcendence as well as for the horizon, and if the two belong together in the transcendental-horizonal essence of the human, then it is also the case that the essence of the human can be inquired into neither transcendentally nor horizonally.

GUIDE: Whoever has once recognized this can no longer evade considering whether the question about the essence of the human could at all be a question about the human; for after what has been thought through it is now necessary to look toward the other of the transcendentally horizonal, the other which is nevertheless the horizonally transcendental itself.

SCIENTIST: If, however, a meditation on the essence of the human cannot consist of a question about the human, then there is some-

38. This "[*sic!*]" appears in the *Gesamtausgabe* edition. —*Tr.*

thing amiss with the vociferous claims of philosophical anthropology in answering the question of what the human is.

SCHOLAR: For with regard to this question philosophical anthropology
not only has nothing to answer, but also no longer anything to ask.
The heretofore authoritative interpretation of the human being
[*Menschenwesen*] as the *animal rationale* is, though, based on an experiencing that immediately looks at the human himself as a living
being [*Lebewesen*] among other living beings.

GUIDE: Nonetheless, this interpretation of the human being is not a
biological interpretation, as one may think; it is not even a biologi-
cally based interpretation. [103]

SCIENTIST: But it is after all based on the initial positing of the human
as *animal* [Latin for "animate being"], as ζῷον, as living being—not
to say with Nietzsche, as animal!

GUIDE: We still know but little about the origin of the determination of
our own essence. How little we know about this should have been
clear to us in the beginning of our conversation, when we considered
whether the determination of the human essence is the answer to a
question, or the answer [*Antwort*] to the word [*Wort*]. It could be the
case, not only that the determination of the human essence does not
originate in a question about the human, but that it does not originate from a question at all, precisely for the reason that this determination cannot be obtained from the human.

SCIENTIST: The origin of the definition of essence that prevails in the
Occident is thus veiled in darkness.

SCHOLAR: And this origin may be difficult to ever illuminate, since we
lack the sources to establish who first pronounced the definition.

GUIDE: Understood in that manner, however, the question about the
origin of the definition of the human essence is unimportant. I understand something else by the origin of the determination of the
human essence.

SCHOLAR: Do you mean perhaps the horizon and the initial positing of
the horizon, within which the essence of the human interpreted as
animal rationale is caught sight of?

GUIDE: What I mean lies in this direction. In meditating on the origin
of the interpretation of essence, what is at issue is knowing whether
in general a horizon, and if so in what sense and in what manner
the horizon is what is determinative, that is to say, is what provides
the measure, in the experience of the essence of the human as
ζῷον. [104] Yet I also mean this: as long as we think with regard to
the horizon without knowing its essential origin, we don't yet think
the question of origin itself originarily.

SCIENTIST: I don't understand why you are so set on the question of
origin.

GUIDE: You are not alone if you don't understand this. But perhaps we could reflect for a moment—by way of another course on the country path—on the strange matter that the human does not think about and is not acquainted with the provenance of his essential determination. Not at home in his own essence, he arrogantly purports to master the world and to rule over and bring to order the various realms of humanity [*Menschentümer*].[39]

SCHOLAR: But how is the human ever supposed to be able to know his provenance?

GUIDE: Pay close attention to a distinction. I do not mean that the human is supposed to first discover where he stems from. I only think that he might meditate on what the now-prevailing determination of his essence is based in.

SCHOLAR: In place of the question of where the thinking animal called the human comes from, you put a meditation on what is really prevailing in the interpretation of the human that experiences him as a thinking animal.

GUIDE: This is what I mean; and thus I spoke not of the provenance of the human, but rather of the provenance of the interpretation of the essence of the human.

SCIENTIST: And so you assume that the heretofore definitive interpretation of the essence of the human does not have absolute validity.

GUIDE: Can you somehow prove that it does possess absolute validity?
[105]

SCIENTIST: No.

GUIDE: Then we are both in the same condition [*im selben Fall*].

SCHOLAR: Or this time only in a similar condition [*im gleichen*].

GUIDE: Even that is enough.

SCIENTIST: So what you will is to get out to a new definition of the human.

GUIDE: You have forgotten what we thought about "new" and "old." Moreover, I do not will to get out to a "definition." As you know, I will only non-willing.

SCHOLAR: And we are meditating on the horizon in which this non-willing could encounter us.

SCIENTIST: We are asking about the essence of the horizon and the possible determination of this essence.

---

39. *Menschentümer* is an unusual plural form of *Menschentum,* which is the common word for "humankind." In the sense that *Griechentum* refers to the (ancient) Greek world, presumably Heidegger is thinking here of "Western humanity" together with the other geographically and historically determined realms of humanity. (Also see below, pp. 136, 154.) —*Tr.*

GUIDE: Insofar as the human as *animal rationale* is the transcendental-horizonal being, then, with this question about the essence of the horizon, we are discussing the essence of the human and the manner and provenance of this determination of essence.

SCIENTIST: And on this occasion you last asserted that the question about the essence of the human is not a question about the human.[40]

GUIDE: I only said that it would be unavoidable for us to consider whether the question about the essence of the human would need to be put in this manner.

SCIENTIST: All the same, it is to me incomprehensible that the essence of the human could ever be found by looking away from the human.

GUIDE: It is incomprehensible to me as well; and so I seek to attain clarity about the extent to which this is possible or even necessary. [106]

SCIENTIST: To catch sight of the essence of the human without looking at the human?

GUIDE: Yes. And if thinking is the distinguishing mark of the essence of the human, then what is essential to this essence, namely the essence of thinking, can be first properly caught sight of only insofar as we look away from thinking.

SCHOLAR: Yet thinking, conceived of in the traditional manner as representing, is a willing; even Kant conceives of thinking in this manner when he characterizes it as spontaneity. Thinking is willing, and willing is thinking.

SCIENTIST: The assertion that the essence of thinking is something other than thinking, then, says that thinking is something other than willing.

GUIDE: That is why, in answer to your question as to what I really will in our meditation on the essence of thinking, I replied: I will non-willing.

SCIENTIST: Meanwhile this expression has clearly shown itself to be ambiguous.

40. The revised excerpt from this text which was published in 1959 (hereafter referred to as the "1959 excerpt") begins here and, while excluding several sections and passages, continues to the end. See "Zur Erörterung der Gelassenheit: Aus einem Feldweggespräch über das Denken," in *Gelassenheit* (Pfullingen: Neske, 10th ed. 1992), pp. 29–71 (reprinted in *GA* 13, pp. 37–74); "Conversation on a Country Path about Thinking," *Discourse on Thinking*, trans. John M. Anderson and E. Hans Freund (New York: Harper & Row, 1966), pp. 58–90. Parenthetical citations of the 1959 excerpt in subsequent notes will refer to the pagination of the German text (abbreviated as *G*) followed by a slash and the pagination of the English translation (abbreviated as *DT*). I have retranslated all of the text which appeared in that excerpt, but will make note of any significant alterations that Heidegger made to the German text in 1959.—*Tr.*.

SCHOLAR: Non-willing still signifies, on the one hand, a willing, in that a *No* prevails in it, even if it is in the sense of a *No* that directs itself at willing itself and renounces it. Non-willing in this sense means: to willfully renounce willing. And then, on the other hand, the expression non-willing also means: that which does not at all pertain to the will.

SCIENTIST: Which can therefore also never be accomplished or achieved by a willing.

GUIDE: But perhaps we come nearer to it through a willing in the first sense of non-willing.

SCHOLAR: So you see the one and the other non-willing in a definite relation to one another. [107]

GUIDE: I not only see this relation. Let me confess that it has appealed to me, if not indeed called on me, ever since I began attempting to reflect on what moves our conversation.

SCIENTIST: Am I right to assume the following determination of the relation between the one and the other non-willing: You will a non-willing in the sense of a renouncing of willing, so that through this renouncing we can let ourselves engage in—or at least prepare ourselves for an engagement in—the sought-for essence of that thinking which is not a willing.

GUIDE: Not only do you assume correctly, but you have—"by the gods," I would say, if they had not flown from us—found something essential.

SCHOLAR: If any of us were in a position to mete out praise, and if this were not to run contrary to the style of our conversations, I would be tempted to say now that you have surpassed both us and yourself with this interpretation of the ambiguous talk of non-willing.

SCIENTIST: That I succeeded in this was not due to me, but rather to the night which has in the meantime fallen upon us, and which compels concentration without using force.

SCHOLAR: By slowing down our pace, it allows us time to ponder.

GUIDE: Which is why we are also far away from human habitation.

SCIENTIST: Ever more relaxed, I am coming to trust the inconspicuous escort who takes us by the hand or, more aptly said, by the word in this conversation.

SCHOLAR: This escort is also needed, since the conversation is becoming ever more difficult. [108]

GUIDE: If by difficult you mean what is unaccustomed, which consists in the fact that we are disaccustoming ourselves to the will.

SCHOLAR: To the will, you say, and not just to willing—

SCIENTIST: —and so you pronounce a rousing proposal in a relaxed [*gelassen*] manner.

GUIDE: If only I already had the necessary releasement [*Gelassenheit*],[41] then I would soon be relieved of this disaccustoming.

SCHOLAR: Insofar as we can at least disaccustom ourselves to willing, we contribute to the awakening of releasement.

GUIDE: Or rather to the remaining-awake for releasement.

SCHOLAR: Why not, to the awakening?

GUIDE: Because we do not awaken releasement in ourselves from out of ourselves.

SCIENTIST: So releasement is effected from somewhere else.

GUIDE: Not effected, but rather allowed [*zugelassen*].

SCHOLAR: Although I don't yet know what the word releasement means, I do have a vague sense that it awakens when our essence is allowed to let itself engage in that which is not a willing.

SCIENTIST: You talk everywhere of a letting, such that the impression arises that what is meant is a kind of passivity. At the same time, I believe I understand that it is in no way a matter of impotently letting things slide and drift along.

SCHOLAR: Perhaps concealing itself in releasement is a higher activity than that found in all the doings of the world and in all the machinations of the realms of humankind. [109]

GUIDE: Only this higher activity is in fact not an activity.

SCIENTIST: Then releasement lies—if we may still speak of a lying here—outside the distinction between activity and passivity.

SCHOLAR: Because it does not belong to the domain of the will.

SCIENTIST: The transition out of willing into releasement is what seems to me to be the genuine difficulty.

GUIDE: And all the more so, when for us the essence of releasement is still concealed.

SCHOLAR: And this above all as a result of the fact that even releasement can be thought of still within the domain of the will, as happens with the old masters of thought such as Meister Eckhart.[42]

GUIDE: From whom, all the same, many good things can be learned.

SCHOLAR: Certainly; but what we are calling releasement evidently does not mean the casting-off of sinful selfishness and the letting-go of self-will in favor of the divine will.

41. See the foreword at the front of this volume (pp. xii–xv) for comments on this key notion of releasement (*Gelassenheit*).—*Tr.*

42. See Eckhart's use of the term *gelāzenheit* in his "Talks of Instruction" ("Councils on Discernment"), no. 21; Meister Eckehart, *Deutsche Predigten und Traktate*, ed. and trans. Josef Quint (Munich: Carl Hanser, 1963), p. 91; *Meister Eckhart: The Essential Sermons, Commentaries, Treatises, and Defense*, trans. Edmund-Colledge and Bernard McGinn (Mahwah, N.J.: Paulist Press, 1981), p. 277. Colledge translates *gelāzenheit* here as "surrender to God's will." See also Heidegger's quotations from Eckhart below, on p.103.—*Tr.*

GUIDE: No, not that.

SCHOLAR: In many respects it is clear to me what the word "releasement" should *not* name. At the same time, I know less and less what we are talking about. We are attempting, after all, to determine the essence of thinking. What does releasement have to do with thinking?

GUIDE: Nothing, if we conceive of thinking according to the heretofore prevailing concept—that is, as a representing. But perhaps the essence of the thinking that we are now searching for is engaged in releasement [*in die Gelassenheit eingelassen*]. [110]

SCIENTIST: Even with my best will to do so, I cannot representationally set before myself[43] this essence of thinking.

GUIDE: Because precisely this best will and the manner of your thinking—namely representing and the will-to-represent—are hindering you.

SCIENTIST: Then what in the world should I do?

SCHOLAR: I am asking myself this too.

GUIDE: We should *do* nothing at all, but rather wait.

SCHOLAR: That is a poor consolation.

GUIDE: Poor or not, we should also not expect any consolation, which we still do when we merely sink into disconsolateness.

SCIENTIST: What then should we wait upon? And where should we wait? I hardly know anymore where I am and who I am.

GUIDE: None of us know this anymore, as soon as we cease fooling ourselves.

SCHOLAR: And yet we still have our path?

GUIDE: To be sure. Yet by forgetting it too quickly, we give up thinking.

SCIENTIST: What should we still think about, if we are to cross over to and enter into [*über- und eingehen*] the as yet unexperienced essence of thinking?

GUIDE: About that from which alone this transition [*Übergang*] can happen.

SCHOLAR: Then you would not like to discard the established interpretation of the essence of thinking?

GUIDE: Have you forgotten what I said about what is revolutionary? [111]

SCIENTIST: Forgetfulness really seems to me to be a particular danger in such conversations.

SCHOLAR: If I understand correctly, we should now see what we are calling releasement in connection with what was spoken of as the

---

43. The phrase *sich vorstellen* would idiomatically be translated as "to conceive of" or "to imagine." However, here I have combined the sense of "representing" with the literal meaning of the phrase, "to set before oneself."—*Tr.*

essence of thinking, although we are hardly acquainted with it and, above all, are not properly accommodating it anywhere.

GUIDE: I mean exactly that.

SCIENTIST: Most recently we presented thinking to ourselves in the form of transcendental-horizonal representing.

SCHOLAR: This representing sets before and toward us, for example, the treeness of the tree, the jugness of the jug, the bowlness of the bowl, the stoniness of the stone, the plantness of the plant, or the animality of the animal, as that outward view into which we see when one thing stands over against us with the outward look of a tree, another thing with the look of a jug, yet another with the look of a bowl, several with the look of stones, many with the look of plants, and many with the look of animals.

SCIENTIST: The horizon, which you are once again describing, is the circle-of-vision which encircles the outward view.

GUIDE: It surpasses the outward look of objects.

SCHOLAR: Just as transcendence passes beyond the perception of objects.

GUIDE: Thus we define what is called horizon and transcendence by this surpassing and passing beyond.

SCHOLAR: Which relates itself back to objects and to the representing of objects.

GUIDE: Horizon and transcendence are thereby experienced from objects and from our representing, and are determined only in regard to objects and our representing. [112]

SCHOLAR: Why do you stress this?

GUIDE: In order to suggest that, in this manner, what lets the horizon be what it is does not yet get experienced at all.

SCIENTIST: What are you thinking of here?

GUIDE: We say that we see into the horizon. The circle-of-vision is thus something open, which does not have its openness from the fact that we see into it.

SCHOLAR: Likewise, it is also not the case that we place the outward look of objects, which the outward view of the circle-of-vision offers, into this open.

SCIENTIST: Rather, the look of objects comes out of this open to encounter us.

GUIDE: What has the character of a horizon is thus only the side turned toward us of a surrounding open, an open which is filled with outward views into outward looks of what to our representing appear as objects.

SCIENTIST: The horizon is therefore something other than a horizon. But, according to what has been said, this something other is the other of itself and thus the selfsame as what it is. You say, the horizon is the open which surrounds us. What is this open itself, if we disregard that it can also appear as the horizon of our representing?

GUIDE: This open seems to me to be something like a region, by means of whose enchantment everything which belongs to it returns to that in which it rests.

SCHOLAR: I am unsure if I understand anything of what you just said.

GUIDE: I do not understand it either, if by "understanding" you mean the capacity to represent [*vorzustellen*] what is offered in such a manner that it is, as it were, set down [*untergestellt*] in what is familiar and thus [113] secured; for I too lack something familiar in which I would be able to accommodate [*unterbringen*] what I attempted to say about the open as region.

SCIENTIST: That is perhaps impossible here, since presumably what you call "region" is itself what first grants all lodging.

GUIDE: I mean something like this; but not only this.

SCHOLAR: You spoke of "a" region in which everything returns to itself. Strictly speaking, a region for everything is not one region among others, but rather the region of all regions.

GUIDE: You are right; it is a matter of *the* region.

SCIENTIST: And the enchantment of this region is perhaps the prevailing of its essence, the *regioning,* if I may call it that.

SCHOLAR: According to the word, the region [*Gegend*] would be that which comes to encounter [*entgegenkommt*] us. Indeed we also said of the horizon that, from the outward view which is delimited by it, the outward look of objects comes to encounter us. If we now comprehend the horizon from the region, then we take the region itself to be that which comes to encounter us.

GUIDE: In this manner we would of course be characterizing the region—just as we earlier characterized the horizon—in terms of its relation to us, while what we are in fact seeking is what the open that surrounds us is in itself. If we say this surrounding open is, in itself, the region, then this word must name something other than what comes to encounter us.

SCIENTIST: Moreover, this coming-to-encounter is in no way a—and even less the—basic trait of the region. What then does this word signify? [114]

SCHOLAR: The word *gegnet*[44] means the free expanse. Does this allow anything to be gleaned from it for the essence of what we would like to call the region?

---

44. The special term Heidegger introduces here, *gegnet,* is a Middle High German form of *Gegend* which is still used in some South German dialects. (Note that, after its first mention, Heidegger capitalizes *Gegnet,* as is done with all nouns in modern German.) *Gegnet* is derived from a contraction of *gegenôte* (-ôte is a sub-

GUIDE: The region gathers—just as if nothing were happening [*gleich als ob sich nichts ereigne*]⁴⁵ —each to each and everything to everything else, gathering all into an abiding while resting in itself. Regioning is a gathering re-sheltering into an expansive resting in the abiding-while.

SCHOLAR: Thus the region is itself at once the expanse [*die Weite*] and the abiding-while [*die Weile*]. It abides into the expanse of resting. It expands into the abiding-while of what has freely turned toward itself. And in view of the accentuated usage of this word, we can also henceforth say "open-region" [*Gegnet*] instead of the familiar term "region" [*Gegend*].

GUIDE: The open-region is the abiding expanse which, gathering all, opens itself so that in it the open is held and halted, letting each thing arise in its resting.

SCIENTIST: This much I believe I see, that the open-region draws itself back, goes away from us [*uns entgeht*], rather than coming to encounter us [*uns entgegenkommt*].

SCHOLAR: Such that things, which appear in the region, also no longer have the character of objects [*Gegenständen*].

GUIDE: Not only do they no longer stand counter to us, they no longer stand at all.

SCIENTIST: Do they lie, then, or how are they situated?

GUIDE: They lie, if by that is meant the restful reposing [*Ruhen*] which was implied in our talk of resting in [*Beruhen*].

SCIENTIST: But where do things rest [*ruhen*], and in what does resting consist? [115]

stantive ending, similar to -*heit* or -*keit*). Both *Gegend* and *Gegnet* bear the sense not only of a "surrounding region" (*Umgegend*), but also of the direction toward (*gegen*) which one is moving, or the direction in which something lies "over against" (*gegenüber*) one. However, Heidegger takes pains here to distinguish his (re)thinking of *Gegend/Gegnet* from anthropocentric notions of a horizonal environment that is centered on and oriented toward the human. His retrieval of the unusual word *die Gegnet* in the present context is intended primarily, it seems, to mark a terminological distinction between this or that limited region on the one hand, and "the region of all regions" on the other. Since Heidegger associates *die Gegnet* with what "the open" (*das Offene*) is in itself, and following his explanation of it as "the free [i.e., open] expanse" (*die freie Weite*) which surrounds the limited or restricted openness of human horizons—both holding them within itself and withholding itself from them (compare *der Enthalt*, "the with-hold," in the second conversation [see p. 118], and also "the open and yet veiled expanse" in the third conversation [see p. 132])—I translate *die Gegnet* as "the open-region."—*Tr.*

45. Given that the gathering spoken of here recalls what Heidegger speaks of elsewhere as the "event of appropriation" (*Ereignis*), it is tempting to translate *gleich als ob sich nichts ereigne* as "just as if no appropriating event were taking place."—*Tr.*

GUIDE: Things rest in the return to the abiding-while of the expanse of their self-belonging.

SCHOLAR: Can there then be a rest in the return, which is after all a movement?

GUIDE: Indeed there can, if the rest is the hearth and the reign of all movement.

SCIENTIST: I must confess that I cannot quite representationally set before myself all of what you said about the region, the expanse and the abiding-while, and about return and resting.

SCHOLAR: It is perhaps not at all to be represented, insofar as through representing everything already becomes an object [*Gegenstand*] standing-counter [*entgegensteht*] to us in a horizon.

SCIENTIST: Then we also cannot really describe what has been named?

GUIDE: No. Any description would have to objectively bring forth the named.

SCHOLAR: Yet does it nevertheless let itself be named and, being named, be thought?

GUIDE: Only if thinking is no longer a representing.

SCIENTIST: But then what should it be?

GUIDE: Perhaps we are just now close to being let into the essence of thinking.

SCHOLAR: In that we are waiting upon its essence.

GUIDE: Waiting, all right; but never awaiting; for awaiting is already involved with representing and latches itself onto what is represented.

SCHOLAR: Waiting, however, lets go of that; or rather I should perhaps say: Waiting does not at all let itself get engaged in representational setting-before. Waiting has, properly speaking, no object. [116]

SCIENTIST: And yet if we wait, we always wait upon something.

SCHOLAR: Certainly; but as soon as we represent to ourselves and bring to a stand that for which we wait, we are no longer waiting.

GUIDE: In waiting we leave open that upon which we wait.

SCHOLAR: Why?

GUIDE: Because waiting lets itself be involved in the open itself.

SCHOLAR: In the expanse of the far.

GUIDE: In whose nearness it finds the abiding-while in which it remains.

SCIENTIST: Remaining is, however, a turning-back.

SCHOLAR: The open itself would be that upon which we could purely only wait.

SCIENTIST: The open itself, however, comes out of the open-region.

GUIDE: Into which we are let while waiting, when we think.

SCIENTIST: Thinking would then be a coming-into-nearness to the far.

SCHOLAR: That is an audacious determination of its essence, which occurs to us here.

SCIENTIST: I have only summarized what we have just named, without representing anything to myself.

GUIDE: And yet you have thought something to yourself.

SCIENTIST: Or rather, in fact, waited upon something, without knowing upon what.

SCHOLAR: And how did you come to be able to suddenly wait? [117]

SCIENTIST: As I now see more clearly, for a long time in our conversation I have been waiting upon the arrival of the essence of thinking. But now waiting itself has become clearer to me, and, together with this, the fact that we have all become more waitful, presumably along the way.

GUIDE: Can you tell us how this is the case?

SCIENTIST: I'll try, if I don't have to run the risk that you will right away pin me down to particular words.

GUIDE: That is really not the custom in our conversations.

SCHOLAR: Rather, we see to it that we freely move in words.

GUIDE: Because the word never represents something, but rather signifies something, and that means brings it to abide[46] in the expanse of what it can say.

SCIENTIST: I am to say how I came to waiting and in what way a clarification of the essence of thinking came to me. Because waiting goes into the open, without representing anything, I attempted to release myself from all representing. And because what opens the open is the open-region, I, released [*losgelassen*] from representing, attempted to remain purely released over to [*überlassen*] the open-region.

GUIDE: So you attempted, if I surmise correctly, to let yourself be involved in releasement [*sich auf die Gelassenheit einzulassen*].

SCIENTIST: To be honest, I did not really think of this, even though we had previously talked about releasement. The occasion which led me to let myself into waiting in the manner mentioned was more the course of the conversation, rather than the representation of any specific objects we considered. [118]

SCHOLAR: We can hardly come into releasement more fittingly than through an occasioning which allows us to let ourselves into an involvement [*Veranlassung zum Sicheinlassen*].

GUIDE: Above all when the occasion is still as inconspicuous as the silent course of a conversation that moves us.

SCHOLAR: Which indeed means that it brings us onto that path which seems to be nothing other than releasement itself.

---

46. Although *verweilen,* "to abide" or "to linger," is normally used only as an intransitive verb, Heidegger uses it here and elsewhere as a transitive verb. In such cases, where it is used with a direct object and an accusative *in,* I have translated *verweilen* as "to bring to abide."—*Tr.*

GUIDE: And yet releasement is something like rest.

SCHOLAR: From this it has suddenly become clearer to me how movement on a way [*Be-wegung*] comes from rest and remains engaged in rest.

GUIDE: Then releasement would not just be the way [*Weg*], but rather the movement (on a way) [*Bewegung*].

SCHOLAR: Where does this strange way go, and where does the movement befitting it rest?

GUIDE: Where else than in the open-region, in relation to which releasement is what it is?

SCIENTIST: I must now finally go back and ask: to what extent is it really releasement into which I attempted to let myself?

SCHOLAR: With this question you bring us into an awkward predicament.

GUIDE: It is that predicament in which we have constantly found ourselves on our path.

SCIENTIST: How so?

GUIDE: Insofar as whatever we in each case name with a word never has that word hanging on it like a name plate.

SCIENTIST: What we name is before that nameless; and this is also the case [119] with that which we call releasement. What do we orient ourselves by, in order to asses whether and to what extent the name is fitting?

SCHOLAR: Or does every naming remain an arbitrary act over against the nameless?

GUIDE: But is it really established that there is the nameless at all? Much is for us often ineffable, but only because the name that it has does not occur to us.

SCHOLAR: By virtue of what naming does it have the name?

GUIDE: Perhaps these names do not come from a transitive naming [*Benennung*]. They owe themselves to an intransitive naming [*Nennung*], an event in which at once the namable, the name, and the named appropriate one another [*sich . . . ereignen*].

SCIENTIST: What you last said about intransitive naming is unclear to me. It would seem that it must be connected with the essence of the word. On the other hand, your remarks on transitive naming, and about there not being the nameless, are clearer to me.

SCHOLAR: Because we can test it in the case of the name "releasement."

GUIDE: Or have already tested it.

SCIENTIST: How so?

GUIDE: What is that which you (transitively) named [*benannten*] with the name "releasement"?

SCIENTIST: If I may say so, it was not I that brought forth the name, but rather you.

GUIDE: I carried out the (transitive) naming just as little as you did.

SCHOLAR: Who then was it? None of us? [120]

GUIDE: Presumably, for in the region in which we stay everything is in the best order when it has been no one's doing.

SCIENTIST: An enigmatic region, where there is nothing for which we can answer.

GUIDE: Because it is the region of the word that alone answers for itself.

SCHOLAR: For us it remains only to hear the answer befitting the word.

GUIDE: That is enough; even when our telling is only a retelling of the answer heard.

SCIENTIST: And nothing depends on he who first attained to such retelling, especially since he often does not know whose tale he retells.

GUIDE: So we don't want to quarrel over who first introduced the name "releasement" into the conversation; we just want to consider what it is that we so name.

SCIENTIST: Speaking from the previously mentioned experience of mine, it is waiting.

GUIDE: And so not something nameless, but rather something already named. What is this waiting?

SCIENTIST: Insofar as it relates itself to the open, and the open is the open-region, then we can say: waiting is a relationship to the open-region.

GUIDE: Perhaps even *the* relationship to the open-region, insofar as waiting lets itself be involved in the open-region and, in letting itself be involved in it, lets the open-region purely prevail as open-region.

SCHOLAR: A relationship to something would accordingly be the true relationship if it is brought into its own essence and held therein by that to which it relates itself. [121]

GUIDE: The relationship to the open-region is waiting. And "waiting" means: to let oneself into an involvement in the open of the open-region.

SCHOLAR: And so: to go into the open-region.

SCIENTIST: That sounds as if we were previously outside the open-region.

GUIDE: That we were, and yet we were not. We are not and are never outside the open-region, insofar as we stay, after all, as thinking beings—and that means as transcendentally representing beings—in the horizon of transcendence. The horizon, however, is the side of the open-region turned toward our representational setting-before. The open-region surrounds us and shows itself to us as the horizon.

SCHOLAR: I find that the open-region rather veils itself as horizon.

GUIDE: Certainly. But nevertheless we are in the open-region as we, representing transcendentally, step out into the horizon. And yet again we are not in the open-region, so far as we have not yet let ourselves be involved in it itself as the open-region.

Scientist: Which happens, however, in waiting.

Guide: As you have already said, in waiting we are released from the transcendental relation to the horizon.

Scientist: This being-released-from is the first moment of release-ment, but not, as it seems to me, releasement in its primary sense.

Scholar: Why not?

Guide: Because releasement in the sense of being-released-from can only occur if the being released from horizonal transcendence is already let into proper releasement.[47]

Scholar: But what is this? Insofar as proper releasement is supposed to be the befitting [122] relationship to the open-region, and if such a relationship determines itself purely from that to which it relates itself, then proper releasement must rest in the open-region, and must have received from it the movement toward it.

Guide: Releasement comes from the open-region, because release-ment properly consists in the human remaining released to the open-region, and doing so by means of the open-region. The human is released to it in his essence, insofar as he originally belongs to the open-region. He belongs to it, insofar as he is inceptually a-propri-ated to the open-region, and indeed by the open-region itself.

Scholar: In fact, waiting upon something—provided this is an essen-tial, and that means an all-decisive, waiting—is also based in the fact that we belong to that upon which we wait.

Guide: Out of the experience of waiting, and indeed out of the experi-ence of waiting upon the self-opening of the open-region, and in relation to such waiting, this waiting was spoken of, addressed [an-gesprochen], as releasement.

Scholar: This is therefore a befitting naming of waiting upon the open-region.

Scientist: But now if transcendental-horizonal representing—from which releasement releases itself into the open-region on the basis of belonging—is the heretofore prevailing essence of thinking, then in releasement thinking transforms itself from such representing into waiting upon the open-region.

Guide: The essence of this waiting is, however, releasement to the open-region. Yet because it is the open-region which now and again lets releasement belong to itself, in letting it rest in itself, the essence of

47. In the 1959 excerpt this sentence was altered to read: "Insofar as proper releasement can occur without necessarily being preceded by this being-released-from horizonal transcendence" (G 49 / DT 73).—Tr.

thinking rests in the fact that, if I may say so, the open-region enregions releasement in itself. [123]

SCHOLAR: Thinking is releasement to the open-region, because its essence rests in the enregioning of releasement.

GUIDE: But by this you are saying that the essence of thinking is not
determined from thinking, and that means not from waiting as
such, but rather from the other of itself, that is, from the open-region, which essentially occurs by enregioning.

SCIENTIST: In a certain manner, I can follow all that we just said about
releasement, open-region, and enregioning; all the same, I can represent nothing of it to myself.

SCHOLAR: You are probably also not supposed to, if you think what
was said in accordance with its essence.

SCIENTIST: You mean that, in accordance with the transformed essence of thinking, we wait upon it.

SCHOLAR: Namely upon the enregioning of the open-region, so that this
lets our essence into the open-region, that is, into belonging to it.

GUIDE: But what if we are already appropriated to the open-region?

SCIENTIST: How does that help us if we are not in fact truly appropriated?

SCHOLAR: Thus we are and thus we are not.

SCIENTIST: Once again this restless to and fro between yes and no.

SCHOLAR: We are suspended, as it were, between the two.

GUIDE: Yet staying in this betweenness is waiting.

SCHOLAR: And waiting is the essence of releasement.

SCIENTIST: So this is no restless suspension, but rather a restful resting.[48] [124]

SCHOLAR: And thus no suspension at all.

GUIDE: Just as little are there the supposedly fixed hooks of yes and
no, on and between which we are supposedly suspended.

SCHOLAR: We are appropriated to the open-region; but we do not yet
experience it as the open-region.

SCIENTIST: Which is why we need to clarify that upon which we are
perhaps waiting. I think this is possible, because after all we succeeded in a clarification of releasement [Gelassenheit].

GUIDE: Whose essence of course remains engaged [eingelassen] in the
open-region.

SCHOLAR: Thus everything depends on a clarification of the essence of
the open-region. And I feel that we passed too quickly over and
away from the essence of the open-region when it first came up in
our conversation.

---

48. The text from this line until the bottom of p. 89 is not included in the 1959
excerpt (see G 52 / DT 75).—Tr.

SCIENTIST: This is also my impression, namely that we passed over much of what should have been considered.

GUIDE: Yet take into consideration that we are in a transition from the heretofore familiar essence of thinking to a perhaps more originary essence.

SCIENTIST: Precisely for this reason we should proceed with more cautious consideration.

GUIDE: Certainly. But perhaps it belongs to such a transition [*Übergang*] that it must at first pass over [*übergehen*] much, in order to retrieve later it.

SCHOLAR: You speak as if this later retrieval [*Nachholen*] is preferential [*Vorzug*].

GUIDE: It is indeed. [125]

SCIENTIST: Presumably because we can more purely retrieve what was passed over if we come back to it from where it belongs.

SCHOLAR: That makes sense to me. But it makes our going [*Gang*] only more difficult, insofar as we have now passed over [*übergegangen*] what belongs to the essence of the open-region, and since it is, however, the open-region which lets all things belong to one another. Although by saying this, I don't mean to broach now the adjacent question of wherein the open-region itself belongs.

GUIDE: Upon the answer that will satisfy that question, we can calmly wait, since this answer will first reveal itself to a releasement to the open-region, and will itself name for us that wherein the open-region belongs—if, that is, it can belong in somewhere else at all.

SCHOLAR: Although the later retrieval [*Nachholen*] as a purer taking in [*Einholen*] deserves preference, and thus the passing over is justified, it still seems to me that in naming the open-region we have passed over that which may not be passed over without endangering the transition into the essence of thinking in the sense of releasement to the open-region.

SCIENTIST: What are you thinking of?

SCHOLAR: We said that the open-region lets each thing belong to each thing, in that it brings all to abide in the expanse of the abiding-while and lets everything rest in the return to itself.

SCIENTIST: In this connection we pointed out that things within the open-region lose the character of objects, or rather never acquired this character in the first place. This can only be due to the manner in which the open-region enregions things, if I may here use the word that occurred to us earlier when we were concerned with naming the relationship of the open-region to the human. [126]

SCHOLAR: If the human is not a thing, and yet enregioning [*Vergegnen*] names precisely the manner according to which the open-region [*die Gegnet*] regions [*gegnet*] what is distinctive in the essence of the human, then we may not say that the open-region enregions things.

SCIENTIST: We will come to know how matters stand in this regard when we clarify the open-region and its regioning in relation to things.

SCHOLAR: But, in my opinion, precisely this is what we may not pass over now; otherwise the clarification of the open-region will likely remain lopsided.

GUIDE: I agree with you entirely. But the task is difficult, and our preparation for it is meager. Above all, our capacity to purely experience the regioning of the open-region in relation to things is hardly awakened.

SCHOLAR: Perhaps it will suffice if we clarify what is vague with an appropriate example.

SCIENTIST: We have already named things such as bowls and jugs.

GUIDE: What is a jug?

SCIENTIST: A container, that is, a holder [*Gefäß*]. What contains or holds are its sides and bottom, and this holder can itself in turn be held by its handle.

SCHOLAR: If it is, for example, a clay jug, this holdable holder is manufactured by the potter. The jug consists of specially prepared and shaped earth.

GUIDE: The jug not only consists of earth, but it can also only first stand—directly or indirectly—on the earth by means of that of which it consists.

SCHOLAR: This consisting [*Bestehen*] and standing [*Stehen*] make it possible that the jug can be an object [*Gegenstand*] for us. [127]

SCIENTIST: Yet we of course do not want to represent the jug as object, but rather to experience and think it as thing.

GUIDE: Now, is what we have just said of the jug said of it as thing or of it as object?

SCHOLAR: I would like to say that it is true of the jug as a thing subsisting by itself; for its subsistence [*Bestehen*] is that of which it consists [*besteht*] and how it consists of this, that is, its material and its form. This subsistence, as well as the standing (on a table, for example) based on this, belong to the jug itself; and this is also the case when humans do not represent it and make it into an object.

SCIENTIST: That of which the jug consists as manufactured and by means of which it also stands, is precisely also that in which it subsists as a jug-thing. And, as I now suddenly realize, something like the open-region is not also needed in order to characterize this standing-in-itself, that is, the thing-character of the thing.

GUIDE: Yet have we not examined the jug exclusively in view of its manufacture?

SCHOLAR: Certainly; how else should we experience it, since after all it is not a plant, like a rosebush, but rather a human construct?

GUIDE: But to its manufacture belongs that pro-duction or setting-forth of an outward look, which we have become acquainted with as the essence of τέχνη.

SCIENTIST: Yet the essence of technology is supposed to be objectification; thus we have grasped the jug in advance as object when we encounter in it a human construct.

GUIDE: Perhaps you go too far when you say that it is grasped as object, even though it is looked at in view of its [128] outward look. From the viewpoint of τέχνη, the Greeks caught sight of the presencing jug in the circle-of-vision of its outward look, and yet did not experience it as object.

SCIENTIST: There, where τέχνη determines the regard, is it not also the case that technology in the modern sense already rules, and with technology objectification?

GUIDE: The objectiveness of objects cannot be grasped from τέχνη, but rather first from technology.

SCIENTIST: Which is why at the next opportunity we must ask how τέχνη and technology differ from one another, and how the one becomes the other.

SCHOLAR: For the moment it suffices to notice that the potter must have the jug in front of himself in view of its outward look; because the material and form, which make up the construct, are determined according to the look of jugness.

GUIDE: The potter looks into a horizon of outward looks.

SCIENTIST: And we with him, when we have the jug before us as container and construct.

SCHOLAR: Then we don't experience the jug in its relation to the open-region.

SCIENTIST: Unless we take the horizon as the side of the open-region turned toward us.

GUIDE: But then we don't grasp the open-region as open-region or the jug as a thing that belongs to it.

SCIENTIST: You are right; and I am beginning to see that a clarification of the relation between open-region and thing is extraordinarily difficult.

GUIDE: Presumably this is because we only represent objects and seldom ever experience a thing. [129]

SCHOLAR: When we attempt this, as a result of firmly rooted habituation we unawares end up looking at the intended thing in a horizon of outward looks and manufacturing.

SCIENTIST: Manufacturing is nevertheless only a kind of causal effecting [Bewirkung].

GUIDE: We are bewitched by what is actual [*vom Wirklichen*] and its effects [*Wirkungen*].

SCHOLAR: Thus we deviate from the path on which we experience the jug as thing.

GUIDE: Or perhaps we have not yet succeeded in even getting on this path.

SCIENTIST: Then we would probably do well to go back along the way to the thing-essence of the jug which we have attempted to take up till now, and pay attention to the point at which we looked out into the horizon of outward looks and manufacturing.

SCHOLAR: We started by examining the jug as container.

SCIENTIST: The jug is in itself what contains. And that in it which contains are the sides and bottom, the formed earth.

SCHOLAR: After all that we have said about the regioning of the open-region, the clarification of the thing-essence of the jug must evidently start with that of the container which contains [*Fassenden des Gefäßes*], consisting in itself and standing there. We talked of how the open-region brings each thing to abide in the expanse of resting in the return to itself.

SCIENTIST: We may not let out of our sight what contains [*Das Fassende*] of the jug that consists in itself as container [*Gefäß*].

GUIDE: If we have ever had it in our sight at all. [130]

SCHOLAR: But we did speak constantly of sides and bottom, even if at the outset in view of manufacturing. We can now disregard manufacturing, since it is the completed jug standing there that is first the jug-thing.

GUIDE: But are sides and bottom, this formed bit of earth, that of the jug which holds?

SCIENTIST: Why would they not be this?

GUIDE: When we fill the jug with wine, do we pour the wine into the sides and into the bottom of the jug?

SCHOLAR: No, rather into the jug.

GUIDE: We fill an empty jug and can never fill a full jug, even though there are sides and a bottom standing there in it.

SCIENTIST: You are noting something obvious.

GUIDE: Not to say something trivial.

SCHOLAR: And yet you indicate something astonishing about the jug.

GUIDE: If such was indicated, the jug said this to us. Now what do you find astonishing?

SCHOLAR: That the emptiness between the sides and bottom and rim is evidently that of the container which contains.

GUIDE: But if this is how matters stand, then the jug, as the container standing there in itself, consists not in that out of which it consists, the formed bit of earth, but rather in its emptiness.

SCHOLAR: This nothingness of the jug is really what the jug is.

SCIENTIST: This emptiness is, however, also that which the potter does not and altogether cannot manufacture. Emptiness is the ungraspable [*das Unfaßliche*]. [131]

GUIDE: But the potter grasps, that is, contains [*faßt*] precisely the emptiness and only the emptiness in the shape of sides and bottom and rim.

SCIENTIST: So he does not shape the clay, but rather the emptiness.

SCHOLAR: He must shape this, if indeed it is that of the container which contains [*das Fassende des Gefäßes*].

GUIDE: But we would like to speak of the jug as container and not of the container as a construct.

SCIENTIST: Your signal to remain with the meditation on that of the container which contains, gives me the opportunity I had wished for to bring up something decisive—something from which we will easily gather that we merely let ourselves be deceived for a moment by the appearance of something astonishing.

GUIDE: I am eager to hear what you will bring up.

SCIENTIST: It is almost as obvious, even if not nearly as illuminating, as what you said about emptiness.

GUIDE: Namely?

SCIENTIST: That the jug, even when it seems to be empty, is not truly empty, and can never be empty. Even the allegedly empty jug is filled with air and with all the mixture that makes up the air and with what that mixture itself is composed of.

SCHOLAR: You are now talking about the jug not as a drinker of a drink, but rather as a physicist.

GUIDE: And, according to your statement, physicists have the advantage of being able to always sit before full jugs.

SCIENTIST: Your friendly mockery cannot dissuade me from asserting that what is actual is first grasped and determined by means of [132] the observations of physics. This assertion will make more sense to you when I add that the filling of a jug does not consist in filling out an emptiness.

SCHOLAR: But rather in what?

SCIENTIST: In an exchanging of the full. When we pour wine into the jug, the air that fills its alleged emptiness is displaced by a liquid.

GUIDE: I do not deny that your statement is correct, nor at all that your correct statement grasps what is actual. But I offer for consideration the question of whether or not what we are talking about has anything to do with what is actual.

SCIENTIST: Then you doubt that the jug is something actual?

GUIDE: In no way. But I doubt whether the actual is the jug.

SCIENTIST: I cannot attach any weight to this question.

SCHOLAR: Because you have forgotten the jug.

GUIDE: And something else too, which the jug now needs if it is supposed to be able to show its thing-essence, such that we also recognize the relation between thing and open-region, as well as the
latter's regioning, which enregions the human into releasement.

SCHOLAR: And it is this releasement that we presage to be the essence
of thinking.

SCIENTIST: Which I myself, after all, experienced as waiting.

GUIDE: Only to hastily forget it once more. [133]

SCIENTIST: Perhaps you mean that I should not only think of the jug,
but also of thinking in the sense of releasement to the open-region?

GUIDE: We should all think of the jug in accordance with this essence
of thinking.

SCIENTIST: That is to say, to wait upon its thing-essence.

GUIDE: Instead of pouncing upon it as an object with the explanations
of physics.

SCIENTIST: Then what you will to do is to completely discard the observations of physics and the scientific explanation of the world?

GUIDE: I will—as you know—only non-willing.

SCIENTIST: That I know and yet do not know. This nighttime conversation on a country path is showing me ever more clearly that we
are moving entirely outside of the workshop of science, so that here
I must put my scientific work and its horizons off to the side; and
this calls forth in me a feeling of emptiness. On the other hand, it is
precisely in the hesitancy of the conversation that I sense that we
are going toward something by drawing back from it. But then suddenly, as happened just now in the case of the jug, I am overcome
once again by an impatience with our tedious talking. I then prefer
to stick with the clarity of scientific questioning, only in the end to
once more let myself engage in waiting.

SCHOLAR: We wait upon the thing-essence of the jug and upon the
relation between thing and open-region.

GUIDE: And really upon the open-region—which, as we said, brings
the thing to abide in its abiding-while, whereas we mostly rush
things. We are also already rushing things when we objectively
represent them. The scientific clarification of things is just one manner of such representing. [134]

SCIENTIST: Following this suggestion, I would be grateful to you if you
would show me precisely the point at which I rushed the jug-thing.
For it seems to me that it is with regard to the essence of the thing
that we should learn what thinking is, rather than by means of a
methodological analysis of thinking in physics.

SCHOLAR: Insofar as we become more waitful before the thing by paying attention to the point at which things are rushed. In meditating

on the jug we said that its emptiness is what holds or contains, and thus is that in which the container consists.

SCIENTIST: I denied that the empty jug is empty.

GUIDE: And in giving evidence for this you showed something that is indeed correct, something that is valid for every hollow space; but you were no longer speaking of the jug.

SCHOLAR: You took our friendly mockery too lightly.

SCIENTIST: And likewise the emptiness of the jug.

SCHOLAR: If you would only just pay attention to the emptiness of the jug, this would suffice for remaining with the jug.

GUIDE: And what is the emptiness of the jug?

SCIENTIST: What else should it be other than emptiness of drink?

SCHOLAR: This emptiness contains the drink, keeps it and stands ready for keeping it.

GUIDE: So that of the container which contains abides in the drink, whether this drink is at the time filling the jug or leaving it empty.

SCIENTIST: And wherein does the drink abide?

GUIDE: I would like to say, if this may suffice as an answer for you, the drink [*Trank*] abides in the whole gathering involved in the event of drinking [*Getränk*]. This gathering is the belonging-together in the event of drinking [135] of what is offered and received as drinkable. The whole gathering of the drink [*Getränk*] consists of the drink offered [*Trank*] and the drink received [*Trunk*].[49] What is offered as drinkable is among other things wine. The one who drinks is the human. The whole gathering of the drink as what is offered abides in the wine, which abides in the grapevine, which abides in the earth and in the gifts from the sky.

SCHOLAR: So the emptiness of the jug is brought to abide in such an expanse. This expanse is what brings the jug to abide in resting in the return to itself.

SCIENTIST: The jug is therefore itself only when it rests in this expanse, and in a certain manner is the selfsame as grapevine and sunshine.

GUIDE: The jug is not only in a certain manner the selfsame, but rather in truth the selfsame, if you just consider what we already said about selfsameness.

49. *Das Getränk nennt das Zusammengehören des tränkenden Trinkbaren und des trinkbaren Getrunkenen des Trinkens. Das Getränk ist Trank und Trunk.* The word *Getränk* is the usual word for "drink" or "beverage," but Heidegger is here evidently taking its *Ge-* prefix to indicate the *gathering* involved in a drink, including the giving and receiving of it. *Tränken* is commonly used in the sense of "to water" animals, that is, to provide them with something to drink. *Trank* and *Trunk* are both relatively older and more literary expressions for a drink, draft, or potion. Heidegger seems to be using *Trank* here to connote a drink that is offered, and *Trunk* to connote a drink that is received.—*Tr.*

SCHOLAR: The jug abides in itself in that it turns back to itself over and through this expanse.

GUIDE: The return is the abiding, into which the jug is brought to abide by the abiding expanse.

SCIENTIST: We called the abiding expanse the open-region. And we now have a clearer sense of the manner in which it regions. It nevertheless seems to me that we do not yet give broad enough consideration to the expanse that brings to abide, the expanse in which the jug abides, so long as we think of the whole gathering of the drink [*Getränk*] only as the drink offered [*Trank*] and forget the drinking [*Trinken*].

SCHOLAR: I too wanted to point this out right away. But I became puzzled even when by myself I silently tried to think of the drinking just as we thought of the wine.

GUIDE: The selfsame difficulty presumably impedes my speech as well. If pressed one could perhaps say that drinking abides in thirst. But we also drink wine when we don't have any thirst. [136]

SCIENTIST: You mean when we drink beyond thirst.

GUIDE: Yes and no.

SCHOLAR: I'd also like to know how you are making a distinction here.

GUIDE: Although one who is accustomed to drinking beyond thirst is indeed called a drinker, mere drinkers do not know how to drink, which is why we also use a word for their drinking that is used to designate what animals do,[50] even though among animals there are never any drinkers of this type.

SCIENTIST: Then "to drink beyond thirst" signifies not merely to get blind drunk, but rather to go out beyond thirst as the usual occasion for drinking, and to drink to conviviality.

SCHOLAR: Or to drink on the occasion of a farewell, or to a memory, or for other special occasions.

GUIDE: And so on the occasion of a festival.[51]

SCHOLAR: So perhaps we could venture to say: the drink offered [*Trank*] or, better, the drink received [*Trunk*], abides in the festival.

SCIENTIST: The festival belongs in that expanse which brings the drink offered to abide in that wherein the emptiness of the jug abides.

GUIDE: The jug would then be something festive. And to that expanse, in which earth and sky are named, belongs also the festival, which, it seems to me, is itself an expanse that brings the human to abide.

---

50. The word alluded to here, *saufen,* means "to drink" when it is used for animals, but "to booze" when it is used for humans. —*Tr.*

51. Although probably best translated here as "festival," *das Fest* has a somewhat wider semantic range. It can also mean "celebration" or "feast," especially when these take place on a commemorative occasion.

SCHOLAR: And so the festival belongs to the open-region and thus also assists in bringing the jug to abide in its abiding-while. It is perhaps for this reason that you also said that the jug is something festive.

SCIENTIST: The more hesitantly I think along with you, the more wonderful [137] and perhaps also the more enigmatic the jug—and in it the thing—becomes for me.

SCHOLAR: And I have a sense of how thinking itself could be a festival.

GUIDE: The festival of sobriety.

SCIENTIST: Thus, at the risk of not entirely understanding what you mean, I maintain that a sober ascertainment [*Feststellung*] is now necessary, which may be of use to our conversation about thinking. Moreover, I cannot bear for long this reveling in inklings of the wonderful. I need exact determinations.

GUIDE: If this is how you take what is festive [*das Festliche*] of thinking, then probably even your will to exactness is not yet sober enough. Although your pressing for order has indeed often helped us.

SCIENTIST: I only wish to make sure of all that we have discussed up to this point. For the sake of clarifying the essence of the open-region, we delved into the relation of the open-region to the thing. In pursuing the relation of the jug to the open-region, there appeared at the same time—and indeed across the open-region—a relation of the jug to the human; and the human in turn has his relation to the open-region in releasement, a relation that is enregioned by the open-region. In addition to this tangle of relations then also comes the immediate relation of the jug to the human, to which we did not pay any further attention.

GUIDE: Yet perhaps we did—indeed constantly—pay attention to this last-named relation. It is just that we did not immediately represent it; nonetheless, we did consider it.

SCHOLAR: But this indication of the intertwined relations—between open-region and thing, open-region and releasement, releasement and human, [138] human and open-region, thing and human—seems to me to indeed be important.

GUIDE: At once important and correct; and nevertheless dangerous, because we tend to represent these relations objectively in a system, instead of waitfully letting ourselves be involved in what is named as open-region and releasement, open-region and thing. Perhaps the enigmatic character of the simple conceals itself behind the appearance of an indeterminate tangle.

SCIENTIST: Which is why you are probably of the opinion that we should enhance this enigmatic character still further, instead of covering it up with a hasty ordering.

SCHOLAR: How can the enigmatic, which indeed gathers itself in what we call the open-region, be further enhanced?

GUIDE: By taking into consideration that thinking is in no way a releasement subsisting by itself; rather, releasement to the open-region is thinking only as the enregioning of releasement, an enregioning that has let releasement into the open-region.

SCHOLAR: But now the open-region also brings the thing to abide in the abiding-while of the expanse. How should we name the regioning of the open-region in relation to the thing?

SCIENTIST: After all, it presumably cannot be named enregioning since this names the relation of the open-region to releasement; and, whereas releasement is said to shelter in itself the essence of thinking, things do not think.

GUIDE: Things are evidently things by means of the regioning of the open-region, as was shown with the abiding of the jug in the expanse of the open-region. Yet the regioning of the open-region does not cause and effect things, any more than the open-region [139] effects releasement. The open-region is, in enregioning, also not the horizon for releasement; and neither is it the horizon for things, insofar as we don't experience them as objects for ourselves. Yet we also do not experience things as "things in themselves," but rather as things for themselves.

SCHOLAR: What you now say seems to me to be to be so decisive that I would like to try to get a grip on it with scholarly terminology. Of course I know that terminology not only rigidifies thoughts, at the same time it also makes thoughts once again ambiguous, corresponding to the ambiguity that inevitably adheres to customary terminologies.

GUIDE: After that scholarly reservation you may freely speak in a scholarly manner.

SCHOLAR: According to your explanation, the relation of the open-region to releasement is neither a connection of cause and effect nor the horizonal-transcendental relationship. To say it still more concisely and more generally: the relation between open-region and releasement, if it is still a relation at all, can be thought of neither as ontic nor as ontological.

GUIDE: But only as enregioning.

SCIENTIST: Similarly, the relation between open-region and thing is also now neither a connection of cause and effect nor the transcendental-horizonal relationship, and therefore also neither ontic nor ontological.

SCHOLAR: But the relation of the open-region to the thing is evidently also not enregioning, which concerns the essence of the human.

GUIDE: So how should we name the relation of the open-region to the thing, if the open-region lets the thing abide in itself as the thing?
[140]

SCIENTIST: It conditions or rather, literally, bethings [*bedingt*][52] the thing into being a thing [*zum Ding*].

SCHOLAR: And so the relation of open-region to thing is best called conditioning or rather, literally, bethinging [*Bedingnis*].

SCIENTIST: But bethinging is not a making and effecting; neither is it a making-possible in the sense of the transcendental.

GUIDE: It is rather only a bethinging.

SCIENTIST: So we must first learn to think what bethinging is.

GUIDE: By learning to experience the essence of thinking.

SCHOLAR: And thus to wait upon bethinging and enregioning.

SCIENTIST: Nevertheless, this naming is now of some help in bringing a certain transparency to the manifold of relations introduced. Still, precisely that relation whose characterization is to me the most important remains indeterminate: I mean the relationship of the human to the thing.

SCHOLAR: Why are you so doggedly persistent about this relationship?

SCIENTIST: We started, after all, by illuminating the relation between the ego and the object by way of the factual relationship of the thinking in physics to nature. The relation between ego and object, often called the subject-object-relation, which I took to be the most universal, is evidently only a historical variation of the relationship of the human to the thing, insofar as things can become objects.

GUIDE: And they have even become objects before attaining their thing-essence. [141]

SCHOLAR: The same is true of the corresponding historical transformation of the human-essence to egoity.

GUIDE: Which likewise occurred before the essence of the human could return to itself.

SCIENTIST: If, that is, we do not regard as final the molding of the human-essence as *animal rationale.*

SCHOLAR: Something which after today's conversation is hardly possible any more.

SCIENTIST: I hesitate to so rashly make a decision about this. However, something else has indeed become clear to me: that in the relation between ego and object something historical conceals itself, something which belongs to the history of the human essence.

GUIDE: And insofar as the essence of the human does not receive the mold of its character from the human, but rather from what we call the open-region and its enregioning, the history of which you had an inkling occurs as the history of the open-region.

---

52. The dictionary definitions of *bedingen* include "to cause" as well as "to condition," but the word is being redefined here in a quite literal sense.—*Tr.*

SCIENTIST: I am not able to think along with you that far yet. I am content if an obscurity is removed for me by the insight into the historical character of the relation between ego and object. For when I decided in favor of the methodological type of analysis in the mathematical natural sciences, you said that this view was historiological.

SCHOLAR: You vigorously objected to that statement.

SCIENTIST: Now I see what was meant. Mathematical projection and experiment are based on the relation of the human as ego to the thing as object.

GUIDE: They even constitute this relation and unfold its historical essence.

SCIENTIST: If any examination that focuses on what is historical [142] is called historiological, then the methodological analysis in physics is in fact historiological.

SCHOLAR: Where the concept of the historiological [*Historischen*] signifies a manner of knowing and is broadly conceived.

GUIDE: Presumably in the direction of the properly historical [*Geschichtliche*], which does not consist in the happenings and deeds of the world.

SCHOLAR: Also not in the cultural achievements of the human.

SCIENTIST: But then in what else?

GUIDE: The historical rests in the open-region and in that which occurs as the open-region, which, sending itself to the human, enregions him into his essence.

SCHOLAR: An essence which we have, however, hardly experienced, assuming that it has not yet fulfilled itself in the rationality of the animal.

SCIENTIST: In such a situation we can only wait upon the essence of the human.

GUIDE: In releasement, by means of which we belong to the open-region, which still conceals its proper essence.

SCHOLAR: We presage releasement to the open-region as the sought-for essence of thinking.

GUIDE: When we let ourselves engage in releasement to the open-region, we will non-willing.

SCIENTIST: Releasement, as the releasing of oneself from transcendental representing, is in fact a refraining from the willing of a horizon. This refraining also no longer comes from a willing, unless a trace of [143] willing is required to occasion the letting-oneself-into a belonging to the open-region—a trace which, however, vanishes in the letting-oneself-into, and is completely extinguished in authentic releasement.

SCHOLAR: But how is releasement related to what is not a willing?

GUIDE: After all that we have said about the bringing-to-abide of the abiding expanse, about the letting-rest in the return, and about the regioning of the open-region—the open-region can hardly be spoken of as will.

SCHOLAR: That the open-region's enregioning and bethinging essentially exclude themselves from all effecting and causing already shows how decisively all that pertains to the will is foreign to them.

GUIDE: For every will wills to effect [wirken] and wills to have actuality [Wirklichkeit] as its element.

SCIENTIST: How easily could someone who now heard us say this fall into the opinion that releasement floats in ineffective unreality and thus in nullity, and, devoid of any power to act, is a will-less allowing of everything and basically a denial of the will to live!

SCHOLAR: So you think it is necessary for us to counter this possible suspicion regarding releasement by showing how something like a power to act and resoluteness prevail in it as well?

SCIENTIST: That is what I mean—though I don't fail to recognize that all these names at once misinterpret releasement as pertaining to the will.

SCHOLAR: One would then have to think the word "resoluteness," for example, as it is thought in the book mentioned earlier: as the self-opening for the open.[53] [144]

GUIDE: Which we think of as the open-region.

SCHOLAR: And if we experience the essence of truth according to Greek saying and thinking as unconcealment and revealing, we remember that the open-region is presumably that which essentially occurs in concealment [das verborgen Wesende], or, as I would like to say, the essential occurring [Wesung] of truth.

SCIENTIST: And the essence of thinking, namely releasement to the open-region, would then be a resolute openness to the essential occurring of truth.

GUIDE: In releasement there could be an endurance concealing itself, one which rests purely in the fact that releasement enters ever more purely into an intimate awareness of its essence [ihres Wesens inne wird] and, enduring it, stands within it.

SCHOLAR: That would be a comportment [Verhalten] which would not become an attitude [Haltung], but which would rather gather itself

53. Here as elsewhere, Heidegger understands Entschlossenheit—a word commonly (and in Being and Time) translated as "resoluteness"—literally as a "de-closedness" (Ent-schlossenheit), that is, as a self-opening. In the 1959 excerpt, "the book" is specified as Being and Time and the last phrase of this passage was rewritten thus: "as the specifically [eigens] undertaken self-opening of Dasein for the open" (G 59 / DT 81). Below, Entschlossenheit is translated as "resolute openness."—Tr.

in a restraint [*Verhaltenheit*] that would constantly remain the restraint of releasement.

GUIDE: So releasement as a restrained enduring would be the reception of the enregioning of the open-region.

SCIENTIST: And restrained enduring, by means of which releasement rests in its essence, might be what corresponds to the highest willing; and yet it may not be that. For this resting-in-itself of releasement, which lets releasement belong precisely to the enregioning of the open-region—

GUIDE: —and in a certain manner to bethinging as well—

SCIENTIST: —for this endurance of the belonging to the open-region, a belonging which rests in itself, we do not yet have a word.

SCHOLAR: Perhaps the word "indwelling" could name some of this. At a friend's place I once read a few lines which he had copied down for himself somewhere, and which contained an explanation of this word. I memorized the lines. They read: [145]

> Indwelling
> Never one truth alone
> to receive intact
> the essential occurring of truth
> for far-extending constancy,
> place the thinking heart
> in the simple forbearance
> of the single magnanimity
> of noble recollecting.

GUIDE: Indwelling in releasement to the open-region would accordingly be the genuine essence of the spontaneity of thinking.

SCHOLAR: And thinking [*Denken*], according to these lines, would be commemorating [*Andenken*], akin to what is noble.

GUIDE: The indwelling of releasement to the open-region would be noble-mindedness itself.

SCIENTIST: It seems to me that this incredible night tempts you both to enthuse.

GUIDE: Yes—if you mean enthusing in waiting, whereby we become more waitful and more sober.

SCHOLAR: Poorer according to appearances and yet richer in coincidental occurrences.

SCIENTIST: Then in your strange sobriety, please say how releasement can be akin to what is noble.

SCHOLAR: Noble is what has provenance.

GUIDE: Not just has, but abides in the provenance of its essence.

SCIENTIST: Now indeed, proper releasement consists in that the human in his essence belongs to the open-region—that is, he is released precisely to it. [146]

SCHOLAR: Not occasionally, but rather—how should we say it—previously [*im vorhinein*].

SCIENTIST: In advance [*Zum voraus*], out to which we really cannot think.

GUIDE: Because the essence of thinking begins there.

SCIENTIST: It is thus in the unprethinkable[54] that the essence of the human is released to the open-region.

SCHOLAR: Which is why we also at once added: and indeed by the open-region itself.

GUIDE: The open-region appropriates [*ereignet*] the essence of the human to its own [*eigenen*] regioning.

SCIENTIST: This is how we explained releasement. Yet at the same time it occurs to me that we have also neglected to consider why the essence of the human is enregioned to the open-region.

SCHOLAR: Evidently the essence of the human [*Wesen des Menschen*] is released to the open-region because this essence so essentially belongs to the open-region that the latter cannot essentially occur as it does without the human-being [*Menschenwesens*].

SCIENTIST: This is hardly thinkable.

GUIDE: It cannot be thought at all so long as we will to represent it to ourselves, and that means to violently bring it before ourselves as an objectively present-at-hand relation between an object called "human" and an object called "open-region."

SCIENTIST: That may be. But even if we are mindful of that, nevertheless, in the statement about the essential relation of the human-being to the open-region, doesn't there remain an insurmountable difficulty? We just characterized the open-region as the concealed essence of truth. If for a moment, to be concise, we say [147] "truth" instead of "open-region," the statement about the relation between open-region and the human-being says this: The human-being is

54. This striking and unusual term, "the unprethinkable" (*das Unvordenkliche*), was probably first used by Schelling (see for instance, F. W. J. Schelling, *The Ages of the World,* trans. Jason M. Wirth [Albany: SUNY Press, 2000], p. 12), and has been variously translated in other contexts as "the immemorial" and "the unpreconceivable." For Heidegger, the word presumably indicates both "that which cannot be thought in advance (i.e., that which cannot be preconceived)" and "that prior to which we cannot think." In other words, as what he calls "the coming" (see below, p. 150), the unprethinkable is that before and beyond or behind which we cannot think.—*Tr.*

appropriated over to truth, because truth requires [*braucht*][55] the human. But is it not the distinguishing characteristic of truth, and indeed precisely regarding its relation to the human, that it is what it is independent of the human?

SCHOLAR: I think you touch upon a decisive difficulty here, which we can of course discuss only after we have explained the essence of truth as such and have more clearly determined the essence of the human.

GUIDE: To both we are just getting under way; nevertheless, I would like to attempt to rephrase the statement about the relation of truth to the human in order to clarify what we have to meditate on if we are to consider this relation as such.

SCIENTIST: What you want to say about this remains, therefore, at first just an assertion.

GUIDE: Certainly; and I mean this: the essence of the human is released into the open-region and accordingly required by it, solely because the human by himself has no power over truth, which remains independent of him. Truth can only therefore essentially occur independently of the human, because the essence of the human as releasement to the open-region is required by the open-region for enregioning and bethinging. The independence of truth *from* the human is after all then a relation *to* the human, a relation which rests in the enregioning of the human-being into the open-region.

SCHOLAR: If this were so, then the human, as the indweller in releasement to the open-region, would abide in the provenance of his essence, which we may thus rephrase [148] as: The human is he who is required in the essential occurrence of truth. Abiding in this fashion in his provenance, the human would be touched [*angemutet*] by what is noble [*vom Edlen*] of his essence. He would surmise [*vermutete*] noble-mindedness [*das Edelmütige*].[56]

---

55. As a key term for the relation of being to human being in Heidegger's later writings, *brauchen,* translated here as "to require," conveys at once the double sense of "to need" and "to use."—*Tr.*

56. Heidegger here and throughout *Conversations* draws on a number of words relating to the root word *Mut.* One of the most frequently appearing *Mut* cognates is the apparently innocuous expression *vermutlich,* "presumably." I have sometimes translated *Zumutung* as "audacious demand," although this generally does not bear "negative" connotations for Heidegger. Perhaps the most deliberately used and important of the *Mut* cognates in *Conversations* is *vermuten,* translated as "to surmise." Drawing on its relation to *Mut,* which today means "courage" and which is etymologically related to "mood" and "mind," Heidegger rethinks *Vermuten* or "surmising" to mean something like a mindful and courageous attempt to follow a hunch or pursue an inkling. Surmising is thus thought here not as a groundless conjecturing, but rather as an attentive dedication to following pre-

SCIENTIST: This surmising could hardly be anything other than waiting, which we think of as the indwelling of releasement.

SCHOLAR: And if the open-region were the abiding expanse, forbearance could surmise the furthest, surmising even the expanse of the abiding-while itself, because it can wait the longest.

GUIDE: And forbearing noble-mindedness [*der langmütige Edelmut*] would be a pure resting-in-itself of that willing which, renouncing willing, has let itself engage in what is not a will.

SCHOLAR: Noble-mindedness would be the essence of thinking and thus of thanking.

GUIDE: Of that thinking which does not first express gratitude for something, but rather simply thanks for being allowed to thank.

SCHOLAR: With this essence of thinking we would have found what we seek.

SCIENTIST: Supposing, of course, that we would have indeed found that in which all that has been said seems to rest, and this is the essence of the open-region.

GUIDE: It is because this is only supposed that, for some time now, as you have perhaps noticed, we have said everything merely in the manner of supposition.

SCIENTIST: All the same I can no longer refrain from confessing that the essence of the open-region has come nearer to us, while the open-region itself seems to me to be farther than ever. [149]

SCHOLAR: You mean that you are in nearness to the essence of the open-region and yet far from the open-region itself?

SCIENTIST: But the open-region itself and its essence cannot after all be two different things, if one can speak of things at all here.

SCHOLAR: The self of the open-region is presumably its essence and the selfsame of itself.

GUIDE: Then perhaps our experience during this conversation can be expressed by saying that, insofar as we are those who think, we come into the nearness of the world,[57] yet, due to such nearness, we at the same time remain far from it; although this remaining is at the same time a return in the sense of a turning to enter into releasement.

---

sentiments, to presaging pathways of thought that are opened up by intimations of being. Indeed, when *Vermuten,* along with other *Mut* cognates, is specifically thematized in the following passages, it is identified explicitly with the attentiveness of "waiting." *Vermuten* is thus being thought in contrast to the willful projection of a horizon—that is, as an alternative to thinking as willing (see also below, pp. 106-107).—*Tr.*

57. This and several of the following passages are modified and abbreviated in the 1959 excerpt (see *G* 65-66 / *DT* 86). Among the changes is the substitution of "open-region" (*Gegnet*) for "world" (*Welt*).—*Tr.*

SCHOLAR: In what you say, only the essence of waiting would be named as the essence of thinking, which unveils itself in this form as commemorating.

SCIENTIST: But how then does it stand with nearness and farness, within which the world opens up and veils itself, draws near and recedes?

SCHOLAR: This nearness and farness can be nothing outside the world.

GUIDE: Because the world, insofar as it worlds, gathers everything, each to the other, and lets everything return to itself in its own resting in the selfsame.

SCIENTIST: Then the world itself would be what nears and furthers.

SCHOLAR: The world would itself be the nearness of farness and the farness of nearness.

SCIENTIST: That sounds of course very dialectical; as if nearness and farness would have to be represented here as two ideas in one. [150] But they are not objects, and thus are not representable. This is, after all, what our meditation came to—if I followed along correctly.

GUIDE: Indeed.

SCHOLAR: Nearness is here not a part of its counterpart, farness. Nearness is that wherein and where-into farness draws near and so essentially occurs as farness. To this farness, which first arrives in nearness, corresponds only a comportment in which arrival is not preemptively anticipated as something present-at-hand, but rather is allowed as arrival.

SCIENTIST: We have come to know waiting as this comportment.

SCHOLAR: In terms of this waiting, we defined thinking as commemorating, distinguishing it from a mere representing.

GUIDE: Then what is the essence of thinking, if it is defined in terms of this comportment to the world, and if world is the nearness of farness?

SCIENTIST: Thinking would then be a kind of relationship [Verhältnis] and comportment [Verhalten] to nearness. How should we grasp this?

SCHOLAR: This probably no longer allows itself to be said in a single word. However, I know a word that until a moment ago still appeared to me as appropriate to name the essence of thinking and therewith also cognition in a fitting manner.

SCIENTIST: I would like to hear this word.

SCHOLAR: It is a word that occurred [einfiel] to me already in our first conversation. This idea [Einfall] is also what I had in mind when, at the beginning of our conversation today, I remarked that I had our first country path conversation to thank for a precious inspiration. In the course of today's conversation I also often wanted to bring forth this [151] word. But each time, it seemed to me less suitable for what was coming nearer to us as the essence of thinking.

SCIENTIST: You are making a secret of your idea, as if you did not want to give away too early a discovery you yourself made.

SCHOLAR: I did not discover the word I am thinking of myself; it is only a scholarly idea that occurred to me.

SCIENTIST: And so, if I may say so, a historiological reminiscence?

SCHOLAR: Certainly. It would also have fit in well with the style of our conversation today, in the course of which we often threw in words and sentences that stemmed from the thinking of the ancient Greeks. But now this word will no longer suit what we are attempting to name with a single word.

GUIDE: That is, the essence of thinking which, as an indwelling releasement to the worlding of the world, bears that relationship by means of which the human dwells in nearness to farness.[58]

SCIENTIST: Even if the word you have in mind is now no longer suitable, you could still divulge it to us at the conclusion of our conversation; for we have again neared human habitation and must in any case break off the conversation.

GUIDE: And this word which is now no longer fitting, yet which was earlier esteemed by you as a precious inspiration, could make clear to us that in the meantime we have come before something ineffable.

SCHOLAR: It is a word from Heraclitus.

SCIENTIST: From which of the fragments handed down by tradition have you taken the word? [152]

SCHOLAR: The word occurred to me alone and by itself, namely because it stands alone. It does not come *out of* a fragment. It itself as this One Word makes up the fragment which is counted with the number 122.

SCIENTIST: I don't know this shortest of Heraclitus's fragments.

SCHOLAR: And it is scarcely paid attention to by anyone else either, since there is little one can begin to do with a single word.

GUIDE: It seems to me entirely questionable that what philology and the historians of philosophy take as "fragments" are broken-off pieces. These words may be this if we set them forth from out of the whole of a text; in themselves, however, they are hardly broken-off pieces. Indeed, it is they that have brought into language intact what is essential of the thoughts which are thought by a thinker.

SCIENTIST: Yet this word of Heraclitus, which is designated as fragment 122, how does it read?

SCHOLAR: Ἀγχιβασίη.

SCIENTIST: What does this mean?

---

58. This passage is replaced in the 1959 excerpt with the following: "You mean the essence of thinking which, as the indwelling releasement to the open-region, is the essential human relation to the open-region, which we presage as nearness to farness" (G 68 / DT 87).—Tr.

SCHOLAR: The Greek word is translated into German as *Herangehen*, "going-up-to."

SCIENTIST: I regard this word as an excellent name for naming the essence of cognition; for the character of actively going-forward [*Vorgehens*] and going-to [*Zugehens*] objects is strikingly expressed in it.

SCHOLAR: It also seemed to me that Ἀγχιβασίη, translated as "going-up-to," is an apt word to characterize what we first made of cognition. This is probably also why the word occurred to me when, in our first conversation, we spoke of the action, achievement, work, [153] and implementation of modern research.

SCIENTIST: One could use this Greek word precisely in order to make clear that research in the natural sciences is something like an attack on nature, but one which nevertheless lets nature speak. Ἀγχιβασίη, "going-up-to"—in fact, I could think of this word of Heraclitus as a motto [*Leitwort*] for a treatise on the essence of modern science, historiological science no less than physical science in the broadest sense.

SCHOLAR: This is why I just now hesitated to pronounce this word yet, since it does not at all suit that essence of thinking which we surmised along the way today.

SCIENTIST: Since the waiting of which we spoke is indeed almost the counter-movement to going-up-to.

SCHOLAR: Which is not to say the counter-rest.

GUIDE: Or simply rest.—Yet is it then decided that Ἀγχιβασίη means "going-up-to"?

SCHOLAR: Translated literally, it says: "going-near."[59]

SCIENTIST: If this word of the Greeks says just as little about the modern age as do others of its kind, what then should we make of it? If we try to merely set forth its opposite, then, rather than "going-up-to" and "going-near," the word would have to mean so much as "remaining-away."

SCHOLAR: Of that there is nothing in the least indicated in the word; for what is spoken of is ἀγχί, "near," and βασίη, βαῖνειν, "to stride," "to go."

SCIENTIST: We are thus ill-advised if, in order to interpret the word, we flee into the mere opposite of what is modern. [154]

SCHOLAR: Moreover, against our own intentions, by positing the opposite we just entangle ourselves yet further in a dependence on that from which we want to free ourselves.

SCIENTIST: Yet what does the word Ἀγχιβασίη say if we think it in a Greek manner?

---

59. The following page and a half (up to the discussion of "going-into-nearness" on p. 102) do not appear in the 1959 excerpt (see *G* 70 / *DT* 89), and much of the remaining text was substantially abbreviated and in places rewritten.—*Tr.*

GUIDE: And presuppose that it is—as the word of a thinker—an essential word.

SCHOLAR: Ἀγχιβασίη names "going" [*das Gehen*].[60] If it is thought with regard to the movement [*Bewegung*] that constitutes the essence of the human, then going means the mobile [*bewegliche*] relationship of the human to that which is.

GUIDE: *Where* does the human go if, thought in a Greek manner, he moves within his relationship to that which *is*? *How* must we think in a *Greek* manner that which *is*?

SCHOLAR: As what presences.

GUIDE: What presences [*Das Anwesende*] essentially occurs [*west*] in unconcealment.

SCIENTIST: Insofar as he goes around in relationship to that which *is*, the human goes *within* unconcealment. The going [*Gehen*] in the word Ἀγχιβασίη then means the course of going [*Gang*] within the unconcealment of what presences.

SCHOLAR: Why then is ἀγχί spoken of, which like ἐγγύς signifies near, in nearness?

GUIDE: What presences in unconcealment—παρόντα—is that which is not away but rather essentially occurring here in nearness. In all presencing, nearness prevails. What is unconcealed is something which has drawn near.

SCIENTIST: Accordingly, nearness belongs just as much to "being," thought in a Greek manner—that is, to εἶναι as presencing—as it does to truth thought in a Greek manner, to Ἀλήθεια. [155]

GUIDE: Which brings us to surmise that Ἀλήθεια and εἶναι could name the selfsame.

SCHOLAR: But if the early Greek thinkers thought solely toward the Ἀλήθεια and the εἶναι of ὄν, toward what presences as such and toward unconcealment; and if just as essentially in the one as in the other, nearness occurs; is it then still surprising if in one word—a word which names the essential relation of the human to what presences within unconcealment—what specifically names "near" (ἀγχί) is indicated?

GUIDE: It is not surprising, provided we learn to think what is Greek in a Greek manner; but it does remain astonishing. Yet what essentially occurs in "what is near" [*im »Nahen«*] is presumably not what is at certain times here or there near, such that we might approach [*annähern*] it. What essentially occurs in the "near" [*im »nah«*], in ἀγχί, would rather be nearness [*die Nähe*] itself.

---

60. Given the context of this "country path conversation," it should be borne in mind that *gehen* means specifically "to walk" as well as generally "to go."—*Tr.*

SCHOLAR: Ἀγχιβασίη may thus mean neither "going-up-to" nor "approaching," because in that case only what is near would be represented, without however nearness being thought.

SCIENTIST: That makes sense. Yet you are only establishing what Ἀγχιβασίη does *not* mean.

GUIDE: Perhaps we can think that it might mean so much as: going-into-nearness.

SCHOLAR: You understand this literally in the sense of: letting-oneself-into-nearness.

GUIDE: That is how I think it.

SCHOLAR: Then in the isolated word Ἀγχιβασίη, going-into-nearness, something like a claim could also be heard resounding.

SCIENTIST: And so it would be easier to understand why this word stands entirely by itself. [156]

GUIDE: But *where* does it stand? *How* do matters stand with this word?

SCHOLAR: It has long ceased to resound.

GUIDE: Faded-*away* [Ver*klungen*] perhaps already at the time it *began* to resound [er*klungen*].

SCHOLAR: But perhaps the resounding [*Widerhall*] of its early resonance [*Halles*] was sheltered at a place that might remain not entirely inaccessible even to us today.

SCIENTIST: Insofar as we *now* perceive something of its resounding-*forth* [An*klang*].

GUIDE: So that we could even use it to name that which we are on the trail of as long as we are thoughtfully pursuing the essence of thinking.

SCHOLAR: Ἀγχιβασίη—going-into-nearness—the word of course in no way means the essence of modern research, be it that of the natural sciences or be it historiological research. But the word can, entirely from afar, stand as name over our walking course [*Gang*] today—

GUIDE: a course which escorted us deep into the night—

SCIENTIST: a night which gleams forth ever more magnificently—

SCHOLAR: and over-astonishes the stars—

GUIDE: because it brings near the distances of the stars to one another.

SCIENTIST: At least in the mind [*Vorstellung*] of the naïve observer, but not so for the exact scientist.

GUIDE: For the child in the human, the night remains the seamstress [*Näherin*] who brings near [*nähert*], so that one star next to the other gleams in silent light.

SCHOLAR: She joins the lights together without seam or hem or yarn. [157]

SCIENTIST: The night is the seamstress who in sewing brings near [*nähernd näht*]. She works only with nearness, which furthers farness.

SCHOLAR: If she ever works and does not rather rest—

GUIDE: while she *a*stonishes the depths of the height—

SCHOLAR: and in astonishment opens up what is closed shut—

SCIENTIST: and so like waiting harbors the arrival—
GUIDE: if it is a released waiting—
SCHOLAR: and the human-being remains *a*-propriated *into* there—
GUIDE: *from* where we are called.

*   *   *

An essential thought, which was touched on during this conversation, has not yet been further considered. It concerns the question of in what way nature, in allowing the objectification of its domain, defends itself against technology by bringing about the annihilation of the human-essence. This annihilation in no way means the elimination of the human, but rather the completion of his will-essence.

Messkirch, 7 April 1945   Martin Heidegger

Supplements

On Letting Go of Things

"Where I will nothing for myself, there wills instead my God."
Eckhart, *Talks of Instruction* (n. 1)[61]

"For whoever has let go of his own will and of himself, has let go of the whole world as truly as if it were his free property, as if he possessed it with full power of authority. Everything that you expressly do not desire—that you have forsaken and let go of for the sake of God. *'Blessed are the poor in spirit,'* our Lord has said; and this means: those who are poor in will." (n. 3, p. 79)

"As far as you yourself go out of all things, just this far—not one step less or more—does God go in with all that is His." (n. 4, p. 80)

Being of Great Essence

"May God become great in us." (n. 5, p. 81)

"Do not think that holiness is to be attributed to a manner of acting: one should attribute holiness to a manner of being."[62] [159]

---

61. Cf. *Deutsche Mystiker*, vol. 3: *Meister Eckhart*, selected and translated [into modern German] by Joseph Bernhardt (Kemten and Munich: Jos. Kösel'sche, 1914), *Die Reden der Unterweisung*, n. 1, p. 77. [For the context of, and for alternative translations of this and the following three quotations, see *Meister Eckhart: The Essential Sermons, Commentaries, Treatises, and Defense*, trans. Edmund Colledge and Bernard McGinn (Mahwah, N.J.: Paulist Press, 1981), pp. 247–251.—*Tr.*]

62. *Deutsche Mystiker des vierzehnten Jahrhunderts*, edited by Franz Pfeiffer, vol. 2: *Meister Eckhart* (Leibzig, 1857), p. 546.

Regioning-

To grant return into the repose [*Ruhe*] in which everything rests [*beruht*].

The abiding-while of the expanse of self-belonging—(A-propriated)

The word does not represent something, but rather brings something to abide in the expanse of what it can say.

The Horizon

is the open which surrounds the human, filled with outward views into outward looks of objects.

The Conversation

Where else could the unspoken be purely kept, heeded, other than in true conversation.

Of all goods the most dangerous is language,[63] because it cannot keep safe the unspoken—(not because it veils too much, but rather because it divulges too much).

---

63. This is an allusion to a line from Hölderlin, which Heidegger quotes and comments on in GA 4: 33, 37–38; *Elucidations of Hölderlin's Poetry*, trans. Keith Höller (Amherst, N.Y.: Humanity, 2000), pp. 51, 55–56.—*Tr.*

2. The Teacher Meets the Tower Warden at the Door to the Tower Stairway

TEACHER: So I have come then too late.

TOWER WARDEN: For what?

TEACHER: To solve the wondrous, which has held me in unrest throughout the day.

TOWER WARDEN: And that is?

TEACHER: Surely you must know.

TOWER WARDEN: Hardly, for I scarcely still think of paying attention to something wondrous in order to solve it.

TEACHER: And this, even though so much that is worthy of thought has been handed down to us.

TOWER WARDEN: Indeed; for everything worthy of thought measures itself out to us [*mißt sich uns zu*] in accordance with [*gemäß*] the manner of thinking within which we move.

TEACHER: You mean that thinking would no longer seek after the wondrous and would keep itself free from wondering. Would not all willing-to-know then be shaken from the ground up? How then should an examination of the world remain passable and capable of providing measure?

TOWER WARDEN: Perhaps we overestimate the role to be played by such an examination of the world, and what we ourselves contribute to it, by holding it to be the work of our representing, and by remaining insensitive to that which touches us inconspicuously. He who lives in the height of a tower feels the trembling of the world sooner and in further-reaching oscillations.

TEACHER: The fact that you think from out of such an experience reveals itself ever more clearly to me each time we converse. And yet why should we not hold fast to the wondrous in order to fathom it and thereby appropriate it? [164]

TOWER WARDEN: Because, prior to that, the strange is there for us to find.

TEACHER: And we are to be satisfied with a mere find?

TOWER WARDEN: A true find is never a mere find, which still lacks something else. It is everything.

TEACHER: That is what you take the strange to be, as opposed to the wondrous.

TOWER WARDEN: The latter arouses our questioning; the former hints back into itself.

TEACHER: I understand what you say of the wondrous, for we are in the habit of questioning.

TOWER WARDEN: Since habituation follows our will to fathom [*Ergründen*] and substantiate [*Begründen*].

TEACHER: And we hold this willing to be thoroughly natural.

TOWER WARDEN: Yet we leave what is natural to itself, as though it has always been what is right.

TEACHER: That it is indeed. It is only that nature as such belongs in the wondrous.

TOWER WARDEN: Perhaps even in the strange.

TEACHER: And is therefore nothing less than natural.

TOWER WARDEN: The same goes for the fathoming and substantiating that live in the will of questioning.

TEACHER: Said more precisely: in questioning as willing.

TOWER WARDEN: And so you hold another manner of questioning to be possible.

TEACHER: Certainly—though I cannot represent it to myself. [165]

TOWER WARDEN: It would be more necessary to attain to it.

TEACHER: Which would involve giving up the wondrous—

TOWER WARDEN: in favor of the strange.

TEACHER: Of which you said, just now, that it hints back into itself. I am not able to follow this indication; I would define the strange [*das Seltsame*], rather, in terms of its rarity [*Seltenheit*].

TOWER WARDEN: As what is infrequent [*das nicht Häufige*]—what does not come about in heaps [*Haufen*] and masses, but rather singularly and then suddenly.

TEACHER: Unsurmised.

TOWER WARDEN: And yet the unsurmised always reaches only those who surmise.[1]

---

1. Compare Heraclitus, fragment 18: "If one does not expect the unexpected one will not find it out, since it is not to be searched out, and is difficult to compass" (G. S. Kirk, J. E. Raven, and M. Schofield, *The Presocratic Philosophers*, 2nd edition [Cambridge: Cambridge University Press, 1983], p. 193). Another translation of this fragment reads: "Unless he hopes for the unhoped for, he will not find

TEACHER: But does this not mean: to grope around in uncertainty and murkiness?

TOWER WARDEN: And to search for grounds, whereby we would once again fall back into questioning as the will-to-a-ground [*den Willen zum Grund*].

TEACHER: Far removed from the way to the strange.

TOWER WARDEN: Indeed.

TEACHER: I take it, then, that you think of surmising differently.

TOWER WARDEN: Neither in terms of the character of uncertainty, nor at all as a representing.

TEACHER: Then this surmising is just as strange as the strange.

TOWER WARDEN: Presumably [*Vermutlich*]. But although the unsurmised [*das Unvermutete*] is suddenly and entirely the near itself, surmising [*Vermuten*] remains forbearing [*langmütig*], on the way; it looks far into the distance and prepares a forecourt for the arrival of the unsurmised. [166]

TEACHER: This surmising requires, if I see correctly, no assurance. Its forbearance is maintained by a peculiar confidence that knows no hastiness.

TOWER WARDEN: Hastiness nevertheless remains a danger.

TEACHER: What you say surprises me. If there is something unsettling for me with regard to what you call the surmising of the unsurmised, it is the question of what supports the confidence of such surmising.

TOWER WARDEN: You ask this because once more, and ever again, you are seeking after supports and foundations.

TEACHER: You mean to say, after grounds.

TOWER WARDEN: That and something else. We hardly ever escape from the persistency of the question about the ground of surmising and its confidence. This question nevertheless remains uncertain. But our long habituation in the will-to-fathom tears us away ever again. When we attempt to free ourselves from this habituation, then we all too easily fall into hastiness.

TEACHER: Instead of?

TOWER WARDEN: Instead of patiently [*langmütig*] awakening surmising [*Vermuten*] in ourselves.

TEACHER: That is to say, a sense for the strange.

TOWER WARDEN: This is the case even if it may be that some mortals are native to the strange.

TEACHER: We, on the other hand, would have to let the wondrous, and the craving to fathom it, pass by.

---

it, since it is not to be hunted out and is impassable" (Richard D. McKirahan, *Philosophy Before Socrates* [Indianapolis: Hackett, 1994], p. 120). On "surmising," see the text and footnote above on pp. 96-97.—*Tr.*

TOWER WARDEN: This word is fitting. To let pass by, but not to will to go beyond and overcome.

TEACHER: And, you mean to say, it is this will that is the danger. [167]

TOWER WARDEN: Indeed. I myself fell prey to it when we met a moment ago. You came to solve the wondrous that had unsettled you all day long.

TEACHER: And you pulled me away from that.

TOWER WARDEN: Because of a haste that is difficult to recover from, a haste which never once wishes to abide with, to behold, what this wondrous might be.

TEACHER: I said of this wondrous, moreover, that you would know it.

TOWER WARDEN: How should I?

TEACHER: My perplexity last night cannot have remained hidden from you.

TOWER WARDEN: In the tower room?

TEACHER: Yes.

TOWER WARDEN: In front of the picture?

TEACHER: Yes. It is on account of it that I have come here to climb up to you.

TOWER WARDEN: In the meantime I have climbed down.

TEACHER: Heraclitus teaches us that the way up and down is the same. You know fragment 60: ὁδὸς ἄνω κάτω μία ὠυτή.

TOWER WARDEN: A stimulating thought for a tower warden.

TEACHER: Indeed, if we carefully translate the saying: "The way upwards downwards one, and that means: the selfsame."

TOWER WARDEN: We experience something of the selfsame in looking at such a way.

TEACHER: Upwards and downwards belong to one another, not as two separated pieces, but rather in the sense that to the upwards belongs already [168] the downwards, and the downwards in its manner unfolds in itself the upwards.

TOWER WARDEN: Climbing up and down, stairway and landing [Stieg und Steg],[2] show their dynamic configuration.

TEACHER: Inside the tower.

TOWER WARDEN: Only inside? Only in the tower? It may be that the selfsame of which we speak gathers itself in the tower in a unique manner, such that its strangeness comes to an unapparent appearing.

TEACHER: What you are now indicating as the strangeness of the tower remains in the dark for me.

---

2. Whereas *Stieg* is presumably referring to the vertical incline of a stairway, *Steg* is presumably referring to the horizontal landing where one reverses direction when ascending or descending a staircase. —Tr.

TOWER WARDEN: This does not allow itself to be easily said from the foot of the tower. It would be better for us to catch sight of the tower from a distance.

TEACHER: "We," you say—and yet at the same time you must admit that in this view of the tower from a distance belongs an experience of the Tower Warden.

TOWER WARDEN: Who looks out into the distance from the tower—

TEACHER: so that here the selfsame would prevail, as in the selfsame of the upwards and downwards.

TOWER WARDEN: The selfsame flows everywhere through us. Because this flowing is no dark and muddled urging, but rather rests in the simplicity of the selfsame, everything thus becomes at once bright and wide when thinking finds itself specially let into the selfsame.

TEACHER: Then that strange unrest of surmising is awakened, which I believe to have just now noticed in you. You do not wish to linger here any longer. I see that I am holding you up.

TOWER WARDEN: But you are not disturbing anything, and so please come along with me.

TEACHER: With pleasure, as long as we don't go too far. [169]

TOWER WARDEN: Just up to the country path.

TEACHER: It will provide the distance from which we can catch sight of the tower.

TOWER WARDEN: Till then we can consider anew the saying of Heraclitus.

TEACHER: Why only up to the country path, why not onto the path itself? Since already on many a walk it has led to insights beyond what was hoped for.

TOWER WARDEN: For just that reason it should remain free for another conversation, one in which you too shall participate, since matters are turning out to be so favorable to you.

TEACHER: You shall always find me ready [*bereit*], even if often not prepared [*vorbereitet*], for the paths onto which you venture.

TOWER WARDEN: And also for the steps, since you often visit me in the tower and effortlessly deal with the climb up and down.

TEACHER: Only yesterday evening I would have shied away from the step, if I had known that I would be faced with the sight of the picture in your tower room. But let us leave the picture. I would rather remain with you in anticipation of the conversation on the country path.

TOWER WARDEN: If so, then let us *not* leave the picture.

TEACHER: You mean, not go—

TOWER WARDEN: yes, but rather first come.

TEACHER: In what way?

TOWER WARDEN: The guest, whom I am going out to meet, recently brought me the picture in the tower room.

TEACHER: So he will be able to give me some direct information about the picture. [170]

TOWER WARDEN: I fear that you will be disappointed if you expect that the guest could, as you wish [*wollen*], solve what is wondrous in the picture.

TEACHER: But perhaps he will show us the strange.

TOWER WARDEN: Presumably not that either, that least of all.

TEACHER: Yet if he gave you the picture, he must have certainly had an acquaintanceship [*Kundschaft*][3] with it.

TOWER WARDEN: How did you come upon this word?

TEACHER: I once found it used in your speech. At the time I was unable to hear it with sufficient clarity, but since then it has continued to strike a chord in me.

TOWER WARDEN: The guest surely must have an acquaintanceship in relation to the picture.

TEACHER: You speak now again in your careful manner.

TOWER WARDEN: This is necessary; for we must distinguish whether we mean acquaintanceship *of* [von] the picture or acquaintanceship *through* [durch] the picture.

TEACHER: In the one case, acquaintanceship would amount to as much as expertise [*Kennerschaft*].

TOWER WARDEN: And thus a matter of mortals.

TEACHER: And in the other case?

TOWER WARDEN: The gift of a message [*Kunde*], if not indeed an original testimony [*Ur-kunde*]; I mean by this the message that comes to us inceptually [*anfänglich*].

TEACHER: We could never make such an acquaintanceship, but rather only receive it. [171]

TOWER WARDEN: And even this only if we are already ready for maintaining.

---

3. The modern usage of *Kundschaft* as "clientele" can be traced back to the sense of "acquaintanceship," namely that of a shopkeeper with the customers who frequent his store. In the sixteenth century a *Kundschafter* was a "messenger" or a "spy," and the verb *kundschaften* meant "to inform." The adjective *kund*, meaning "known" or "apparent," goes back to the ninth century, and is reflected in several modern words such as *kundig* (expert, experienced), *kündigen* (to give notice, as in to quit or to fire someone), *bekunden* (to demonstrate or testify), *erkunden* (to explore or find out), *die Erkundung* (reconnaissance), and *die Erkundigung* (inquiry). The modern word *Kunde* means either "customer" or less frequently "message," and is also used as a suffix appended to subjects of study (*Erdkunde* is geography and *Sozialkunde* is social studies). Although the modern usage of *Kundschaft* is restricted to the sense of "clientele," Heidegger is here presumably drawing on the word's etymologically more original sense to suggest a "knowing by means of receiving a message."—*Tr.*

TEACHER: Something that we, in an earlier conversation with the neighbor, considered to remain infinitely distinct from possessing.

TOWER WARDEN: When the moment is favorable, the guest will tell us himself whether and how he has an acquaintanceship with the picture in the tower room.

TEACHER: In the meantime, we already see the tower from a distance—

TOWER WARDEN: and we are drawing near to the country path, without having entered into the interplay between Heraclitus's saying and the essence of the tower.

TEACHER: Because I have again let the feeling of unrest that the picture brings me run its course.

TOWER WARDEN: This letting is good, especially when the picture belongs in the tower room,

TEACHER: —a belonging [Gehören] which, though it still remains concealed at least to me, the guest perceived [hörte] when it occurred to him to bring you the picture.

TOWER WARDEN: So we should not separate the strange of the picture and the strange of the tower.

TEACHER: Then we are nearer to the matter than it would appear.

TOWER WARDEN: You mean the matter of thinking which is never sufficiently emplaced through discussion [erörterte].[4]

TEACHER: This I mean, while knowing at the same time that a successful crossing-over [Übergang] into your manner of thinking continues to evade me.

TOWER WARDEN: This will remain the case so long as you struggle at a crossing-over rather than allowing a turning-back [Rückkehr]. [172]

TEACHER: To where?

TOWER WARDEN: To that place where we truly already are.

TEACHER: Yet over this locale of mortals, as you sometimes name it, lies for me a darkness.

TOWER WARDEN: Be glad. It helps more than the artificial light that one shines today through everything, such that neither light nor darkness remain, not even dimness—

---

4. Although *erörtern* would commonly be translated as "to discuss," I have rendered it here as "to emplace through discussion." Whereas the etymology of "discussion" inappropriately implies an analyzing by way of breaking up into pieces, Heidegger writes that *Erörterung* is to be understood first as "to point toward the place" (*in den Ort weisen*), and then as "to attend to the place" (*den Ort beachten*) (*GA* 12, p. 33; *On the Way to Language*, trans. Peter D. Hertz [New York: Harper & Row, 1971], p. 159, translation modified). It should also be borne in mind that the excerpt from the first conversation published in 1959 was given the title "Toward an Emplacing Discussion [*Erörterung*] of Releasement [*Gelassenheit*]: From a Country Path Conversation about Thinking."—*Tr.*

TEACHER: and we, inundated with information, nowhere find our way.

TOWER WARDEN: Least of all with respect to ourselves; for there, where we truly already are, stands initially our ego [*Ich*] or, if you still wish to name it so, our existence [*Existenz*].

TEACHER: Then when do we experience where we truly already are, if no such greedily drilling dissection of the human ever reaches his essence? Must we not rather look away from ourselves in order to find ourselves where we truly are? But what does "truly" [*eigentlich*] mean here? And toward where should we look?

TOWER WARDEN: Toward everywhere—when we have the look [*Blick*]; only not at ourselves.

TEACHER: From where do we take the look?

TOWER WARDEN: We never take it, yet constantly receive it. It brings us before the unapparent, for example the tower or the picture, if this may still be called thus.

TEACHER: How is it with the tower?

TOWER WARDEN: As for how the matter [*Es*] stands with the tower, the saying of Heraclitus gives us a hint.

TEACHER: The upwards and downwards belong to one another. [173]

TOWER WARDEN: This not only, however, in the case of the up and down of the stairs inside the tower. The upwards and downwards do not present themselves first by means of the stairs, but rather the tower brings these with itself.

TEACHER: So the upwards and downwards come about by means of the tower.

TOWER WARDEN: In no way. The tower merely gathers the upwards and downwards around and in itself.

TEACHER: In what manner does this happen?

TOWER WARDEN: In that the tower gathers the upwards and downwards so that the gathering first gives the belonging-together of both into the free-dimension [*ins Freie*], wherein the appearing of the unapparent plays.

TEACHER: Hardly anyone will understand what you have expounded.

TOWER WARDEN: Because there is nothing here to understand, since everything depends on looking.

TEACHER: I have taken this into consideration; but you cannot bar one from demanding a suitable clarity from words like gathering, the free-dimension, or the appearing of the unapparent.

TOWER WARDEN: A word is clear [*deutlich*] if it is capable of indicating [*deuten*] by pointing toward where it would like to show, and indeed to show within the domain of the saying whereby it became a word.

TEACHER: A dictionary definition [*Wortbedeutung*] is precisely what is not involved in indicating [*Deuten*] and its clarity [*Deutlichkeit*].

TOWER WARDEN: Not at all. As long as one ascribes to words dictionary definitions, one does not let their indicating speak, that is, literally "come to word" [*zu Wort kommen*].⁵

TEACHER: So a mere group of individual words [*Wörter*] are then not a genuine gathering of words [*Worte*]. They say nothing.⁶ [174]

TOWER WARDEN: If "saying" means: a showing-hinting-calling letting-appear of that which is to be caught sight of.

TEACHER: But this is a very arbitrary determination of saying.

TOWER WARDEN: At least it appears so, because one explains saying on the basis of language, and yet represents language as expression.

TEACHER: Along with this, and from ancient times within the tradition of our thinking, attention has also been also given to the sign-character of language.

TOWER WARDEN: You are right. One pays attention to the sign-character of language, but does not consider the manner of showing [*die Art des Zeigens*] of these signs [*Zeichen*]. Presumably the manner of showing in saying remains unique. Its uniqueness [*Einzigartiges*] can itself belong only in the unique one [*das Einzige*].

TEACHER: By that you mean to imply [*andeuten*] that the word and its indicating [*Deuten*], saying and its showing, may not be explained on the basis of something else, for example a formal-universal definition of sign and expression.

TOWER WARDEN: Not only may they not be explained on the basis of something else, but they may not be explained at all; rather, they are only to be caught sight of.

TEACHER: Which demands that we remain with the uniqueness of the matter.

TOWER WARDEN: And this is what is most difficult.

TEACHER: For in order to remain with the matter, it must itself already be abiding with us. It seems to me that we continually get caught in the same difficulty, which happened to me earlier when I attempted to hear what you refer to as the indicating of the word. We can follow the indicating only if we are already held in a preview [*Vorblick*] of that which is to be caught sight of [*das zu Erblickende*]. [175]

TOWER WARDEN: What you now touch on is no mere difficulty. It is a unique state of affairs.

5. The idiom, *zu Wort kommen*, is commonly used in the sense of "to get a chance to speak."—*Tr.*

6. There are two plural forms of "word" in German, *Wörter* and *Worte*. The former is used for a collection of unconnected words, such as is found in a *Wörterbuch*, a dictionary, or in a vocabulary list. The latter is used for a group of coherently connected words, such as when one refers to the words of a poem or a speech.—*Tr.*

TEACHER: And so perhaps a sign of that unique one [*jenes Einzigen*]. But which state of affairs do you have in view?

TOWER WARDEN: I not only catch sight of it and do catch sight of it only insofar as we—you as well as I—stay within it.

TEACHER: Thus it comes constantly and in manifold ways into the world; and this is why I would find it helpful to grasp the state of affairs in a fitting word.

TOWER WARDEN: That remains an ambivalent intention, so decisively so that even this ambivalence corresponds to the state of affairs.

TEACHER: I will come to know this only if you simply say what the state of affairs is for us.

TOWER WARDEN: I already did say this when we came to talk of the matter of thinking.

TEACHER: The matter of the thinking that you follow.

TOWER WARDEN: To which there exists no passageway for crossing-over [*Übergang*] from your manner of thinking, which I would like to call a loosened up metaphysical manner.

TEACHER: Why loosened up?

TOWER WARDEN: Because you showed a predilection to follow my intimations from your manner of thinking.

TEACHER: Which is fundamentally impossible, if there exists no passageway for crossing-over.

TOWER WARDEN: You assert too much, for such a passageway is not required.

TEACHER: You spoke of a turning back, and I immediately [176] asked: to where? Yet it soon became clear to me that this question is insufficient. For it assumes that the course of a thinking should only change its direction, and not its kind.

TOWER WARDEN: But the possible directions are already predetermined by the manner of thinking.

TEACHER: Thus we had best abandon this manner of thinking. One will resist this proposal, not only because it is extreme, insofar as it concerns the entire tradition of Western thought, but also because it is groundless.

TOWER WARDEN: If you equate the groundless with the merely arbitrary, then what you call the proposal, namely the audacious directive to abandon the established manner of thinking, is in no way groundless, for it arises out of a determinative calling [*Bestimmung*]. But not everything that determines [*nicht jedes Bestimmende*] is necessarily a kind of ground.

TEACHER: What determinatively calls on [*bestimmt*] us, then, to abandon the established manner of thinking?

TOWER WARDEN: In order to sufficiently answer your question, an extensive emplacing discussion is required. As you recall, a short time ago we touched on the same question from an entirely different angle in a conversation with our neighbor.

TEACHER: The connection first becomes apparent to me now that you mention it, and it certainly seems to me more pressing than before.

TOWER WARDEN: Let us therefore let this matter rest today, and instead I will repeat more clearly what is involved in a transformation of the manner of thinking: *From everywhere we must continually turn back to where we truly already are.*

TEACHER: What you say sounds even more obscure than your first remark. Every word here calls for an emplacing discussion. [177]

TOWER WARDEN: On a good occasion—since one is required—we would like to attempt this. We shall not come to an end therewith.

TEACHER: But perhaps to an inception?

TOWER WARDEN: Or even to *the* inception.

TEACHER: Human thinking never reaches this far.

TOWER WARDEN: Let us leave the decision on that matter open. We save it, together with the emplacing discussion of my indication, for a later moment.

TEACHER: I thoroughly agree, if for no other reason than since we should avoid always letting new questions push us forward and drive us from the path.

TOWER WARDEN: Do you not notice that we are already walking on the ever reliable country path? If we pause and turn around, the tower has in the meantime receded farther away.

TEACHER: It seems to me that we catch sight of it more clearly now.

TOWER WARDEN: You mean of towerness?

TEACHER: Precisely that. Only I forget now what gave us the occasion to reflect on the essence of the tower.

TOWER WARDEN: Several things. The saying of Heraclitus on the self-sameness of upwards and downwards—

TEACHER: which I myself mentioned.

TOWER WARDEN: But in the context of your question concerning how we would arrive at where we truly already are.

TEACHER: A question you answered with the strange turn of phrase, that in order to arrive at our own essence we must look away from ourselves.

TOWER WARDEN: Whereto? [178]

TEACHER: I see more clearly: everywhere—only not at ourselves.

TOWER WARDEN: Insofar as we represent ourselves as existing egos and have the look that goes along with this.

TEACHER: To everywhere—for example at the tower. What do we catch sight of in towerness?

TOWER WARDEN: You will find it if you look in light of the saying from Heraclitus, and indeed, now from the country path.

TEACHER: But the upwards and downwards of the way of the stairs has become invisible.

TOWER WARDEN: For that reason it shows itself more clearly and even in its belonging-together.

TEACHER: Perhaps the upwards of the entire tower—how it towers [*sich ragt*] up high.

TOWER WARDEN: Its towering up—whereto?

TEACHER: And its downwards.

TOWER WARDEN: How it remains engaged [*eingelassen*]—

TEACHER: wherein?

TOWER WARDEN: We still ask out of habit: whereto and wherein [*wohin*]?

TEACHER: And have long since known—

TOWER WARDEN: or in fact, in the end, we have not known it, if "knowing" means: to have caught sight of,

TEACHER: with that look which is called for in and for our manner of thinking.

TOWER WARDEN: To this look is shown: The tower towers up into the sky and is engaged in the earth.

TEACHER: For this statement a special look is not required; it merely expresses an everyday idea [*Vorstellung*]. [179]

TOWER WARDEN: I would like to suggest that today this idea is no longer everyday, but rather is falling into ruin.

TEACHER: Because it can no longer stand up to the forward march of modern natural science's manner of representation [*Vorstellungsweise*].

TOWER WARDEN: Science on its own could never effect [*bewirken*] this alteration.

TEACHER: If technology did not transpose scientific representations onto actuality [*Wirklichkeit*].

TOWER WARDEN: One is accustomed to thinking in this manner. Yet technology possesses this power to alter actuality only because scientific representations, whose actualization technology is said to achieve, already arise out of the peculiar essence of technology.

TEACHER: I find it difficult to follow your thoughts every time you present the relation of science and technology in this manner.

TOWER WARDEN: This is not only the case for you. It will still take a long time before the human enters into an engagement with the insight that modern science stems from the essence of modern technology.

TEACHER: Why do you place such weight on this insight?

TOWER WARDEN: Because only it allows the experiences through which the human could achieve a befitting relation to the technological world.

TEACHER: If this is the case—which, to be frank, I do not entirely perceive—then there is no time to lose in the project of awakening the essential insight.

TOWER WARDEN: Certainly not—but it is also the case that we cannot force this insight through mere instruction and decree. [180]

TEACHER: Why not? Please excuse this questioning, which draws us further away from catching sight of the tower.

TOWER WARDEN: Leave the tower to its restful standing. It stands how it stands, and perhaps we shall catch sight of it somewhat more clearly once we have clarified the questions that have now been introduced.

TEACHER: For me much would depend on this clarification. But will we have managed to do so by the time we encounter your guest?

TOWER WARDEN: Don't worry. He can listen, and indeed do so with such courteous anticipation that, for me, because of this prevailing gesture and attitude of his, he is the guest *par excellence*.

TEACHER: Then we can freely venture into this digression of our conversation.

TOWER WARDEN: Especially since it will show itself to not be a digression after all.

TEACHER: I shall now intentionally question around the matter, perhaps even passing it by; but your answer will help me. Why is it that one so easily falls prey to the tendency to transpose the relation between science and technology back onto that between theory and praxis?

TOWER WARDEN: Because one thinks all that you have named with these four terms too shortsightedly: namely as acts of human consciousness. You yourself know best, from your knowledge of metaphysics and its history, how this has come to pass.

TEACHER: But this knowledge does not help so long as the view is lacking that would reveal how it is that one thinks too shortsightedly with respect to the four terms. How is this lack to be made up for?

TOWER WARDEN: We are already once again at that place where I can only say: From everywhere we must continually turn back to where we truly already are. [181]

TEACHER: Through its repetition this saying becomes indeed more memorable, but not in any way clearer.

TOWER WARDEN: Where truly are human representing [*Vorstellen*], producing [*Herstellen*], and ordering [*Bestellen*]—if you'll permit me to bring the above-named terms back to these manners of human comportment?

TEACHER: According to the doctrines of philosophy one would clarify: representing, producing, and ordering are, as acts of consciousness, in the human. Where else?

TOWER WARDEN: But representing, producing, and ordering are ways through which what presences reveals itself to us in its presence.

TEACHER: These ways of revealing are as such already there with what presences, which in each case goes to them in its own way.

TOWER WARDEN: The manners of comportment [*Verhaltens*] we mentioned thus belong in a sojourn [*Aufenthalt*][7] of the human.

TEACHER: He who has his place in view of what presences.

TOWER WARDEN: If he, as sojourn, is not himself this place.

TEACHER: It seems to me that you think this sojourn more fully than I am yet able to.

TOWER WARDEN: Indeed. Yet what I could now explain to you will seem to you contrived; this is no wonder, since the human has long forgotten how to listen to the mysteriously working enabling-capacity of language.

TEACHER: Attempt it nevertheless; for I believe that I am now somewhat more practiced in thinking from the matter [*Sache*] and listening to words such that they resound out of the state of affairs [*Sachverhalt*], no longer presenting themselves, as they all too easily have the appearance of doing, as bearers of meanings that we have blindly contrived. [182]

TOWER WARDEN: The state of affairs is shown to us: the human in view of what presences.

TEACHER: For example: Humans on the coast in sight of the ocean. Yet "in sight of" means here: while they receive the ocean to see and look at it.

TOWER WARDEN: Such is also the meaning of the turn of phrase, "in view of what presences." But "in view" properly says that what presences views us, such that we stay [*unsaufhalten*] in this view, indeed such that it at the same time contains [*enthält*] us, harbors us, so that we comport [*verhalten*] ourselves in this with-hold [*Enthalt*] to that which the view holds open for us [*uns aufbehält*]: sojourn-in-the-with-hold [*Auf-ent-Halt*].[8]

TEACHER: A beautiful word.

TOWER WARDEN: And a rich one, if we are fortunate enough to manage to experience what holds in the withhold of the sojourn-in-the-with-hold.

TEACHER: Accordingly, sojourn is both a matter of that which presences to—while viewing—the human, because it contains; and also a matter of the human, who stays [*sichaufhält*] in such a view and containing with-hold.

TOWER WARDEN: Good—but now, who is the human?

---

7. *Aufenthalt* most often means "sojourn" in the sense of staying (*Sichaufhalten*) somewhere temporarily. However, similar to our word "residence," *Aufenthalt* can refer not only to the act of staying, but also to the place where one stays (*Aufenthaltsort*) and the time-period that one stays there (*Aufenthaltszeit*).—Tr.

8. On these key notions of "sojourn" (*Aufenthalt*), the "with-hold" (*Enthalt*), and "sojourn-in-the-with-hold" (*Auf-ent-Halt*), see my foreword, p. xx.—Tr.

TEACHER: We have said it: the one who sojourns by staying in the with-hold [*der sich im Enthalt Aufhaltende*] —

TOWER WARDEN: for which reason he is first of all determined as the self-restraining-comporter [*der Sichverhaltende*].

TEACHER: The human: the self-restraining-comporter.

TOWER WARDEN: But mind you: as what we have named sojourn.

TEACHER: The self-restraining-comporter thus does not mean only: he who behaves in such and such a manner, reacts in different circumstances in this or that manner.

TOWER WARDEN: With this opinion we would fall back into the representation [183] of the human as an organism and subject of consciousness.

TEACHER: To this and this alone belongs also the unconscious. The consciously maneuvered interest in the unconscious is a sign of the last triumph of the conception of the human as a subject of consciousness.

TOWER WARDEN: The human: the self-restraining-comporter as sojourn. A long and careful attentiveness is required to give this determination its due consideration.

TEACHER: It can suffice for us at the moment if you show what determination representing, producing, and ordering, and thus technology and science receive from this.

TOWER WARDEN: We now no longer think these manners of comportment too shortsightedly, but rather in their breadth, that is, as involved [*eingelassen*] in the sojourn.

TEACHER: Out of the with-hold of the sojourn, presencing takes the human into its claim —

TOWER WARDEN: has in each case already taken him, insofar as all of his comporting [*Verhalten*] and sojourning [*Sichaufhalten*] belong in that hold [*Halt*] which we are, to be sure, not yet able to determine.

TEACHER: But I am now catching a glimpse of what you wish to show with respect to the essence of science and technology. Allow me to say what I am thinking in the language that is familiar to me.

TOWER WARDEN: With pleasure — so far as this still suffices not only for the expression of what is thought, but above all for staying in the domain of thinking.

TEACHER: Only a trial can decide this. I would like to attempt it by way of going back as far as possible in the history of thinking, [184] especially now that I have assured myself of your agreement to do this.

TOWER WARDEN: Under one condition of course — namely, that going back to what has historically been becomes a preview of what is yet to come, of what long approaches us.

TEACHER: And which requires no presumptuous prediction.

TOWER WARDEN: And yet also may never be equated with any mere modernization of the historically past.

TEACHER: Even if my efforts were already headed toward experiencing the historical in the manner we just spoke of, it was indeed good that we clarified once more this relation to history.

TOWER WARDEN: For the essence of history [*Geschichte*] is determined from that which is, to us, called "the sojourn." If we are successful in turning to enter this sojourn, then a liberation from history could come about.

TEACHER: And this would happen at the same time as historiology [*Historie*] still looks forward to making great strides in the form of the information industry, among the ranks of which everything that has today become tradable under the name of "culture" must be counted.

TOWER WARDEN: On account of being fitted into to the technological world, we—and I think it is necessary to say this for the moment—must consider the essence of this technological world within the field of view [*Blickfeld*] of what we have called "the strange."

TEACHER: The field [*Feld*] through which the country path [*Feldweg*] leads, where we become aware of just a bit of the abundance—a bit that is shown by its simple vistas [*Ausblicke*].

TOWER WARDEN: Vistas which, against our expectations, bring us to halting stays [*Aufenthalten*] in the course of our conversation.

TEACHER: Which in no way do I feel are delays. [185]

TOWER WARDEN: And even if they were delays, they could still bring us nearer to the proper sojourn [*eigentlichen Aufenthalt*].

TEACHER: Which is what I wish to paraphrase in my language and thereby suggest how we could avoid a superficial thinking of representing, producing, and ordering.

TOWER WARDEN: What do you have in mind?

TEACHER: Something long accustomed, which you know sufficiently, and yet which still insufficiently occurs to me: a return to Heraclitus.

TOWER WARDEN: You evidently don't count him among the mystics who are thought to chase after primal origins.

TEACHER: Mysticism and primal origins are both foreign to the Greek world. All is presencing, gathering, Simple, pure appearing, including the appearing of darkness and pain.

TOWER WARDEN: You hear the language of the true Greek world. So now speak freely.

TEACHER: I shall attempt to do so, even though I must sketch in broad terms the still unresolved question of the relation between science and technology.

TOWER WARDEN: It is better if, rather than unresolved, we say: unquestioned. It is best if you help us into this question, such that you bring us back to the essential provenance of both science and technology.

TEACHER: I have often enough attempted this, each time without successful results: One thoughtlessly holds fast to the idea that technology is the actualization of the knowledge and theories of the natural sciences.

TOWER WARDEN: Since when do you reckon with results and lack of results? [186]

TEACHER: I don't reckon with them. Yet I am disturbed by the stubbornness of the dominant representation of the relation between science and technology.

TOWER WARDEN: And rightfully so. For the dominance of this manner of representation is more threatening than bombs and missiles. We don't need to say much about that.

TEACHER: Yet we must strive to break the dominance of this manner of representation.

TOWER WARDEN: Mortals alone will never be capable of this.

TEACHER: What then can we still do?

TOWER WARDEN: We can think. Thinking and its quiet prevailing nurture with the forbearance [Langmut] of shepherds.

TEACHER: You have now given me the courage [Mut] to bring forward what I am thinking. I am thinking here once again of a saying of Heraclitus. You know fragment 112: τὸ φρονεῖν ἀρετὴ μεγίστη, καὶ σοφίη ἀληθέα λέγειν καὶ ποιεῖν κατὰ φύσιν ἐπαΐοντας.[9]

TOWER WARDEN: By means of this saying of Heraclitus you wish to say: Representing, producing, and ordering are not only each related to what presences, but also, prior to this, they are held into all relations to what presences by the presencing of what presences.

TEACHER: Right. But with this reference there remains for me one reservation: I would like to consider whether going back to ancient thinkers can provide us with a clear explanation of how we are to think that which you have in view when you say that representing, producing, and ordering are held by the presencing of what presences. The critical point lies in this "held" [gehalten]. I know that speaking of a point [Punkt] is not fitting—I mean the focal-place [Ort][10] of the crisis of thinking. [187]

TOWER WARDEN: Whether it follows the track of metaphysics, or—

TEACHER: I have a dim presentiment of this other possibility, but also know that we are not yet decisively and exclusively engaging in a meditative pursuit of it.

---

9. McKirahan translates this fragment as follows: "Right thinking is the greatest excellence, and wisdom is to speak the truth and act in accordance with nature, while paying attention to it" (Philosophy Before Socrates, p. 120).—Tr.

10. Although Ort generally means "place," it originally referred to the "tip" (Spitze) of something, such as a spear. This would not be one point among others, but rather the place where something is gathered, focused.—Tr.

TOWER WARDEN: For we still lack the trust, or even the proper aptitude for this trust in what carries and what calls on non-metaphysical thinking.

TEACHER: Thus you are unable to get by without keeping one eye trained on metaphysics.

TOWER WARDEN: Certainly not, and especially not when it is a matter of a first indication of the other thinking, if you will allow me this naming, which implies no sense of superiority over against metaphysics.

TEACHER: I too have never assessed attempts of the other thinking in this manner. Yet it has always seemed and still seems to me that this other thinking, precisely because it is inceptual thinking, would have to be able to come out with its own wealth and present itself immediately.

TOWER WARDEN: We agree that any countermovement against metaphysics, and any mere turn away from it, always remain still caught in metaphysical representation.

TEACHER: If one does not, like Nietzsche, see in art the countermovement against metaphysics.

TOWER WARDEN: Hence we may also no longer merely include his thinking in metaphysics.

TEACHER: Nietzsche moves on a borderline that he himself drew; yet this borderline is difficult to make out, since the idea of value led his thinking—at least according to its form of expression—to fall back into metaphysics. [188]

TOWER WARDEN: Nevertheless, this seems to me to be more of a minor impediment in contrast to the other issue, namely that Nietzsche interprets art—which he experiences as *the* countermovement to metaphysics—not only in an anti-metaphysical but also in a metaphysical manner.

TEACHER: What else could he have done, when everywhere around him he found only an art that derived from metaphysics.

TOWER WARDEN: Is there then any art that would not have to be metaphysical?

TEACHER: Evidently not, so far as I can follow this train of thought.

TOWER WARDEN: Then what today still appears to be art, namely in the dominant purview of metaphysical representation, is in truth no longer art.

TEACHER: But what is it then? Indeed yesterday the picture in your tower room excited me with this question. I held it to be something wondrous. You, however, called it "the strange."

TOWER WARDEN: Before which all metaphysical representations break down.

TEACHER: Always again metaphysics. It disturbs us even in this conversation on a country path.

TOWER WARDEN: Where it does not belong; but it is also not worth you railing against it so. Metaphysics never disturbs if we don't let it disturb.

TEACHER: Which was just the case.

TOWER WARDEN: Only according to appearances. Insofar as you touched on the critical point, you already saw the other path of thought.

TEACHER: I don't yet see it; I merely have a presentiment of it. [189]

TOWER WARDEN: Having a presentiment, or presaging [*Ahnen*], bears more fruit than alleged seeing, which is all too sure of itself.

TEACHER: If our presaging receives the proper escort.

TOWER WARDEN: If it is capable [*vermag*] of receiving.

TEACHER: For which a mere wanting [*Mögen*] as wishing is insufficient.

TOWER WARDEN: Your meditation on the critical point divulges more than a mere wishing.

TEACHER: All the same my effort needs help.

TOWER WARDEN: This help will come unforeseen, as long as we do not lose our way. We have done enough in this regard if we follow what has already begun and don't let go again of what we have already caught sight of.

TEACHER: You mean to imply that today's path has already shown something that could shed some light for me on the darkness of the critical point.

TOWER WARDEN: That is what I mean. Hence, it would be beneficial if you could once more paraphrase the critical point.

TEACHER: Our representing, producing, and ordering of what presences is held by the presencing of what here and there presences. What is meant here by "held"?

TOWER WARDEN: Probably "supported."

TEACHER: And so "grounded."

TOWER WARDEN: Presencing gives the ground; it is the ground for the fact that what presences can presence as such.

TEACHER: But the ground must be represented by us as ground, [190] not subsequently, but rather prior to all relations with what presences.

TOWER WARDEN: Then these relations would be fundamentally held—grounded—by our representing of presencing. The being-held of our representing and producing is located after all in us. It does not rely on the presencing of what presences. How is this presencing of what presences supposed to hold our representing?

TEACHER: Precisely this is my question.

TOWER WARDEN: Which you cannot answer otherwise than you just did.

TEACHER: Not so long as the presencing of what presences appears as ground.

TOWER WARDEN: Yet this is how it has appeared since ancient times.

TEACHER: Accordingly, all representing, producing, and ordering are held by this: to fathom the ground [*den Grund zu ergründen*], and in each case to substantiate [*begründen*] what presences.

TOWER WARDEN: In the meantime this way of thinking has become so common that one hardly ventures to specifically articulate it.

TEACHER: Despite all this, something unclarified remains in the background.

TOWER WARDEN: What you have called the critical point.

TEACHER: To which I am now—I know not why—coming a bit nearer.

TOWER WARDEN: Speak.

TEACHER: I can only ask. Must presencing, which holds our representing and producing in the relation to what presences, necessarily have the character of ground? How does it stand with presencing itself, such that it is capable of holding? [191] Is this holding necessarily a supporting as grounding? I ask all this because I find nothing of the sort in the old determinations of presencing as φύσις and λόγος.

TOWER WARDEN: And yet you also cannot deny that what presences as such, and our representing and producing relations with what presences, are held by presencing.

TEACHER: Held in what sense?

TOWER WARDEN: Presumably in the sense that our representing and producing depend on [*angewiesen auf*], or better yet, are accommodated into [*eingewiesen in*] the relation to presencing.

TEACHER: Accommodated by what?

TOWER WARDEN: By what else than by presencing itself?

TEACHER: Then presencing is what holds in the sense of what accommodates.

TOWER WARDEN: It can only accommodate [*Einweisen*] if it has already directed [*gewiesen*] representing and producing to itself, indeed inceptually [*anfänglich*] fetched them into [*eingeholt*] itself.

TEACHER: This would mean: there are not first of all human representing and producing, which then happen to be fetched by presencing.

TOWER WARDEN: Rather, this fetching-into [*Ein-holen*] is what essentially occurs in inceptual beginning [*das Wesende im Anfangen*], that is, a taking-on in the sense of a holding [*Haltens*] as safeguarding and harboring, and thus, in the sense of a containing as with-holding [*Enthaltens*].

TEACHER: We spoke of this when we clarified what you named sojourn.

TOWER WARDEN: On the way from there, we can consider how presencing holds. [192]

TEACHER: Sojourn [*Aufenthalt*] means: to stay in the with-hold [*Sich aufhalten im Enthalt*]; as such, presencing presences to our representing and producing—initiating [*anfängt*] them into their essence.

TOWER WARDEN: Yet sojourn at the same time means: with-hold, which determines representing and producing as sojourning [*Sich-aufhalten*].

TEACHER: What is meant here by determining?

TOWER WARDEN: Your question is legitimate, but rushed.

TEACHER: How so?

TOWER WARDEN: In that your question will find its answer sooner if we first remain with what is now given.

TEACHER: You mean the twofold character of that which is for us called sojourn?

TOWER WARDEN: Yes. And I readily acknowledge that we will not easily find our way into the twofold hinting of the words with-hold [*Enthalt*] and sojourn [*Aufenthalt*], that is, into their belonging-together.

TEACHER: But even then, much will remain in the dark for me.

TOWER WARDEN: For me no less—which may attest to the fact that we have reached the darkness that belongs to the domain from out of which we are to think sojourn.

TEACHER: And moreover, out of which we are to think all that our meditation has brought forward—I mean the relation between science and technology, which we have now put in terms of representing and producing.

TOWER WARDEN: Yet we didn't want to speak about that.

TEACHER: Especially since in an earlier conversation we found that the question of the relation between the natural sciences and technology would require an extensive explication.

TOWER WARDEN: And it would require a conception that would remove it from the purview of usual treatments. [193]

TEACHER: In these usual treatments one is reluctant to give up the preeminence of science.

TOWER WARDEN: Because one is resistant to reflecting on the provenance of the essence of technology.

TEACHER: Yet, it seems to me, it is toward this that we were just now under way.

TOWER WARDEN: In a certain sense, yes; but at the same time we are in danger of losing sight of this being-on-the-way.

TEACHER: What do you mean by this?

TOWER WARDEN: To being-on-the-way belongs not only foresight, but also hindsight.

TEACHER: We come from the tower.

TOWER WARDEN: And would like now to catch sight of the tower.

TEACHER: In doing so we find that our view of the tower—according to which it towers up into the heavens and is engaged in the earth—

would belong in a realm of our representing that no longer corresponds to the ruling world-picture of the natural sciences and technology. Yet at the moment, neither foresight nor hindsight reaches far enough for me. I don't know from where and to where we are on the way.

TOWER WARDEN: With this statement you mean to suggest that it remains unclear whether we want to abandon a pre-scientific representation of the tower in favor of a scientific-technological one, or whether we want to hold tight to it.

TEACHER: And whether we are reflecting on the belonging-together of representing and producing precisely in order to metaphysically justify the scientific-technological world-picture, or—here I don't know what more to say.

TOWER WARDEN: You think it is possible that meditating on the [194] essential provenance of science and technology opens vistas through which something shows itself that shakes science and technology's claim to truth.

TEACHER: I would like to surmise this with the help of the indications you have now given. Only I don't see where this shaking that you speak of would lead, because through this shaking, the entire realm wherein the contemporary human runs around pursuing his business without, as it were, staying to sojourn [*ohne Aufenthalt*], would begin to waver and lose all its grounding, and since the human would quickly arrive at explanations of the manner of representation, which you still called pre-scientific, as being merely unscientific. One would then admit that the technological-scientific world is indeed an artificial one, but would nevertheless accept it as the effectively actual [*wirkliche*] world, since it secures the continued existence of the steadily growing masses of humanity on this earth of ours.

TOWER WARDEN: The technological-scientific world is in no way an artificial one, nor is it a natural one; it is rather the consequential configuration of the metaphysical representation of the world,

TEACHER: such that in it nature and art both disappear—

TOWER WARDEN: and are dissolved into what one today calls "cultures." Consider for a moment what today's dominant information industry presents under the title "cultural truths."

TEACHER: Thus all cultural critique is fruitless.

TOWER WARDEN: It is senseless. Which is why we would do well to pass it by.

TEACHER: What drove us into it?

TOWER WARDEN: As is so often the case in our conversations, the always too-shortsighted effort to remain with what is actual by dealing with what is contemporary. [195]

TEACHER: Which is not what we are properly concerned with.

TOWER WARDEN: Hence I was previously so pleased when you attained to surmising,

TEACHER: when I referred to the possible shaking of the contemporary world-picture.

TOWER WARDEN: Yes—the mere shaking brings about nothing, unless it soon swings within an older, sturdy bringing-to-rest.

TEACHER: From where would this come to us, and to where can the shaking lead?

TOWER WARDEN: In both questions you are surmising the selfsame.

TEACHER: You are speaking obscurely.

TOWER WARDEN: Yes and no. No—insofar as we might think that the shaking of the scientific world-picture could bring back the pre-scientific one—

TEACHER: and in this manner rescue.

TOWER WARDEN: Little would be achieved thereby. For the natural world-picture—as one still calls it for short, without being clear about what is here called nature—was presumably pillaged from the technological-scientific world-picture, because it did not have its own provenance as its own.

TEACHER: And so it did not know it.

TOWER WARDEN: Perhaps was even unable to know it, never having been permitted to know it. And when I make mention of this, I have to agree that my speech is obscure.

TEACHER: What could be the reason for this?

TOWER WARDEN: If I knew this, then my speech would no longer be obscure. [196]

TEACHER: But you do surmise something with respect to the provenance of the natural world-picture.

TOWER WARDEN: That the appropriation [*Aneignung*] of its provenance remained distant, because the provenance itself kept itself concealed.

TEACHER: You speak in mere surmises.

TOWER WARDEN: To be sure. We may even let this surmising come yet further into the open [*ins Freie*].

TEACHER: How so? We are speaking of the provenance of the natural world-picture.

TOWER WARDEN: I prefer to avoid this label, since it is rooted in modern metaphysical representation, and to speak rather of the sturdy relationship of things to us.

TEACHER: And the provenance of this relationship would be concealed?

TOWER WARDEN: Indeed, and with it also the thing-character of things.

TEACHER: So it would have happened that things came to presence without their thingness having been properly considered.

TOWER WARDEN: That is what I mean; I also surmise that, because thingness remained concealed, things were susceptible to being changed into objects [*Gegenständen*] —

TEACHER: which in the meantime have become mere standing-reserves [*Beständen*]. What really changed with this change? Surely not the things.

TOWER WARDEN: Rather their thing-character, in that it, instead of coming to appearance and into appropriation itself, in a concealed manner allowed room for the object-character of what presences. [197] What I say here are sheer surmises.

TEACHER: I take them in this way and in this sense ask: where does the object-character come from?

TOWER WARDEN: Always the question of provenance!

TEACHER: We also do not know where this question comes from—

TOWER WARDEN: and we cannot know this, so long as we do not tell ourselves what is meant here by "provenance."

TEACHER: The unclarity about this was already disturbing to me when we considered the provenance of science and technology, namely their derivation from representing and producing.

TOWER WARDEN: Which led us to reflect on the provenance of representing and producing.

TEACHER: Yet it seems to me that we omitted doing just that.

TOWER WARDEN: It is good that you noticed this yourself.

TEACHER: We want to retrieve what was neglected.

TOWER WARDEN: Even if we are able to do this, it is not enough.

TEACHER: Enough for what?

TOWER WARDEN: For the elucidation of what you surmised with regard to the shaking of the claim to truth made by science and technology.

TEACHER: I surmised that this shaking opens vistas, yet onto what I cannot now say.

TOWER WARDEN: Perhaps onto the provenance of the object-character of what presences and its advent. [198]

TEACHER: Such that an insight would be given into the concealment of the thing-character of things.

TOWER WARDEN: You mean the insight that such a concealing was at play—

TEACHER: and is still at play; otherwise the characterization of the towerness of the tower would not be so arduous and circuitous. The tower is, after all, a thing.

TOWER WARDEN: Yes. Only I don't find anything arduous and circuitous on our path of thought; I agree much more with "he who is far greater" than both of us combined, who said that thinking is a festival.[11]

---

11. The phrase "he who is far greater" is presumably an allusion to John the Baptist's reference to Jesus (see Mathew 3.11, Mark 1.7, Luke 3.15, and John

TEACHER: To a festival belong guests.

TOWER WARDEN: I see our guest coming from over there.

TEACHER: Almost too early, since we have not succeeded in getting very far in our attempt to catch sight of the tower as thing.

TOWER WARDEN: Where then would we like to get to?

TEACHER: Not at all—if I am following along with your line of thought—to a purportedly better concept of tower and of thing.

TOWER WARDEN: We would much rather get to the tower and into my room—

TEACHER: and indeed in front of the picture, which for me is no longer an object ever since I encountered its wondrousness.

TOWER WARDEN: We called it the strange.

TEACHER: And since then we have distanced ourselves ever farther from it, as from the tower itself.

TOWER WARDEN: And instead brought ourselves nearer to the guest.

TEACHER: Who perhaps brings us the festive. [199]

TOWER WARDEN: His claim is not so lofty. But he could—as far as I know him—awaken sooner the festive of our country path.

TEACHER: If it were for us already a sufficiently clear path of thought—which, for me at least, it is not yet.

TOWER WARDEN: Why not?

TEACHER: Because I am beset by too many questions, and find no sufficient answers. Even by means of what little we have discussed on our short stretch of path today, I do not foresee that our conversation could swing out into a simple meditation on what genuinely unsettles me.

TOWER WARDEN: You mean the picture in my room.

TEACHER: Only this.

TOWER WARDEN: We are nearer to the simple than you think.

TEACHER: This may be because my thinking does not yet reach it.

1:27). It is not as clear to whom Heidegger is attributing the idea *"das Denken sei ein Fest"* (*Fest* could also be translated as "feast" or "celebration"). Plato—who often speaks of festivals, feasts, and symposia, and sometimes of a "feast of *logos*" (see *Phaedrus* 227b, *Timaeus* 20c)—might seem to be a likely candidate, as might Nietzsche, whose poem that speaks of "the festival of festivals" to which Zarathustra arrives as "the guest of guests" Heidegger quoted in a lecture course in the fall of 1944 (GA 50: 125). Yet given that, for Heidegger, Plato and Nietzsche represent the inception and completion of metaphysics, it seems more likely that Heidegger has in mind Hölderlin, whose poetic word calls for and corresponds to a non-metaphysical thinking. It is certainly in his readings of Hölderlin that Heidegger most often reflects on "the festival" (see especially *Elucidations of Hölderlin's Poetry*, translated by Keith Hoeller [Amherst, NY: Humanity Books, 2000], pp. 125–130). Heidegger himself used the expression "the festival of thinking" (*das Fest des Denkens*) in "The Origin of the Work of Art" (*GA* 5: 3); see also the suggestion that "thinking itself could be a festival" in the first conversation (above, p. 89). —*Tr.*

TOWER WARDEN: More likely because we are not yet sufficiently intimate with that into which our thinking is nevertheless already initiated.

TEACHER: How can we recognize this?

TOWER WARDEN: By paying attention to how we ask everywhere about the selfsame.

TEACHER: You mean the question of provenance?

TOWER WARDEN: Yes, and I mean not only what we ask about, but also how.

TEACHER: The question of the where-from is so familiar to us that it seems to be innate. [200]

TOWER WARDEN: You mean that it belongs to the nature of the human.

TEACHER: I thought this for a fleeting moment, but now I must admit that we gain nothing by appealing to the nature of the human.

TOWER WARDEN: At most we become aware that this nature, which is often appealed to, itself means nothing other than the provenance.

TEACHER: We would then find ourselves led into the question of the provenance of provenance, and thereby into the well-known infinite regress [endlosen Prozeß].

TOWER WARDEN: Certainly, if we neglect to first of all clarify what is called "provenance."

TEACHER: To that I might be able to contribute something. It suffices to fundamentally think through what is given in the course of Greek thought; I need only mention the terms ἀρχή and αἰτία.

TOWER WARDEN: And we would at once be in the whole realm of that which we generally designate as ground [Grund].

TEACHER: If we attempt to fathom [ergründen] its essence, then we seek the ground of ground and end up in emptiness—

TOWER WARDEN: If that is what you want to call what is always identical, which presents itself to us whenever we are not in the right moment to see—or to allow the surmise—that what we call "ground" does not coincide with what is called "provenance."

TEACHER: Every kind of ground provides a provenance; but not every provenance is a kind of ground. And so provenance would have to be in play where no ground is given.

TOWER WARDEN: Not even abysses [Abgründe], which prevail only within a looking backward toward grounds [Gründe].

TEACHER: Thus we would have to think provenance as [201] remaining in the same manner both groundless and abyssless—an audacious demand [Zumutung], to be sure, on the customary manner of representing, which has long provided the authoritative standard of measure for thinking. How do you intend to force such a long-accustomed manner of thinking to acquiesce to this audacious demand?

TOWER WARDEN: We cannot force something to acquiesce to an audacious demand, but rather can only free something for it.

TEACHER: So that we let it come to us.

TOWER WARDEN: But there is the guest coming around the bend in the path.

TEACHER: Whereby you also mean to tell me that we should save the conversation we have begun about the essential occurring and prevailing of the provenance for another occasion.

TOWER WARDEN: Not at all; I told you rather that the guest would like to listen.

TEACHER: Even when it is a matter of such a general and wide-ranging question as that of the provenance of provenance?

TOWER WARDEN: If you wish, let us leave the question, as it were, lying under way.

TEACHER: The guest shall speak to us of his own accord about what concerns him.

TOWER WARDEN: You may be mistaken.

TEACHER: Then we must ourselves initiate the course of another conversation.

TOWER WARDEN: If you like—but here he is; let me at once introduce you to him. In a certain sense he in fact knows you already, since yesterday evening in the tower room I first told him something about what has moved us for years.

GUEST: I am pleased to encounter both of you in [202] conversation— after having already heard a lot about what it is that you speakof.

TOWER WARDEN: My teacher friend was admittedly about to break off our conversation.

GUEST: Whatever for?

TEACHER: For your sake.

GUEST: That was a mistake.

TEACHER: But you don't even know what we are speaking about.

GUEST: That I don't know.

TOWER WARDEN: Although you can guess what it is from what I told you.

TEACHER: That we have long been moving ourselves [*wir uns . . . bewegen*] on a between-field [*Zwischenfeld*].

GUEST: You mean between fields on the country path [*Feldweg*]?

TEACHER: That would be splendid.

TOWER WARDEN: But it is not so; to walk on the country path [*auf dem Feldweg gehen*] does not yet necessarily mean to celebrate this path [*diesen Weg begehen*][12]—

TEACHER: such that it moves us [*er uns bewegt*].

GUEST: Then the three of us are in the same condition, and there is no reason to break off the conversation you have begun.

---

12. The verb *begehen* is sometimes used synonymously with *feiern*, meaning to celebrate, as in to celebrate a festival (*ein Fest begehen*). —*Tr.*

3. Evening Conversation: In a Prisoner of War Camp in Russia, between a Younger and an Older Man

YOUNGER MAN: As we were marching to our workplace this morning, out of the rustling of the expansive forest I was suddenly overcome by something healing. Throughout the entire day I meditated on wherein this something that heals could rest.

OLDER MAN: Perhaps it is what is inexhaustible of the self-veiling expanse that abides in these forests of Russia.

YOUNGER MAN: You probably mean that the capacious, which prevails in the expanse, brings to us something freeing.

OLDER MAN: I do not only mean the capaciousness in the expanse, but also that this expanse leads us out and forth.

YOUNGER MAN: The capaciousness of the forests swings out into a concealed distance, but at the same time swings back to us again, without ending with us.

OLDER MAN: It is almost as if, out of the open and yet veiled expanse, something could never break in that sets itself in the way of our essence and blocks its course. So nothing is encountered that bends our essence back on itself and confines it to a narrowness by means of which it is made rebellious in itself.

YOUNGER MAN: The expanse carries us to what is objectless, and yet also keeps us from dissolving into it. The expanse delivers our essence into the open and at the same time gathers it into the simple, as though the expanse's abiding were a pure arrival for which we are the inlet.—

OLDER MAN: This expanse provides us with freedom. It frees [206] us while we here—between the walls of these barracks, behind barbed wire—incessantly run up against and wound ourselves on what is objective.

YOUNGER MAN: At first this morning, I in fact also thought that this experience of what is healing [*das Heilsame*] came only from a feel-

132

ing of contrast to the unwholesome [*heillosen*] narrowness of the camp, as if it were nothing other than the fleeting appearance of a blessing that for a short time is afforded to such self-deceptions. Yet since early this morning this expanse has abided around me in such a releasing, signifying, and gathering manner that I am no longer able to understand it as a mere deception.

OLDER MAN: The healing expanse is not that of the forest, but rather, the forest's own expanse is let into [*eingelassen*] what heals.

YOUNGER MAN: But the forest does not become a mere symbol of the healing expanse; it is probably also something other than what merely occasions its appearing, although the enigma of the occasioning which allows for something to happen [*Veranlassung*] does indeed give enough to be thought, so as to keep us from all too rashly explaining such experiences in terms of what is commonplace. Indeed, I cannot say what was experienced otherwise than in view of what the forest occasioned.

OLDER MAN: And yet you will presumably be able to name some sign in which what heals shows itself to you. I don't want to press you any further, however, since I know how strictly you bury in your silence all the adversities that have befallen us here these past months. Nevertheless, in order to comprehend what has become healing for you, I would have to know what is wounded in you. And what is not all wounded and torn apart in us?—us, for whom a blinded leading-astray of our own people is too deplorable to permit wasting a complaint on, despite the devastation that covers our native soil and its helplessly perplexed [*ratlose*] humans. [207]

YOUNGER MAN: But you are still thinking about our decision on the march into captivity, the decision not to talk any more about this devastation for a long time. Whenever it might become unavoidable to talk about it, however, such talk should take place only in a collected manner, according to the highest standards, and without false passion. For the devastation we are thinking of has not, after all, existed just since yesterday. And it is not exhausted by what is visible and tangible. It can also never be accounted for by an enumeration of instances of destruction and the obliteration of human lives, as if it were only the result of these.

OLDER MAN: Yet because the essence of the devastation is deeper and comes from farther away, our reflections return to it again and again. In so doing, we may recognize ever more clearly that the devastation of the earth and the annihilation of the human essence that goes with it are somehow evil [*das Böse*] itself.

YOUNGER MAN: By evil, of course, we do not mean what is morally bad, and not what is reprehensible, but rather malice.

OLDER MAN: But may we then, if we think clearly, say that evil is malice? Rather, as the name says, malice [*das Bösartige*] is of the nature [*Art*] of evil [*Bösen*], and is an outflow of it.

YOUNGER MAN: But as long as with the name "evil" one always means only the morally reprehensible, then the statement, evil is malice, may very well have a sense, assuming that we think of malice on the basis of something other than morality [*dem Sittlichen*].

OLDER MAN: On the basis of what else should we think it?

YOUNGER MAN: On the basis of precisely that toward which the word "malicious" [*»bösartig«*] refers us. Malice is insurgency, which rests in furiousness, indeed such that this furiousness [*Grimmige*] [208] in a certain sense conceals its rage [*Ingrimm*], but at the same time always threatens with it. The essence of evil is the rage of insurgency, which never entirely breaks out, and which, when it does break out, still disguises itself, and in its hidden threatening is often as if it were not.

OLDER MAN: It could thus have a profound sense to say that evil is malice.

YOUNGER MAN: The fury which essentially prevails in evil lets loose the insurgency and the turmoil that we presage on all sides, where we encounter a dissolution that seems to be unstoppable.

OLDER MAN: If, however, evil rests in malice—which in itself is infuriated about its own fury, and thereby becomes ever more furious—then I could almost think that malice is something pertaining to the will.

YOUNGER MAN: Perhaps in general the will itself is what is evil.

OLDER MAN: I shy from even surmising something so audacious.

YOUNGER MAN: I too only said "perhaps," and what I said is also not my thought, even though it has not let go of me ever since I once heard it. On that occasion too, this thought was expressed only as a surmise.

OLDER MAN: The reference to evil has helped me to see a bit more clearly what we said about the devastation, above all in regard to how we can encounter the devastation—I mean, how we may in no way encounter it.

YOUNGER MAN: What you are now thinking of is not clear to me.

OLDER MAN: The devastation that we have in mind, and that we [209] surely must begin to think still more rigorously, is not evil in the sense of a moral badness of the supposed originators of this devastation. Rather, evil itself, as malice, is devastating. Hence, a moral indignation, even if it makes the world's general public into its mouthpiece, is not capable of doing anything against the devastation.

YOUNGER MAN: And why not then?

OLDER MAN: Because moral superiority is not in a position to grasp, much less abolish or even mitigate, evil.

YOUNGER MAN: For it could be the case that even morality [*die Moral*], for its part, together with all the peculiar attempts to envision a world-order and make certain of a world-security for the national peoples [*Völkern*] by means of morality, are only a monstrous offspring of evil; just as the much-appealed-to "world's general public," in its essence and in its manner of emergence, presumably remains a construct and product of the process that we are calling the devastation.

OLDER MAN: While I do not entirely see these interconnections, it seems to me that something similar concerning the origin of morality was said already by Nietzsche.[1]

YOUNGER MAN: And yet you also know the suspicion of his metaphysics that dwells in us. Nietzsche of course interpreted morality—that is to say, the Platonic-Christian ethical doctrine [*Sittenlehre*] together with its later secularized forms, for example the rational ethics of the Enlightenment and socialism—as appearances of the will to power. He situated his own thinking in a "beyond good and evil." But Nietzsche did not recognize that this "beyond" or "thither side" [*»Jenseits«*]—as the realm of a pure will to power, that is, of a will to power that has come into its own—would have to remain only the counter-world to the Platonically thought world. Thus his doctrine of "discipline [210] and breeding" is also only the extreme affirmation of morality. Assuming, however, that the will itself is what is evil, then the realm of pure will to power is least of all a "beyond good and evil"—if there otherwise can at all be a beyond-evil.

OLDER MAN: I see that it was careless of me to now mention the name Nietzsche. We have indeed often reflected on the fact that a thought about Nietzsche's philosophy should only be expressed with the highest degree of rigor and from out of the richest and most far-reaching vision into the entirety of occidental thinking. Over against his philosophy, moral indignation and moral haughtiness are capable of just as little as they are with regard to the process of devastation.

YOUNGER MAN: And this devastation, after all, concerns our own essence and its world in a manner that we are only just now beginning to presage.

OLDER MAN: Therefore I also feel that it is again and again necessary for me to speak of this devastation, even though the contrary will of an aversion [*Widerwille*] would rather stop me from doing so,

1. See Friedrich Nietzsche, *Beyond Good and Evil*, especially parts V and IX, and *On the Genealogy of Morals*, both in *Basic Writings of Nietzsche*, trans. and ed. Walter Kaufmann (New York: The Modern Library, 2000). See also Friedrich Nietzsche, *The Will to Power*, trans. Walter Kaufmann and R. J. Hollingdale (New York: Vintage, 1967), especially the second part of book II ("Critique of Morality"), and book IV ("Discipline and Breeding").—*Tr.*

pressuring me to seek out a standpoint of superiority in an attitude
that no longer pays heed to the devastation.

YOUNGER MAN: But as long as we let ourselves be driven by a will of
aversion, we are morally evaluating the devastation.

OLDER MAN: We are not yet standing truly free in the midst of its
essence.

YOUNGER MAN: Which we are first able to do when we are truly capable of thinking it.

OLDER MAN: So you mean that we must first be granted the privilege
of this thinking.

YOUNGER MAN: Perhaps we are both here in this camp, involved in such
conversations, in order to receive this privilege. [211] We agreed earlier on the thought that the devastation is probably a far-reaching
event through which any and all possibilities for something essential
to arise and bloom in its dominion are suffocated at the root.

OLDER MAN: And that which inflicts the suffocating hides itself behind something insidious, something which announces itself in the
form of the purportedly highest ideals of humanity: progress, un-
restrained escalation of achievement in all areas of creating, equal
employment opportunities for everyone, and above all the allegedly
highest rationale—the uniform welfare of all workers.

YOUNGER MAN: What is really devastating, and that means what is
malicious, consists here in the fact that these goals for humanity
lead the various realms of humanity to become obsessed with de-
voting everything to their realization, and so with unconditionally
driving the devastation onward while increasingly reinforcing it in
its own consequences.

OLDER MAN: We said once—it was at an old village well, by which our
troop of prisoners was resting—that this devastation is in no way a
consequence of the World War, but rather the World War is for its
part only a consequence of the devastation that has been eating
away at the earth for centuries.

YOUNGER MAN: Therefore, human individuals and gangs—who indeed
must instigate and sustain such consequential phenomena of the
devastation, though never the devastation itself—can always only
be of a subordinate rank. They are the angry functionaries of their
own mediocrity, who stand lower in rank than the small and
wretched who stand within their genuine limits.

OLDER MAN: "Devastation" [»Verwüstung«] means for us, after all,
that everything—the world, the human, and the earth—will be
transformed into a desert [Wüste]. [212]

YOUNGER MAN: While this desert, however, does not first of all arise
little by little as a result of the spread of the devastation. The desert
is already previously there, and I mean as though in an instant [im

Nu], in order to then draw everything into itself, which is to say, to desert-ify [*ver-wüsten*].

OLDER MAN: Yet what then is the desert? With this name we associate the idea of a waterless sandy plain and a process of increasingly turning to sand, although one also speaks of the "watery desert" of the ocean, by which is probably meant its immeasurable surface as a plain of lifelessness.

YOUNGER MAN: The desert is the wasteland [*die Öde*]: the deserted [*verlassene*] expanse of the abandonment [*Verlassenheit*] of all life. And this abandonment extends to such depths that the wasteland allows for nothing that emerges [*aufgeht*] of itself, in its emergence unfolds itself, and in unfolding calls others into a co-emerging.[2] The desolation [*Verödung*] extends so far that it no longer even allows any perishing [*Untergehen*].

OLDER MAN: We are thus transferring the geographical idea of a desert, for example the Sahara, onto the process of the desolation of the earth and of human existence [*menschlichen Daseins*].

YOUNGER MAN: So it appears. It seems to me, however, that the geographical concept of the desert is just the not yet sufficiently thought-out idea of desolation, which proximally and thus mostly comes into our view only in particular circumstances and conditions of the surface of the earth.

OLDER MAN: And so we are thinking the desert as the deserted [*verlassene*] expanse of the abandonment [*Verlassenheit*] of all life. The desert is what really devastates. Hence devastation consists in that everything—world, human, and earth—enters into the abandonment of all life.

YOUNGER MAN: Here we are thinking the word "life"—as has often been done since ancient times in occidental thinking—in such breadth that its sphere of meaning coincides with that of the word "being." [213]

OLDER MAN: But now, insofar as the devastation consists in the abandonment of being, then after all it no longer allows for any beings, such that anything whatsoever that could be affected by it is lacking. Or may we call a historical age in which a form of "life" still in some manner holds sway, "the age of devastation"?

YOUNGER MAN: If we may or even must do this, then world, human, and earth can be—and yet, having entered into the devastation, they can nevertheless remain abandoned by being.

---

2. What emerges of itself, *was von sich aus aufgeht,* is for Heidegger one of the essential traits of the Greek notion of *physis*. While *physis* gets translated into Latin as *natura* (nature), according to Heidegger it was one of the principal early Greek words for "being" as such.—*Tr.*

OLDER MAN: The being of an age of devastation would then consist precisely in the abandonment of being. Such a matter is, however, difficult to think.

YOUNGER MAN: To be sure, it is difficult currently and for the contemporary human, who hardly gives thought to the fact that, under the appearance of a secured and improving life, a disregard—if not indeed a barring—of life could occur.

OLDER MAN: If we give room to this thought, then we must think the following: the being of all that is, remains ambiguous to the core.

YOUNGER MAN: And we must think this without initially being able to find out wherein this ambiguity is based, and whether with this characterization the slightest thing is said of being itself. Presumably we are speaking here only of a predicament of human understanding [Deutens] in relation to being, but not of being itself. It is enigmatic.

OLDER MAN: And so more mysterious than common sense is accustomed to thinking, which rashly assesses history and historical ages according to rise and fall, and tallies all historical phenomena in terms of what is desirable and undesirable. [214]

YOUNGER MAN: This kind of historiological reckoning could already even be a consequence of the fact that the human is devastated in his essence, which now means for us, abandoned by being.

OLDER MAN: And of the fact that the human, so abandoned, nonetheless is, but is in such a manner that with all his doing and having he rolls into nothing.

YOUNGER MAN: With this you are concisely saying that nihilism can only ever be something historically actual when something like the abandonment of beings by being occurs, an abandonment which nonetheless still lets beings be.

OLDER MAN: Nietzsche had indeed then caught sight of the appearances of nihilism; but he did not yet grasp its essence.

YOUNGER MAN: Because for essential reasons he was not at all yet able to think this essence,

OLDER MAN: Which is why Nietzsche's own thinking remained caught in nihilism.

YOUNGER MAN: And so conclusively so that his metaphysics first prepares for complete, unconditional nihilism.

OLDER MAN: And therefore, his metaphysics itself belongs in the process of the devastation.

YOUNGER MAN: The malice of this devastation reaches its extreme when it settles into the appearance of a secure state of the world, in order to hold out to the human a satisfactory standard of living as the highest goal of existence [Daseins] and to guarantee its realization.

OLDER MAN: The process of devastation will thus not be warded off, much less ended, with the setting up of a morally grounded world order. [215]

YOUNGER MAN: Because here the "measures" [»*Maßnahmen*«] that humans take—however massive their "extent" [»*Ausmaß*«] may be—are capable of nothing. For malice, as which the devastation occurs, may very well remain a basic trait of being itself.

OLDER MAN: If in fact the devastation rests in the abandonment of beings by being, and if this abandonment comes forth from being itself. But don't you also find that this thought—that being is in the ground of its essence malicious—is an awful demand on human thinking?

YOUNGER MAN: Certainly, and especially when thinking should also refrain from regarding this thought, that evil would dwell in the essence of being, as "pessimistic" or in any way evaluating it.

OLDER MAN: All this is of course not easy.

YOUNGER MAN: That this, namely thinking what is essential, is supposed to be easy is also a demand that comes only from the spirit of the devastation.

OLDER MAN: Because the devastation, insofar as it comes forth from being, is a world-event that beleaguers the earth, humans may never presume to pass judgment on it. For not only is the purview of everyday opining among individuals and groups always too narrow, but also the person who passes judgment too easily falls prey here to a quarreling and an annoyance that gnaw at him; or he becomes a slave to self-righteousness who no longer sees out beyond the façade that he has hurriedly built around himself.

YOUNGER MAN: And since enough of the misfortune has been given to us to bear, we ourselves would now like to keep mind and heart free from the disturbing aura exuded by all ill-humored thinking. The more essential an insight is, the greater must also be the tact with which it awakens in fellow humans the knowledge that grows from it. [216]

OLDER MAN: I do not entirely understand why you now stress precisely this.

YOUNGER MAN: Because one day, from a more clarified insight into the essence of the devastation, we will recognize that the devastation reigns also and indeed precisely there, where country and people have not been affected by the destruction of the war.

OLDER MAN: And so there, where the world shines with the gleam of advancement, advantages, and fortune; where human rights are respected, where civil order is maintained; and above all where the supply for the continual repletion of an undisturbed contentment is secured, so that everything remains overseeable and arranged and accounted for so as to be useful.

YOUNGER MAN: Where, above all, the unnecessary never impedes the daily routine and brings the dreaded empty hours, in which the human becomes boring to himself.

OLDER MAN: How it is that nevertheless there—indeed, even to the highest degree there—what we mean by the devastation of the earth is supposed to hold sway, is difficult to experience and even more difficult to think. But what will be most difficult is to show, without haughtiness, the devastation to those who are affected and, without the slightest trace of paternalism, to give them advice for the long meditation which is required to become familiar with the devastation as an event that prevails outside of human guilt and atonement.

YOUNGER MAN: Thus we will also never—merely on account of hearing the news that the devastation is just a matter of fate [*Schicksal*]—fall victim to the obvious temptation to get over it; especially since we are guarding ourselves above all else against getting over something.[3]

OLDER MAN: We would rather learn to simply wait until our own essence has become noble and free enough to aptly [*schicklich*] comply with the mystery of this destiny [*Geschickes*]. [217]

YOUNGER MAN: To simply wait, as though this compliance were to consist in waiting; and to wait for so long, as though waiting would have to outlast death.

OLDER MAN: Death is itself like something that waits in us.

YOUNGER MAN: As though it waits upon our waiting.

OLDER MAN: And upon what do we wait?

YOUNGER MAN: May we even ask this, if we are properly waiting?

OLDER MAN: Insofar as we wait for something [*auf etwas warten*], we attach ourselves to something awaited. Our waiting [*Warten*] is then only an awaiting [*Erwarten*]. Pure waiting is disturbed—because in pure waiting, it seems to me, we wait upon nothing.

YOUNGER MAN: If we specifically wait upon Nothing, then we have already fallen back again into awaiting, which in this case clings to there never in fact being anything awaited. So long as we wait upon nothing in this manner, we do not purely wait.

OLDER MAN: How strange this is, to wait neither upon something nor upon nothing, and yet nevertheless to wait.

YOUNGER MAN: That is, to wait on that [*dessen zu warten*][4] which corresponds to pure waiting. More fittingly let us say: to wait on that which answers pure waiting.

---

3. The phrase "getting over something" translates here the similarly colloquial *mit etwas fertig zu werden*, which is also commonly translated as "to cope with something" or "to put up with something."—*Tr.*

4. The verb *warten* (to wait) generally takes the preposition *auf*, as in to wait *for* or *upon* something. Yet here Heidegger uses a genitive pronoun, *dessen*, without a

OLDER MAN: You speak of waiting on something, and thus think of waiting as something like a safeguarding and tending or servicing. And yet the question remains—what does "waiting" then mean, if it is not simply to be equated with safeguarding?

YOUNGER MAN: Since early this morning I am now able to say to you: Waiting is letting come.

OLDER MAN: Letting what come?

YOUNGER MAN: In pure waiting, what else do we let come other than the coming? [218]

OLDER MAN: And so not something that comes—even if in waiting we also, but only secondarily, think of the coming of what comes.

YOUNGER MAN: No; that which we think of, in letting come, is the coming. To think toward the coming [*An das Kommen denken*]—this is an enigmatic commemorating [*Andenken*].

OLDER MAN: If letting come characterizes waiting, then waiting is a future-directed and thus reversed commemorating, assuming that by commemorating we first of all mean a relation to what is past.

YOUNGER MAN: But perhaps this opinion is arbitrary. Perhaps we must also first consider whether pure waiting is directed toward the future. Presumably that is only valid for awaiting. What is enigmatic about waiting as a commemorating rests in that it remains directed neither toward something futural nor toward something past, and evidently also not toward something already present.

OLDER MAN: We would almost like to surmise that waiting reaches—I don't know if I should I say *in* or *out*—to a still-concealed dimension of time.

YOUNGER MAN: And, as letting come of the coming, waits in the sense of safeguarding.

OLDER MAN: But after all, we can only safeguard what has already been entrusted to our guardianship and is thus present.

YOUNGER MAN: Yet it could be entrusted to us and at the same time still held in reserve.

OLDER MAN: Everything that you are now saying about waiting is so simple and yet so mysterious, which is why I must ask you, how is

preposition. While this is unusual in German, such a construction is used with a synonymous verb, *harren*, for example, *Ich harre seiner:* "I am waiting on him." The genitive rather than the prepositional construction evidently suggests a less objectifying and more openly attentive relationship. Here and below, when *warten* is used with a genitive object, it is translated as "to wait on." It may be helpful to draw an analogy here with the manner in which a good waiter waits on tables, namely, with a comportment of attentive assistance which is neither simply active nor simply passive.—*Tr.*

it that you can know this with such clarity and just since this morning?

YOUNGER MAN: Because in the experience of the coming, and in the experience that it [219] is what we are waiting on, and that in such waiting our essence first becomes free—because in the simple experience of all this, what is healing draws near and is granted to us.

OLDER MAN: You say "to us," and yet this healing was granted only to you.

YOUNGER MAN: But on this same day I would like to share it now with you, because I have long sensed clearly enough in our often-interrupted conversations during breaks in the fighting, in our quarters, on marches, and now here in this camp, that you are pained by the same wound.

OLDER MAN: Yet I myself do not now know the wound that aches in you in such a peculiar manner.

YOUNGER MAN: Since having been allowed to experience what is healing early this morning, I can also name for you the wound that is beginning to heal. Throughout all the years of military service in the war, indeed in a certain sense already prior to that during my study at the university, it was as if my essence were walled up and wholly expelled from the open expanse of thinking. At the same time, however, I was allowed to presage and learned to presage this thinking like a distant land.

OLDER MAN: For years now, how many of us have not had to forfeit their stay in the world of the mind? How many have been forever snatched away from that world?

YOUNGER MAN: I do not mean so much the relinquishment of intellectual activity, but much more the withdrawal of the human existence [Dasein] that rests on the ground of thinking. The burning pain is that we were not permitted to be there [da sein] for the unnecessary.

OLDER MAN: We were barred from being young.

YOUNGER MAN: Even though we were told that we should lay claim to the rights of youth, whereupon everything [220] ended merely with the inexperience of adolescents challenging the knowledge of elders.

OLDER MAN: And then overnight these adolescents were proclaimed to be "men."

YOUNGER MAN: Such that all concepts and words were turned around, because everything already sprang from turmoil.

OLDER MAN: The devastation was already at work before the destruction began.

YOUNGER MAN: Indeed; otherwise the destruction could not even begin.

OLDER MAN: And nevertheless there was among many of us a genuine kind of youth. Like all genuine youths, at any given time they could have thought out beyond those who were older, if only they had been permitted to just be youths.

YOUNGER MAN: And that means, if they had been permitted to purely wait. To be sure, one says that youths are impetuous and incapable of waiting. Yet it seems to me that youthful impetuosity for what is coming arises only from a still-incompliant waiting and is its first blossoming, which those who are older should protect from untimely frost; they should do this by purifying the youth's waiting and bringing it onto the path, instead of nipping it in the bud and falsifying it into mere expectations [*Erwartungen*] and then abusing it.

OLDER MAN: The obsession of mere expecting and the greed of accumulating always cling only to what is purportedly necessary.

YOUNGER MAN: They make the eyes of our essence blind to the unnecessary.

OLDER MAN: And to the fact that the unnecessary remains at all times the most necessary of all.

YOUNGER MAN: Only one who has learned to know the necessity of the unnecessary [221] can appreciate anything at all of the pain that arises when the human is barred from thinking.

OLDER MAN: Thinking is thus the unnecessary, and yet you attribute to thinking a high rank of honor in the essence [*Wesen*] of the human.

YOUNGER MAN: Even the highest. You also know, of course, that occidental wisdom has since ancient times thought of the human as the thinking being [*das denkende Wesen*].

OLDER MAN: I do indeed know this. But I do not really know the reason [*Grund*] for it. And I could never grasp why this wisdom hastily transposed—through a process that of course took centuries—the essence of thinking into *ratio* and into rationality [*Vernünftigkeit*].

YOUNGER MAN: It is as if the Occident was unable to wait until thinking could find its way into its originary essence, which perhaps consists in pure waiting and the ability to wait.

OLDER MAN: Perhaps it is also precisely therefore that the essence of thinking is especially vulnerable and susceptible to all hastiness.

YOUNGER MAN: For we can only experience pure waiting, and preserve our essence in it, by waiting. To will to take hold of pure waiting in haste would be like trying to scoop water with a sieve.

OLDER MAN: On this favorable opportunity, when you so are so clearly warning against hastiness, I would like to tell you something that has unsettled me for a long time.

Whenever we previously spoke about the essence of the human—and that means about the occidental determination of the essence

[*Wesensbestimmung*] of the human—each time you focused only on the characterization of the human as the living being that thinks. [222] To be sure, this definition [*Bestimmung*] was already common in the ancient Greek world. But in the most ancient Greek world, the human was thought otherwise—namely, as ὁ θνητός, as the mortal in distinction to the immortals, the gods. This characterization of the human seems to me to be incomparably deeper than the one first mentioned, which is gained by means of holding in view the human by himself,[5] isolated and detached from the great relationships in which he properly stands. And among these relationships, the one he has to the gods has priority above all others.[6]

YOUNGER MAN: What is it that you would like to say with this reference?

OLDER MAN: I would like to admit a fear, namely that you hasten by the older and deeper definition of the essence of the human as the mortal being, in favor of the younger and shallower characterization of the human which conceives of him as the thinking being. I believe I also understand what this haste is based in.

YOUNGER MAN: And what do you think it is based in?

OLDER MAN: In that philosophy and the historiological account of its history take into view as a matter of course this definition of the human as the thinking being. Although this definition is common among thinkers, I must admit that I do not know why it is common. The older characterization of the human as the mortal is, by contrast, more typical of [*eigen*] the poets, which you can still see from Hölderlin's poetry.

YOUNGER MAN: What you say touches on something with regard to which I do indeed owe you an answer. But now I would like to also admit to you a fear, namely that we would have to sacrifice our night's rest and the [223] conversation begun this evening were we to elucidate the two definitions of the essence of the human and their relations in even a crude fashion.

OLDER MAN: It was not my intention to suddenly turn our evening conversation toward the multilayered [*vielschichtige*] and thus also ambiguous [*vieldeutige*] question of the essence of the human. It just seemed to me to be a good opportunity to present to you something that had long been on my mind.

YOUNGER MAN: Perhaps your interim question even belongs in our conversation. Thus I would like to answer you in several respects. And to some extent I am probably able do this, since I have to reflect almost constantly on this matter when I think.

5. how? as a ζῷον among other things that presence in ζωή
6. yet along with θνητός and ἀ-θνητός *also* he who presences

OLDER MAN: I'll be satisfied if you tell me your stance toward the older, and in my opinion deeper, definition of the essence of the human, which thinks of him as the θνητός, the mortal.

YOUNGER MAN: I know it very well; but the older definition can only be explained if the younger one is thought through. I would like to call into question the idea that the younger definition remains shallow in comparison to the older one. Only the common interpretation of the definition of the essence of the human as the ζῷον λόγον ἔχον seems to me to be shallow. Yet if we finally learn to think that λόγος originally means gathering, then the definition of the human with regard to λόγος says that his essence consists in being in the gathering, namely, the gathering toward the originally all-unifying One.

OLDER MAN: As you say this, the inner relation of this definition to the older one is already becoming more lucid. Presumably you did not at all hasten past the older definition in favor of the younger, but rather only more carefully considered the younger in order to be able to then more purely wait upon the truth of the older. [224]

YOUNGER MAN: So it is; for the older is, like everything inceptual, more difficult to think.

OLDER MAN: If the human as the mortal is experienced in distinction to the immortals, he is obviously thought with regard to the gods and the divine. And if λόγος means the gathering toward the originally all-unifying One, whereby the One is the divine itself, then the two essential definitions—which initially appear as almost incompatible, or at least as foreign to one another—basically think the selfsame.

YOUNGER MAN: While your elucidation of the belonging-togetherness of the two oldest occidental definitions of the essence of the human is indeed splendid, it seems to me to hasten by the allegedly older one, which experiences the human in his mortality.

OLDER MAN: How so?

YOUNGER MAN: Insofar as you take this definition of the human, namely that he is a mortal, only as a hallmark for what essentially distinguishes him from the immortals. But in the definition ὁ θνητός, which one is accustomed to translating as "mortal," it is not so much the relation of the human to the immortals that is named, but rather the relation to death: ὁ θνητός is that being which can die.

OLDER MAN: But the animal can also do that, and to that extent the characterization as θνητός would not at all be a distinguishing trait of the essence of the human.

YOUNGER MAN: If this is in fact a distinguishing trait, then we must attend to the fact that the animal cannot die. The animal cannot die, that is, if to die means: to go toward death, to *have* death. [225]

OLDER MAN: Only one who is acquainted with [*kennt*] death is capable of this.

YOUNGER MAN: Or rather, only one who can at least know [*wissen*] of death. And if indeed death is what waits upon us, this is possible only for one who can, according to his essence [*Wesen*], wait on that which, like death, waits upon our entire being [*Wesen*].

OLDER MAN: The human is, as that being which can die, the being that waits.

YOUNGER MAN: This is what I think.

OLDER MAN: You have thought something beautiful. However, with *this* interpretation of the older definition of the essence of the human, now I don't really see any relation to the younger one.

YOUNGER MAN: Yet if you consider that in λόγος, as the gathering toward the originally all-unifying One, something like attentiveness prevails, and if you begin to ask yourself whether attentiveness is not in fact the same as the constant waiting on that which we named the pure coming, then perhaps one day you will sense that, also in the allegedly younger definition, the essence of the human as the being that waits is experienced. To be sure, this waiting essence of the human remains here, as it does there, in what is unspoken. And I would not like to assert that what was just now said was already specifically [*eigens*] thought by the ancients—just as little as I would like to decide which of the two definitions, thought out toward their truth, is the older. It seems to me that they are both equally old, because equally originary and in their origin equally concealed. Yet take what was said only as a surmise.

OLDER MAN: You know what?—

YOUNGER MAN: What?

OLDER MAN: I am glad that I confessed to you my thoughts about the supposed priority of the supposedly younger definition of the essence of the human. [226]

YOUNGER MAN: And I am thankful that I was able to explain something in that regard. Yesterday I would not yet have been capable of this.

OLDER MAN: Because early this morning that which heals was first granted to you, that which is beginning to heal you and—as I now experience—me as well, by letting us become those who wait.

YOUNGER MAN: Those for whom everything far is near in the nearness of what is held in reserve, and everything near is far in the farness of what is dear.

OLDER MAN: And so for those who wait, the near and the far is the selfsame, although precisely for them the difference of the near and the far holds itself open most purely.

YOUNGER MAN: Hence, those who wait will also guard themselves against straightaway inquiring into what that which heals is in itself. Throughout this entire day I still felt the urge to ask this. And now I see that such questioning remains unbefitting to that on which we wait.

OLDER MAN: It seems to me that those who wait first learn the right kind of humble contentment.

YOUNGER MAN: So that they can be the teachers of great poverty.

OLDER MAN: Those who know what heals without investigating it.

YOUNGER MAN: What else could that which heals be, other than that which lets our essence [*Wesen*] wait. In waiting, the human-being [*das Menschenwesen*] becomes gathered in attentiveness to that in which he belongs, yet without letting himself get carried away into and absorbed in it.

OLDER MAN: In waiting and as those who wait, however, we do listen-out into the undetermined and so, as it were, abandon ourselves. And now you mean to say that, in waiting and as those who wait, we are rather on the path that leads us into our own essence. [227]

YOUNGER MAN: Waiting is a footbridge which supports our going, a footbridge on which we become who we are without already being who we are: those who wait.

OLDER MAN: And so, if a human were capable of this, pure waiting would be like the echo of pure coming.

YOUNGER MAN: This coming essentially occurs all around us and at all times, even when we are not mindful of it. Waiting is a capacity that transcends all power to act. One who finds his way into the ability to wait surpasses all achieving and its accomplishments, although waiting never reckons on an overtaking.

OLDER MAN: This cannot at all be thought of in terms of something like a competition. As those who wait, we are the inlet [*Einlaß*][7] for the coming. We are in such a manner as though we were to first come to ourselves, in letting in [*einlassend*] the coming, as those who are themselves only by abandoning themselves—this, however, by means of waiting toward [*entgegenwarten*] the coming.

YOUNGER MAN: In waiting, we are purely "present" as literally "waiting-toward" [*Gegenwart*].[8]

OLDER MAN: And nothing else. We are this so purely that from nowhere else does something stand over against us, to which we could cling and into which we would still want to escape.

YOUNGER MAN: In waiting, we are in such a manner as though we were to have passed away unnoticed and unnamed—not there for all who still await [*erwarten*] this or that and still expect [*erwarten*]

---

7. Here "inlet" is meant literally, as what "lets in" (*einläßt*).—*Tr.*

8. Here Heidegger is thinking *entgegen* and *gegen*, not in the sense of "contrary" or "against," but rather in the sense of "toward," as in *entgegengehen*, "to go toward, approach, go out to meet."—*Tr.*

from this or that something for themselves. Waiting is in essence otherwise than all awaiting and expecting, which are basically unable to wait.

OLDER MAN: In waiting we have indeed entirely gone away, namely to our essence, which is required by pure coming as the inlet that answers it.

YOUNGER MAN: As those who are required in this manner, we are like a string instrument of the most ancient provenance, in whose sound the primordial play of the world resounds. [228]

OLDER MAN: Such that this instrument is probably also—think of the oldest definition of the essence of the human—aptly taken up and preserved [*aufgehoben*][9] in what is concealed. Incidentally, when you say that we are in essence the answering inlet and so the answer to the coming, is not "answer" [*»Antwort«*], even in word [*Wort*], the selfsame as "present as waiting-toward" [*»Gegenwart«*]?

YOUNGER MAN: Yes, however not only "even in word," as you say, but rather precisely and previously already in word.

OLDER MAN: If now the present as waiting-toward is related to time, while the answer is related to the word, then time and the word are in their essence more intimately kindred than humans may have yet sensed.

YOUNGER MAN: Insofar as we are to have a basis for making this surmise, however, we would probably need to learn to think the essence of time according to what has now been thought as the "present as waiting-toward," and to think the essence of the word [*Wort*] in view of the answer [*Antwort*].

OLDER MAN: Perhaps we are already learning this by being those who wait, that is, by being those who have time for the long time in which one day the true will occur [*das Wahre sich ereignet*].

YOUNGER MAN: Those for whom the long lingering of the coming never becomes boring.

OLDER MAN: Why might this be?

YOUNGER MAN: Presumably it has to do with the fact that we already, in waiting on the coming, also grant to each thing an inlet.

OLDER MAN: Into where? Surely not into our interior, for then we would be setting ourselves up over against things as those who have dominion over the essence of things. In this manner we would be making things into objects for subjects, assuming for ourselves the role of the latter.

---

9. Depending on the context (or, as in Hegel's dialectical thinking, all at once) the verb *aufheben* can mean "to cancel," "to lift up," and/or "to preserve." Here it should also be noted that *aufgehoben sein* is commonly used in the sense of "to be in [good] hands."—*Tr.*

YOUNGER MAN: We, however, are precisely not such subjects and are no longer such subjects [229] when we become those who wait. Rather, in waiting, we release things precisely into where we—as those who wait—let ourselves into, namely into that in which we belong.

OLDER MAN: And wherein do things belong?

YOUNGER MAN: In that in which they rest [*beruhen*].

OLDER MAN: And wherein do they rest?

YOUNGER MAN: In the return to themselves.

OLDER MAN: So when the human sets things toward himself as objects, and only lets them stand as such and subsist in this sense, he does not let things be in their restful repose [*Ruhe*].

YOUNGER MAN: The human chases things around in an unrest that is foreign to them by making them into mere resources for his needs and items in his calculations, and into mere opportunities for advancing and maintaining his manipulations.

OLDER MAN: By not letting things be in their restful repose, but rather—infatuated by his progress—stepping over and away from them, the human becomes the pacesetter of the devastation, which has for a long time now become the tumultuous confusion of the world.

YOUNGER MAN: If we are those who wait, then we do not, as it were, have things come to us; in this manner we would straightaway change from those who wait to those who await and only will something of things.

We are those who wait when we let things return to themselves. Out of such a return to themselves, they bring their own presence [*Gegenwart*] from themselves toward [*entgegen*] us; so in advance they fill out the emptiness that seems to gape around us when we wait on the pure coming, and do not just now and then await something that comes. [230]

OLDER MAN: We would have to properly say that the things that are in this way present do not allow for an emptiness in the first place, and so there is also no possibility of filling out this emptiness.

YOUNGER MAN: The pure coming, on which we wait, is also not something blurry and indeterminable. It is the unique and the simple itself, to which we humans, however, adapt ourselves only slowly, because we are seldom capable of letting something be in that in which it rests.

OLDER MAN: But as soon as we are capable of this, namely of letting something be in that into which—as into its own essence—it is let, then we are truly free. Freedom rests in being able to let [*Lassenkönnen*], not in ordering and dominating.

YOUNGER MAN: This freedom alone is the true superiority, which does not need to have something under it, on which it must support itself in order to remain above.

OLDER MAN: Perhaps the essence of freedom, however, is still more mysterious than we think.

YOUNGER MAN: As long as we are still thinking of it in terms of ruling and effecting.

OLDER MAN: Yet I am also learning now to more clearly sense how it was possible for that which frees to be occasioned for you by the abiding of the expanse of the forest, and how in that which frees what is healing could draw near.

YOUNGER MAN: Which heals by soothing, but never removing, the pain.

OLDER MAN: However, as you yourself said, what was painful was that you remained barred from thinking. But it seems to me now that what was painful consisted rather in that you were no longer able to know in what sense you are one who thinks—and that means, after all that we have said, one who waits. You [231] were already one who waits whenever the event of the devastation distressed you. If we were not already in essence those who wait, then how could we ever become so?

YOUNGER MAN: According to an old saying, we only become who we are.

OLDER MAN: And according to a young saying, we are only what we seek.

YOUNGER MAN: And we seek only that on which we wait.

OLDER MAN: And we wait on that in which we belong.

YOUNGER MAN: Yet we belong to the coming as *the* present-waiting-toward [*Gegenwart*], which in answering [*antwortend*] lets in the coming.

OLDER MAN: As this present-waiting-toward, we release ourselves to the coming, because our essence is already released to it.

YOUNGER MAN: And so in thus releasing ourselves, we first come into our own.

OLDER MAN: Each of these sentences, which call to one another, says the selfsame.

YOUNGER MAN: And none can be preconceived [*unausdenklich*] because each thinks ahead [*vordenkt*] into the coming.

OLDER MAN: The coming is presumably that before [*vorauf*] which nothing more can be thought: the unprethinkable [*das Unvordenkliche*].[10]

YOUNGER MAN: Hence, what heals can also never be set forth in propositional statements.

OLDER MAN: But rather can only be conversationally surmised, as happened just now with us.

YOUNGER MAN: Or perhaps also in the manner in which I initially attempted to say it for myself, when, without their being willed, the following words spoke themselves to me: [232]

10. See the footnote above on p. 95.—*Tr.*

First in waiting
do we come into our own,
granting to every thing
the return into resting.

Like the tender
sound of old master violins,
which passed away unheard
from instruments in hidden cases.[11]

OLDER MAN: I have often pondered whether your thinking is not in fact a concealed poetizing.

YOUNGER MAN: You mean that I poetize because I now express what we are attempting to say with the help of verses and rhymes.

OLDER MAN: I do not in fact mean that; for I know very well that verses and rhymes do not attest to what is poetical, and that even genuine poets can fall prey to their verses and rhymes. Jacob Burckhardt,[12] whose letters we have often read together, once wrote a sentence that I memorized and have often reflected on, and thus can recite from memory. It reads: "There are things written by very renowned poets that are inwardly completely null and void, and that walk along merely on the crutches of rhymes."

YOUNGER MAN: And yet I spoke just now in rhymes.

OLDER MAN: But I surmise that the poetizing of your thinking lies rather in that it is a waiting, and it basically already was so, even before this was raised to the level of clear knowledge for you today.

YOUNGER MAN: Perhaps those among a people [Volk] who poetize and who think are none other than those who in the noblest manner

---

11. This is a rather literal translation of the poem, which in German reads:

> Erst im Warten
> werden wir uns selbst zu eigen,
> gewähren allem Ding
> die Rückkehr ins Beruhen.
>
> Gleich dem zarten
> Klange alter Meistergeigen,
> der ungehört verging
> den Instrumenten in verborgnen Truhen.—Tr.

12. Jacob Burckhardt (1818–1897) was an influential historian of culture and art, known especially for his writings on the Italian Renaissance and on ancient Greek civilization, and for his prescient reflections on modern historical developments. A professor in Basel, he was admired by Nietzsche, who became one of his occasional correspondents. A selection of his correspondence has been published in English as *The Letters of Jacob Burckhardt,* ed. and trans. Alexander Dru (Indianapolis: Liberty Fund, 2001).—Tr.

wait, through whose present-waiting-toward the coming [*Gegenwart zum Kommen*] the word attains to [233] the answer of the human-being [*Menschenwesens*] and thus is brought to language.

OLDER MAN: Then the people of poets and thinkers would be in a unique sense the people that waits.

YOUNGER MAN: The people that still must first, and perhaps for a long time, wait upon the arrival of this essence of theirs, so that this people would become more waitful for the coming, in which the devastation, as something past, is already passed over.

OLDER MAN: This waiting people would—especially during a time when its essence still eludes it, and precisely because of this still-unexperienced waiting essence—be endangered like no other.

YOUNGER MAN: And indeed, this people would be endangered not by threats from the outside, but rather by the fact that it would tyrannize itself with its own ignorant impatience, and so would spur itself on to continual mistakes.

OLDER MAN: And it would even do all this in the opinion that it is thereby following its essence, which would have to finally fight to win recognition from the side of other peoples.

YOUNGER MAN: While in fact this rash pseudo-essence remains a perpetually maladroit imitation of the foreign.

OLDER MAN: If this people were to ever become a people that waits, then it would have to remain indifferent to whether others listen to it or not.

YOUNGER MAN: This people could also never, so long as it would know its essence, insist on its waiting essence as on a special calling and distinction.

OLDER MAN: Having found its pure essence, this people could never have any time left over for comparing itself with others, be this in an overestimating or in an underestimating manner. [234]

YOUNGER MAN: The waiting people would even have to be entirely unusable to others, because of course what always only just waits, and constantly waits moreover on the coming, yields nothing tangible that could be of use for progress and raising the achievement curve, and for the brisk pace of business.

OLDER MAN: And this entirely unusable people would have to become the most elderly people, so that no one concerns himself with it and no one makes use of—and so utilizes and prematurely uses up—its strange doing, which is a letting.

YOUNGER MAN: Its fame—if it were to concern itself at all with such a thing—would have to consist in that it could squander its essence purely on the unnecessary. For what is more unnecessary than the waiting that waits on the coming? What is more necessary than getting down to business with the given facts, remaking what is present at hand, and moving forward what has existed heretofore?

OLDER MAN: In other words, that factual sense of reality which they claim lets the human first stand with both feet squarely on the ground.

YOUNGER MAN: That sense which drives peoples to secure a place for themselves on the earth, a place on which they can stand fast and create close to the facts in order to be effective and validated. And yet, nonetheless, this necessary matter [*Nötiges*] of theirs can never be without the unnecessary [*das Unnötige*].

OLDER MAN: Such that the necessity of the unnecessary [*die Notwendigkeit des Unnötigen*] would remain to be thought.

YOUNGER MAN: Do we not think this in waiting? Is not waiting into the coming such thinking—perhaps even the authentic thinking? According to my unmistakable feeling, the healing that befell us rests not in that it freed us personally from an inner need [*Not*], but rather in that it transplanted us into the knowledge that we, as those who wait, are now to begin to turn and enter [*einzukehren*] the still-withheld essence of our vanquished people. [235]

OLDER MAN: You mean that by becoming those who wait, we first become German?

YOUNGER MAN: Not only is this what I mean—since early this morning, it is what I know. Yet we will not become German so long as we plan to find "the German" by means of analyzing our supposed "nature." Entangled in such intentions we merely chase after what is national, which, after all, as the word says, insists on what is naturally given.[13]

OLDER MAN: Why do you speak so severely against the national?

YOUNGER MAN: After what we have said about the event of devastation, it has become unnecessary to still inveigh against the national.

OLDER MAN: I don't quite understand this.

YOUNGER MAN: The idea [*Idee*] of the nation is that representation [*Vorstellung*] in whose circle-of-vision a people bases itself on itself as a foundation given from somewhere, and makes itself into a subject. And to this subject everything then appears as what is objective, which means that everything appears only in the light of its subjectivity.

---

13. The words "nation" and "native" can be traced back to the Latin *nasci*, meaning "be born." The derived noun *natio* "literally meant 'that which has been born,' a 'breed,' but was soon used by extension for a 'species' or 'race,' and then by further narrowing down for a 'race of people, nation'" (Ayato, *Dictionary of Word Origins*, p. 361). Heidegger's critique here is obviously aimed at the racist nationalism of Hitler's National Socialism.—*Tr.*

OLDER MAN: Nationality is nothing other than the pure subjectivity of a people that purports to rely on its "nature" as what is actual [*das Wirkliche*], from out of which and back to which all effecting [*Wirken*] is supposed to go.

YOUNGER MAN: Subjectivity has its essence in that the human—the individual, groups, and the realms of humanity—rises up to base himself on himself and to assert himself as the ground and measure of what is actual. With this rebellious uprising into subjectivity emerges the uprising into work as that form of achieving by means of which the devastation of the earth is everywhere prepared for and ultimately [236] established as unconditional.

OLDER MAN: The national thus remains definitive when nations unite in agreement on the international.

YOUNGER MAN: The national and the international are the selfsame. The international, if it were to genuinely come about, would be what the mountain range [*Gebirge*] is in relation to the individual mountains [*Bergen*]. But can the mountain range ever bring the individual mountains out beyond themselves?

OLDER MAN: In its highest possibility, the mountain range at best holds the individual mountains together in their willful individualism. While the mountain range is indeed different in kind than the sum of its mountains, it is nevertheless only the essential occurrence [*das Wesende*] of the mountains.

YOUNGER MAN: The national and the international are so decidedly the selfsame that both, by basing themselves on subjectivity and insisting on what is actual, know just as little—and above all can know just as little—whose business it is that they are incessantly conducting.

OLDER MAN: The business of the devastation, and that means of work for the sake of increased possibilities for work. Thus we cannot become German—which means those who poetize and think, that is, those who wait—so long as we chase after the German in the sense of something national.

YOUNGER MAN: Yet, if we are German, we also do not lose ourselves in a vague internationalism.

OLDER MAN: Viewed in terms of the national and international, then, we can no longer say at all what we properly are.

YOUNGER MAN: It is indeed unnecessary to say this, because what is essential dwells most restfully and quietly in what is unspoken. On the [237] other hand, we can know that, as those who wait, we have the longest historical time [*Geschichtszeit*] before us.

OLDER MAN: You know, it seems to me as though I too am now beginning to feel that which heals. What you just said suggests that the historical existence [*geschichtliche Dasein*] of a people and its duration is not grounded in the fact that humans of its native kind [*Geburtsart*] merely survive the devastation, live on, and perhaps, as one says, rebuild, in order to once again demonstrate in a modified form the worth of what has been. Rather, the pure duration of destiny becomes well-grounded solely by means of the waiting that waits on the coming.

YOUNGER MAN: Therefore, we can do nothing more humble than this humble deed of calmly letting ourselves engage in waiting.

OLDER MAN: And learning to know the need [*Not*] in which everywhere the unnecessary [*das Unnötige*] must still persevere.

YOUNGER MAN: Because we still so little know the necessity of the unnecessary [*die Notwendigkeit des Unnötigen*], it appears as if the unnecessary is cast out into a desolate abandonment.

OLDER MAN: You presumably say deliberately, "it appears as if." For in truth, it is not that the unnecessary is in a state of abandonment, but rather that we—we who do not pay attention to the unnecessary as that which is a necessity—are those who are abandoned.

YOUNGER MAN: You are right, and yet perhaps also not right. The unnecessary requires us and our essence like the sound—even if it should fade away unheard—requires the instrument which gives it off.

OLDER MAN: Thus, we must learn to know the necessity of the unnecessary and, as learners, teach it to the peoples [*den Völkern*].

YOUNGER MAN: And for a long time this may perhaps be the sole content of our teaching: the need and the necessity of the unnecessary. [238]

Now I can also say to you more clearly what gave itself to be known in the healing that was granted to us today. It is the dark and the difficult that such a learning and teaching must bear on it shoulders, insofar as learning and teaching may only ever have their element in waiting.

OLDER MAN: What do you mean by this?

YOUNGER MAN: Learning is waitful when it is a seeking, and teaching is waitful when it remains an advising [*Raten*].

OLDER MAN: We all too eagerly rush past seeking to what is found, and we rush past advising with an arrogant will to have an effect.

YOUNGER MAN: But I am not afraid of the burden of the teaching that learns. I know that there will be kindred ones who will bear this burden together.

OLDER MAN: On many evenings to come in this camp, we will ponder over how to advise those among us and among others, who only know the necessary, on the necessity of the unnecessary—and we will ponder over how to do this in such a way that those being advised do not fall into rashly making this teaching into a belief and a worldview and extolling it as such.

YOUNGER MAN: No matter what content they may want to teach, all "worldviews," according to their essence, belong to the age of, and in the dominion of, the devastation.

OLDER MAN: That is a bold assertion.

YOUNGER MAN: What I said may sound so. What I have in mind could become clear to us by means of a meditation on the essence of modern thinking.

OLDER MAN: For that we would presumably have to be still more practiced in thinking. [239]

YOUNGER MAN: And after this evening that now means: we must learn to wait.

OLDER MAN: And we must attempt to tell friends what is given to them to think for a long time ever anew. Yet we ourselves must have first constantly experienced and examined what is inexhaustibly given to the human to think.

YOUNGER MAN: Only in this way does what steadily endures come into our learning and teaching. Yet I fear that today we have shared our joy about what is healing for too long. Tomorrow the sheer work will once again stand before us.

OLDER MAN: But as a good night parting, and perhaps also as a thanks, I would still like to relate to you now a short conversation between two thinkers. In my student days I copied it down from a historiological account of Chinese philosophy because it struck me, though I did not quite understand it earlier. This evening it first became bright around me, and probably because of that, this conversation also occurred to me. The names of the two thinkers escape me.

The conversation goes like this:

The one said: "You are talking about the unnecessary."

The other said: "A person must first have recognized the unnecessary before one can talk with him about the necessary. The earth is wide and large, and yet, in order to stand, the human needs only enough space to be able to put his foot down. But if directly next to his foot a crevice were to open up that dropped down into the underworld, then would the space where he stands still be of use to him?"

The one said: "It would be of no more use to him."

The other said: "From this the necessity of the unnecessary is clearly apparent."[14]

14. The conversation retold here can be found in chapter 26 of the *Zhuangzi:*
Hui Tzu [Huizi] said to Chuang Tzu [Zhuangzi], "Your words are useless!"
Chuang Tzu said, "A man has to understand the useless before you can talk to him about the useful. The earth is certainly vast and broad, though a man uses no more of it than the area he puts his feet on. If, however,

YOUNGER MAN: I thank you for this conversation. [240]

OLDER MAN: And I you for your poem [*Gedicht*], in which perhaps after all something densely composed [*Gedichtetes*][15] is concealed.

YOUNGER MAN: Let us think of what poetically condenses [*das Dichtende*].

OLDER MAN: A good night to us both and to all in the camp.

YOUNGER MAN: And to the homeland the blessing of its destined assignment.

* * *

Schloß Hausen im Donautal, on 8 May 1945.

> On the day the world celebrated its victory, without yet recognizing that already for centuries it has been defeated by its own rebellious uprising.

SUPPLEMENTS

1. The Need of the Delay of the Unnecessary

Evil, malice, furiousness [*das Grimmige*], rage [*der Ingrimm*], becoming infuriated [*Ergrimmen*].

The War at an end, nothing changed, nothing new, on the contrary. What has long subsisted must now noticeably come out.

> you were to dig away all the earth from around his feet until you reached the Yellow Springs [i.e., the underworld], then would the man still be able to make use of it?"
> "No, it would be useless," said Hui Tzu.
> "It is obvious, then," said Chuang Tzu, "that the useless has its use."
> (*The Complete Works of Chuang Tzu*, trans. Burton Watson [New York: Columbia University Press, 1968], p. 299.) —*Tr.*

15. The noun *Gedichtetes* is formed from the participle of *dichten*. However, there are two etymologically unrelated verbs with the same spelling, *dichten*. On the one hand, obviously involved in this context is the verb meaning "to compose" in the sense of "to poetize." On the other hand, Heidegger is presumably also intending the other verb *dichten*, "to seal," which derives from the adjective *dicht*, "dense" as in "impenetrable," and which is closely related to *verdichten*, "to thicken" or "to condense." This latter sense of *dichten* and *dicht* etymologically carries the sense of "sturdy and reliable" and is related to *gedeihen*, "to flourish," as in a dense growth of vegetation. Perhaps, then, Heidegger is suggesting something such as the following: a poem would densely compose language, sealing its treasury of sense in concealment in order to guard and preserve it, thus letting it flourish as a reliable sustenance for thought.—*Tr.*

The *devastation*—that it goes onward.
Onward? so much as possible.
What initially comes, only the emerging, less and less hiding.
The disruptively inessential of beyng—*evil*—*the will.*[16]

The burning pain that we are unable to be there for the unnecessary and are enslaved only to the useful, which by itself is the nothing [*das Nichts*] and so null [*nichtig*] that it drives forth the deepest degradation of the human-being.

> Even while guarded by violent force
> our one and only concern
> is that we become shepherds
> of our long saved-up essence.

2. A-nihilation—and Forgottenness of Being

Allowing oneself to become absorbed into the nihilating of one's own-most concealed essence, that is, into the forgottenness of being in the form of the presumption of its effect in objectification.

The nihilating of memory in the event of appropriation [*Ereignis*]. [242]

Forgottenness and *subjectivity* (*subjectivity:* humanity, nationality, bestiality, brutality), but in a concealed manner belonging to the truth of beyng.

But still in the terrible non-essence [*Unwesen*] not to be denied as memory in the event of appropriation—namely, as the willing of the will to will.

The will and the idea [die Idee]!

The will a something willed and something effectuated still of willing.

Anthropomorphy and machination. (κοινόν)

The *isolation* into the exclusivity of self-will as the *single willing* and true essence of will.

The isolation into the inevitable violence.

---

16. The phrase "the disruptively inessential" translates *das Unwesen*, a word that literally means "the inessential" yet is generally used to refer to a "nuisance" in the sense of an "excess" or "deformation of essence" that disturbs the essential order of things. While most often found in the phrase, *sein Unwesen treiben*, meaning that someone is "doing mischief" or is "up to their old tricks," it is also commonly used to refer to a "terrible state of affairs." The word "beyng," an antiquated spelling of "being," is used to translate *das Seyn*, an antiquated spelling of *das Sein* (being). In the 1930s, Heidegger began using this older spelling to signify that he is attempting to think "being itself" rather than merely "the being of beings" (*das Sein des Seienden*). See below, p. 160, where he comments on the metaphysical distinction between *das Sein* and *das Seiende* (note that in this case I have translated *das Seiende* as "what-is" rather than as "beings"), and says that the "more inceptual" notion of *das Seyn* cannot be understood in terms of this distinction.—*Tr.*

3. Objectification

Physics as technology—τέχνη—objectification.

Objectification—object.

Objectification—object—world-pictures.

Objectification and the transcendental-horizonal essence of the human.

Objectification and metaphysics.

Objectification and uprising.

Uprising and refusal of attention to the belongingness in beyng.

Uprising *and refusal*—from abandonment as being-released into forgetting.

4. Uprising and Object

Uprising and objectification.

Objectification and representational setting-before [*Vor-stellen*] of the secured standing-reserve.

Representing and securing.

Objectification and achievement. [243]

Achievement and willing of the will.

Success and progress and welfare.

Objectification and arranging of possibility for achievement.

The "neutrality" of technology over against beyng and disaster [*Unheil*], where it in essence drives forward the annihilation of the human essence [*Menschenwesens*].

"From humanity via nationality to bestiality (into brutality)." (Roman terms!)

Objectification and the Barring of Waiting.

It obstructs the free-dimension and open of the open-region.

It blocks the footpath of the attentiveness of gathering [*Sammlung*].

It disrupts human being and drives human being into the uprising.

Human being, elevating itself above itself, seeks only in this manner its self (transcendence, horizon, anthropomorphism).

The *isolation* of the human into the inevitable violence.

This isolation engenders the mass-essence of the human.

5. ἄνθρωπος

1. θνητός = the mortal, the one who dies, having death before oneself, succumbing to it.

(the *immortals*—the gods) in view of duration, presencing, being. Φύσις—*remaining* in what is concealed, but the being-relation not specifically thought.

2. ζῷον λόγον ἔχον
λόγος τῆς ψυχῆς. Heraclitus.
Gathering [*Versammlung*]—unity. [244]

6. Brought into the Extreme

and at the same time in the most extrinsic and only then guarded.
Welfare, unemployment, sheer *continuation.*
Mere *surviving.*
The War decides nothing.
The decision is just now beginning to prepare itself—also and espe-
cially, prior to everything, the decision of whether the *Germans* as the
central heart of the Occident fail in the face of their historically des-
tined assignment and *become* the victim of *foreign ideas.*
The "miserable terrain"—"possession and acquisition."

7. Security (what one understands by this)

arises not from securing and the taking of measures for this; security
rests in repose and by means of this becomes itself superfluous.
But what is repose [*Ruhe*] without that in which what reposes [*das
Ruhende*] rests [*beruht*]?
Where is resting in [*beruhen*] without a belonging in one's proper
realm [*Eigentum*]?
Where is such a belonging without appropriating [*Ereignung*]?
Where is appropriating without the event of appropriation
[*Ereignis*]?

8. The Metaphysical Distinction

between idea and actuality is the ground for the distinction in modern
metaphysics, which comes out in Schelling, between positive and negative philosophy.
Being [Sein] is the idea of being, because being = objectivity of representing. *Representationally-set-out-before-ness* [Vor-gestelltheit].
What-is [Seiende] is what creates, the actual that effectuates being
and actualizes itself. [245]
But more inceptual than this is *beyng,* to which the distinction of
being and what-is (idea and what is actual) is not applicable.
Beyng is more essentially than any "person," which, after all, is only
a person thanks to the relation of *beyng* to it.

Editor's Afterword

The conversations collected in this volume were composed in the winter of 1944/45, as the Second World War was approaching its inexorable end. The date 7 April 1945 was inscribed at the end of "Ἀγχιβασίη," and 8 May 1945 at the end of the conversation in a prisoner of war camp. The conversation between a Teacher and a Tower Warden bears no date, but it was also probably composed during this time. In his *Nachlaß* we find Heidegger's manuscripts and transcriptions with their supplements collected together under the title "Country Path Conversations."

There were clearly far more conversations planned, seeing as we find sketches for continuations of all three conversations.

The basis for the text of "Ἀγχιβασίη" is the transcription by Fritz Heidegger that was reworked and supplemented by hand. This transcription was compared with Heidegger's manuscript; what were obvious errors or misreadings were corrected without notation, and the different speakers were emphasized in order to make the text more reader-friendly. Headings were taken from the manuscript. In the abridged version of the transcription we find appended to the key word "A Guide" [*Ein Weiser*] the phrase: "which means here one who indicates [*ein Weisender*], see pp. [53-54]."

A part—roughly the last third—of the first conversation was published by Heidegger in 1959 under the title *Zur Erörterung der Gelassenheit—Aus einem Feldweggespräch über das Denken* [Toward an Emplacing Discussion of Releasement: From a Country Path Conversation about Thinking], in a small volume entitled *Gelassenheit* (Pfullingen: Neske), pp. 29-73.[1] This text has been reprinted in volume 13, *Aus der Erfahrung des Denkens* [From the Experience of Thinking], pp. 37-74, of Heidegger's *Gesamtausgabe*.

1. An English translation of this excerpt can be found in Martin Heidegger, *Discourse on Thinking*, trans. John M. Anderson and E. Hans Freund (New York: Harper & Row, 1966), pp. 58-90.—*Tr.*

The present edition does not take into consideration the minor revisions that were made to this part of the text when it was first published in 1959.

For the second conversation, "The Teacher Meets the Tower Warden," only a manuscript and a couple of project notes are available. In this case too a continuation was presumably planned.

The composition-remains for the "Evening Conversation" are more extensive: a first draft, two fair transcriptions, and one transcription that was evidently made of the more developed "second fair transcription." The second fair transcription and its transcription were compared with one another, and, as with the other two conversations, the text was prepared in accordance with our editorial guidelines.

From the many fragmentary supplements to this conversation a few interrelated pages, which have a clear construction of key words together with their thematic development, were chosen for inclusion. These can be read as a kind of summary of the main thoughts of the conversations.

* * *

Now, fifty years after the German surrender in May 1945, these thoughts of Heidegger's during that time appear in print for the first time. With the devastation of Germany and Europe before his eyes, in these conversations Heidegger places the forgottenness of being in modern thinking—which is stamped with the character of will, and which manifests itself in the rule of technology—in relation to the "process of annihilation which holds the earth in its grasp." The central themes of his later philosophy are present here.—Yet those who, on account of the dates of these conversations, expect a word from the philosopher concerning the end of the Nazi regime, will find themselves disappointed.

For his thought-paths, Heidegger chose a new form: These are imaginary conversations in various situations, where in each case the conversation takes place between one who indicates (a *Weisender*) and one or two companions who think with and differently from him. In all three conversations what is at issue is an other essence of thinking, one that is even "futural" or "yet to arrive" [*künftige*], and which comes from releasement [*Gelassenheit*]. What is necessary is not a new direction for thinking, but rather a new manner of thinking. Through the form of conversation, the accustomed scientific and everyday manner of thinking, with its consequences that are destructive and even annihilating of the human-essence [*Menschenwesen*], is, in a lively and easily understood manner, broken open and loosened up, so that room is given for the wider dimension of thinking, from which arrive "the hints" of those to come.

In the first conversation, "A Triadic Conversation on a Country Path," Heidegger lets the other way of thinking open up to a Scientist and a Scholar, who represent the heretofore prevailing manner of thinking. In their questioning resistance, with the repeated summaries of each single step in thinking, and led by the Guide's fore-understanding of that which is to come, the reader experiences the thoughtful conversation as a way "into nearness": Ἀγχιβασίη, thinking out of releasement. The key word "releasement" [*Gelassenheit*] is not to be understood here according to contemporary usage; rather, Heidegger's understanding is oriented explicitly from Meister Eckhart's emphasis on two formal essential characteristics of "releasement": letting go [*Ablassen*] of willing, and thereby letting-oneself-into [*Sich-ein-lassen*] and allowing [*Zulassen*]. For Meister Eckhart, it is the divine Will into which one is to let oneself, whereas Heidegger speaks of the "open-region" [*Gegnet*], which opens itself to humans as they open themselves to it. The open-region is the realm of the appearance of the divine, the clearing of beyng. Non-willing appears here from the side of humans as the prerequisite for a transforming essence of thinking.

The conversation between a teacher and a tower warden draws attention to astonishment and an eye for the wondrous, in contrast to modern-objective thinking, which keeps wondering at bay in order to obtain everything in its grasp. The Tower Warden explains that "he who lives in the height of a tower feels the trembling of the world sooner and in further-reaching oscillations." Here too, what is at issue is the essence of the human with respect to the openness of beyng, which should not be distorted.

The third conversation is set in a prisoner of war camp, where Heidegger searched, in thought, for both of his missing sons. The point of departure here is the younger prisoner's experience of something healing with respect to the devastation all around, and together with the older prisoner he seeks to clarify this something.

*   *   *

I would like to sincerely thank Dr. Hermann Heidegger and Prof. Dr. Friedrich Wilhelm von Herrmann for their trusting cooperation and ongoing conversation. I am very grateful to Dr. Luise Michaelsen and once again to Dr. Hermann Heidegger for their help in critically examining the texts and with deciphering difficult passages. I am grateful to them and to doctoral candidate Paola-Ludovica Coriando for assistance with proofreading. I thank Dr. Hartmut Tietjen for looking up citation sources.

Stuttgart, in January 1995   Ingrid Schüßler

Glossaries

English–German Glossary

to abandon	*verlassen*
abandonment	*die Verlassenheit*
abandonment of being	*die Seinsverlassenheit*
to abide	*verweilen, weilen*
abiding	*das Verweilen*
abiding-while	*die Weile*
to abstain	*verzichten*
abundance	*die Fülle*
to accommodate	*einweisen, unterbringen*
to account for	*verrechnen*
accustomed	*gewohnt*
achievement	*die Leistung*
achievement-character	*der Leistungscharakter*
achieving	*die Leistung*
acquaintanceship	*die Kundschaft*
acquisition	*der Erwerb*
activity	*die Aktivität; die Tätigkeit*
actual	*wirklich*
actuality	*die Wirklichkeit*
actualization	*die Verwirklichung*
to adapt (oneself)	*sich schicken*
to address	*zuprechen*
to adorn	*schmücken*
adornment	*der Schmuck*
advance	*fortschreiten*
advancement	*der Fortgang*
to advise	*raten*

age	*das Zeitalter*
agreement	*die Zustimmung*
akin	*verwandt*
to allow (for)	*zulassen*
amazing	*verwunderlich*
ambiguous	*zweideutig*
ambivalent	*zwiespältig*
angry	*wütend*
to annihilate	*vernichten*
annihilation	*die Vernichtung*
to answer to	*verantworten*
appearance	*die Erscheinung*
appearing	*das Scheinen*
approaching	*die Annäherung*
to appropriate	*aneignen, ereignen*
to a-propriate	*vereignen*
a-propriated	*ge-eignet*
to appropriate over	*übereignen*
appropriating	*die Ereignung*
approval	*die Zustimmung*
aptly	*schicklich*
arbitrariness	*die Willkür*
arbitrary act	*die Willkür*
to arise	*entstehen*
to ascertain	*feststellen*
ascertainment	*die Feststellung*
to ask	*fragen*
to assert	*behaupten*
to assign	*zuordnen, zuweisen*
to astonish	*erstaunen*
astonishment	*das Staunen*
attentiveness	*die Achtsamkeit*
attitude	*die Haltung*
audacious demand	*die Zumutung*
authentic	*eigentlich*
to await	*erwarten*
awkward predicament	*die Verlegenheit*
badness	*die Schlechtigkeit*
barring	*die Verwehrung*
to base	*gründen*
basic trait	*der Grundzug*
basis	*der Boden; der Grund*
to be acquainted with	*kennen*

to be mindful	*achten*
to bear	*tragen*
the beautiful	*das Schöne*
beautiful	*schön*
becoming infuriated	*Ergrimmen*
to befall	*widerfahren*
befitting	*gemäß*
to begin	*anfangen, beginnen*
behavior	*das Verhalten*
to behold	*vernehmen*
a being	*Wesen, ein*
being	*das Sein*
being-able-to-let	*das Lassenkönnen*
being-let-loose	*die Losgelassenheit; das Los-Gelassensein*
beings	*das Seiende*
belonging-together	*das Zusammengehören*
belonging-togetherness	*die Zusammengehörigkeit*
to bething	*bedingen*
bethinging	*das Bedingen; die Bedingnis*
beyng	*das Seyn*
a beyond	*ein Jenseits*
blessing	*der Segen*
blind alley	*der Irrgang*
to block	*verschütten*
boring	*langweilig*
to break down	*versagen*
bridgeless	*steglos*
to bring near	*nähern*
to bring to abide	*verweilen*
bringing to rest	*die Beruhigung*
by itself	*für sich*
bypath	*der Seitenpfad*
to calculate	*berechnen, rechnen*
calculation	*die Berechnung*
calmly	*ruhig*
cannot be preconceived	*unausdenklich*
capability	*das Vermögen*
the capacious	*das Geräumige*
careful attentiveness	*die Behutsamkeit*
to carry out	*vollziehen*
carrying capacity	*die Tragkraft*
carrying out	*der Vollzug*

to catch sight of	*erblicken*
to cease	*ablassen*
celebration	*die Feier*
to change	*wechseln*
characterization	*die Kennzeichnung*
characterization of essence	*die Wesenskennzeichnung*
to characterize	*Kennzeichnen*
to chase after	*nachjagen*
cheerful serenity	*das Heitere*
circle-of-vision	*der Gesichtskreis*
circumstances	*die Bewandtnis*
claim	*der Anspruch*
to clarify	*deuten*
clarity	*die Deutlichkeit*
to clear	*sich lichten*
to climb out beyond	*hinaussteigen*
to climb over	*übersteigen*
climbing-over	*das Übersteigen; der Überstieg*
to co-determine	*mitbestimmen*
co-emerging	*das Mitaufgehen*
cognition	*das Erkennen; die Erkenntnis*
cognitive activity	*die Denktätigkeit*
coincidence	*der Zufall*
coincidental occurrence	*der Zufall*
to co-intend	*mitbeabsichten*
to collapse	*zusammenfallen, zusammenstürzen*
to come to encounter	*entgegenkommen*
the coming	*das Kommen*
the coming forth of a coincidence	*der Zu-fall*
coming-into-nearness	*In-die-Nähe-kommen*
command	*der Befehl*
commemorating	*das Andenken*
common sense	*der Menschenverstand*
commonsense understanding	*der gewöhnliche Verstand*
compliance	*die Fügsamkeit*
to comply	*sich fügen*
comportment	*das Verhalten*
to conceal	*verbergen*
concealment	*die Verbergung*
to conceive of	*sich vorstellen*
to concern oneself with	*sich kehren an*
to condition	*bedingen*
conduct	*das Verhalten*
configuration	*das Gefüge; die Gestalt*

to consider	*bedenken*
consideration	*die Überlegung*
to consist	*bestehen*
to construct	*bilden*
construct	*das Gebild*
to contain	*enthalten, fassen*
container	*das Gefäß*
containing as with-holding	*das Enthalten*
the containing with-hold	*das Enthalten*
the contrary will of an aversion	*der Widerwille*
conversation	*das Gespräch*
counter-word	*das Gegenwort*
course	*der Gang*
to cover up	*verdecken*
crossing-over	*der Übergang*
customary	*gewöhnlich*
to decree	*verfügen*
dedication	*die Hingabe*
deeds	*die Taten*
defense	*die Gegenwehr*
to define	*bestimmen*
definition	*die Bestimmung*
deliberately	*mit Bedacht*
deliberation	*die Überlegung*
to delimit	*umgrenzen*
delimitation	*die Abgrenzung; die Umgrenzung*
demand	*die Zumutung*
denial	*die Verneinung*
deployable	*verwendbar*
deployment	*das Verwenden*
desert	*die Wüste*
deserted	*verlassen*
desert-ify	*ver-wüsten*
to designate	*bezeichnen*
desolate	*wüst*
desolation	*die Verödung*
destined assignment	*die Bestimmung*
destiny	*das Geschick*
destruction	*die Zerstörung*
determination	*die Bestimmung*
to determine	*bestimmen*
devastated	*verwüstet*
devastation	*die Verwüstung*

dialogue	*der Dialog*
dictionary definition	*die Wortbedeutung*
difference	*der Unterschied*
the different	*das Verschiedene*
to direct	*verweisen*
to disaccustom	*entwöhnen*
disaster	*das Unheil*
discover	*entdecken*
to discuss	*erörtern*
discussion	*die Erörterung*
to disregard	*absehen*
the disruptively inessential	*das Unwesen*
to distance	*entfernen*
distance	*der Abstand*
distances	*die Fernen*
distancing	*die Entfernung*
the divine	*das Göttliche*
to divulge	*verraten*
domain	*der Bereich*
dominance	*die Herrschaft*
to dominate	*beherrschen*
domination	*die Beherrschung*
dominion	*der Herrschaftsbereich*
to doubt	*zweifeln*
drawnear	*nahen*
drink offered	*der Trank*
drink received	*der Trunk*
to dwell	*wohnen*
to effect	*bewirken, wirken*
effect	*die Wirkung*
to effectuate	*erwirken*
ego	*das Ich*
egoity	*die Ichheit*
to elucidate	*erläutern*
to emplace through discussion	*erörtern*
emplacing discussion	*die Erörterung*
emptiness	*die Leere*
enabling-capacity	*das Vermögen*
enchantment	*der Zauber*
to encompass	*umgreifen*
to encounter	*begegnen*
endurance	*die Ausdauer*
to engage in	*sicheinlassenauf*
engaged	*eingelassen*

enigma	*das Rätsel*
the enigmatic	*das Rätselhafte*
enigmatic	*rätselhaft*
to ennoble	*adeln*
to enregion	*vergegnen*
enregioning	*die Vergegnis*
entanglement	*die Verstrichung*
enthusing	*das Schwärmen*
epistemic side	*die Wissensseite*
to escort	*geleiten*
escort	*das Geleit*
essence	*das Wesen*
essence of the tower	*das Turmwesen*
essential domain	*der Wesensbereich*
essential occurrence	*das Wesen; das Wesende*
essential occurring	*die Wesung*
essential provenance	*die Wesensherkunft*
essential sphere	*die Wesenssphäre*
essential structure	*der Wesensbau*
to essentially occur	*wesen*
to essentially prevail	*wesen*
event of appropriation	*das Ereignis*
evil	*das Böse*
examination	*die Betrachtung; die Untersuchung*
to examine	*erprüfen, prüfen, untersuchen*
expanse	*die Weite*
to expect	*erwarten*
expectation	*die Erwartung*
to experience	*erfahren*
expertise	*die Kennerschaft*
to explain	*erklären, erläutern*
explanation	*die Erläuterung*
factual sense of reality	*der Tatsachensinn*
faculty	*das Vermögen*
fail to recognize	*verkennen*
familiar	*bekannt, vertraut*
the far	*das Ferne*
far, far-extending	*weit*
farness	*die Ferne*
far-reaching	*vorausgreifend*
far-reaching vision	*der Weitblick*
fate	*das Schicksal*
to fathom	*ergründen*

fellow humans	*die Mitmenschen*
festival	*das Fest*
the festive	*das Festliche*
field	*das Gebiet*
field of view	*das Blickfeld*
find	*der Fund*
fitting	*gefügt, gemäß*
focal-place	*der Ort*
footbridge	*der Steg*
forbearance	*die Langmut*
forest	*der Wald*
to forgo	*entsagen*
forgottenness of being	*die Seinsvergessenheit*
to form	*bilden*
foundation	*das Fundament; die Grundlage*
frame of mind	*die Gesinnung*
to free	*be-freien, lösen*
free-dimension	*das Freie*
furiousness	*das Grimmige*
to further	*fernen*
fury	*der Grimm*
to gather	*versammeln*
gathering	*die Sammlung; die Versammlung*
to get off track	*auf einen Abweg geraten*
to give itself to be known	*sich kundgeben*
glimpses of light	*die Lichtblicke*
to go forward	*fortgehen*
to go out beyond	*hinausgehen (über)*
to go up to	*herangehen*
gods	*die Götter*
going-up-to	*das Herangehen*
going-into-nearness	*In-die-Nähe-gehen*
to grasp	*fassen*
the Greek world	*das Griechentum*
to ground	*gründen*
ground	*der Grund*
grounding	*die Begründung*
to guard	*hüten*
guardianship	*die Obhut*
guide	*der Weise*
guilt	*die Schuld*
habitat, habitation	*die Behausung*
habituation	*die Gewöhnung*

to halt	*anhalten*
to harbor	*verwahren*
haste, hastiness	*die Übereilung*
to have a presentiment	*ahnen*
to have dominion over	*gebieten*
the healing	*das Heilende*
to heed	*hüten*
held in reserve	*aufbehalten*
helplessly perplexed	*ratlos*
to hide (oneself)	*sich verstecken*
hint	*der Wink*
historian	*der Historiker*
the historical	*das Geschichtliche*
historical time	*die Geschichtszeit*
historiological	*historisch*
historiology	*die Historie*
history	*die Geschichte*
to hold	*fassen, halten*
to hold fast	*festhalten*
to hold open	*aufbehalten*
to hold sway	*herrschen*
homeland	*die Heimat*
homogeneity	*das Einerlei*
horizon	*der Horizont*
the horizonal	*das Horizontale*
horizonal	*horizonthaft, horizontal*
horizonal character	*das Horizonthafte*
horizonality	*das Horizontale*
horizonally	*horizontal*
horizon-essence	*das Horizontwesen*
horizontal	*horizontal*
the human	*der Mensch*
human-being	*das Menschenwesen*
human essence	*das Menschenwesen*
humanities	*die Geisteswissenschaften*
humanity	*die Menschenheit*
humankind	*das Menschentum*
humble contentment	*die Genügsamkeit*
humble deed	*das Geringe*
idea	*der Einfall; die Idee; die Vorstellung*
idea that has come/occurs to one	*der Einfall*
the identical	*das Gleiche*
identical	*gleich*
identicalness	*die Gleichheit*

idle	*tatenlos*
immortals	*die Unsterblichen*
impatience	*die Ungeduld*
in advance	*zum voraus*
inactivity	*die Untätigkeit*
inception	*der Anfang*
inceptual	*anfänglich*
the indeterminate	*das Unbestimmte*
to indicate	*deuten, nennen, weisen*
indication	*der Hinweis; die Weisung*
the indistinct	*das Unterschiedlose*
indweller	*der Inständige*
indwelling	*die Inständigkeit*
ineffable	*unsagbar*
ineffective unreality	*die Unwirklichkeit*
inexhaustibility	*die Unerschöpflichkeit*
inexhaustible	*unerschöpflich*
information industry	*das Nachrichtenwesen*
inkling	*die Ahnung*
inlet	*der Einlaß*
to inquire	*fragen*
to inquire into	*erfragen, erkunden*
inquiry	*die Frage; die Fragestellung*
insight	*der Einblick*
to insist	*beharren*
to institute	*festsetzen*
insurgency	*der Aufruhr*
intact	*heil*
interim question	*die Zwischenfrage*
to interpret	*deuten*
interpretation of essence	*die Wesensauslegung*
interrelated	*verwandt*
intertwined	*ineinanderlaufend*
to intimate	*andeuten*
intransitive naming	*die Nennung*
to investigate	*erforschen, forschen, untersuchen*
investigation of nature	*die Naturforschung*
to join together	*zusammenfügen*
to keep	*behalten, bewahren, einhalten*
to keep safe	*wahren*
to keep secret	*verheimlichen*
kindred ones	*Verwandte*

to know	*kennen, wissen*
to know one's way around	*sich auskennen*
knowing one's way around	*das Sichauskennen*
knowledge	*die Erkenntnis; die Kenntnis; das Wissen*
leading astray	*die Irreführung*
to leave	*lassen*
to leave something alone	*etwas sich selbst überlassen*
to let, to let be	*lassen*
to let go	*ablassen*
let into	*eingelassen*
to let loose	*loslassen*
to let oneself be involved in	*sicheinlassen auf*
to let oneself engage in	*sicheinlassen auf*
letting come	*das Kommenlassen*
letting-be-unconcealed	*das Unverborgenseinlassen*
letting-oneself-into-nearness	*In-die-Nähe-hinein-sich-einlassen*
to lie at the base of	*zugrundeliegen*
to lie out beyond	*hinausliegen*
lifelessness	*das Leblose*
limit	*die Grenze*
limitless	*grenzenlos*
to linger	*verweilen*
lingering	*das Verweilen*
linguistic usage	*der Sprachgebrauch*
listening-into	*das Hineinhören*
living being	*das Lebewesen*
locale	*die Ortschaft*
to look	*blicken*
look	*der Blick; das Aussehen*
to look ahead	*vorausblicken*
to look at	*anblicken*
to look away from	*hinwegblicken*
to look into	*hineinblicken*
looking out beyond	*das Hinausblicken*
machination	*die Machenschaft*
magnanimity	*die Großmut*
to maintain	*behalten*
malice	*das Bösartige*
malicious	*bösartig*
to manifest (itself)	*sich offenbaren*
manifestation	*die Erscheinung; die Offenbarung*

manifold	*das Mannigfaltige; vielfältig*
manner	*die Weise*
manner of viewing	*die Betrachtungsweise*
manners of comportment	*die Verhaltensweisen*
to manufacture	*anfertigen, verfertigen*
matter, matter at issue	*die Sache*
matter-of-factness	*die Sachlichkeit*
to mean	*bedeuten, meinen*
meaning	*die Bedeutung*
to meditate	*sich besinnen, nachsinnen*
meditating, meditation	*die Besinnung*
mental	*geistig*
message	*die Kunde*
mind	*der Geist*
mindfulness	*das Achten*
misleading	*irreführend*
mobile	*beweglich*
the mold of its character	*das Gepräge*
molding	*die Prägung*
moment, moment of vision	*der Augenblick*
monstrous offspring	*die Ausgeburt*
moral	*moralisch*
morality	*die Moral; das Sittliche*
the mortal	*der Sterbliche*
mortality	*die Sterblichkeit*
mountain range	*das Gebirge*
movement	*die Bewegung*
movement on a way	*die Be-wegung*
mystery	*das Geheimnis*
to name	*benennen, nennen*
the nameless	*der Namenlose*
the national	*das Nationale*
natural forces	*die Naturkräften*
natural science	*die Naturwissenschaft*
nature	*die Natur*
the near	*das Nahe*
to near	*nähern*
near to the facts	*tatsachennah*
nearness	*die Nähe*
the necessary	*das Nötige*
necessity	*die Notwendigkeit*
need	*die Not*
needs	*die Bedürfnisse*

negation	*die Verneinung*
the negative	*das Negative*
nihilating	*das Nichten*
the no	*das Nein*
nobility	*der Adel*
noble	*edel*
noble-mindedness	*der Edelmut*
non-willing	*das Nicht-Wollen*
the not/non	*das Nicht*
not-going-away	*das Nicht-weg-gehen*
the nothing	*das Nichts*
null	*nichtig*
nullity	*die Nichtigkeit*
the numerical one	*die Eins*
object	*der Gegenstand; das Objekt*
objectification	*die Vergegenständlichung*
objectiveness	*die Gegenständlichkeit*
objectivity	*die Objektivität*
observation	*die Betrachtung*
obsession	*die Sucht*
to occasion	*veranlassen*
occasioning which allows	*die Veranlassung*
the Occident	*das Abendland*
occidental	*abendländisch*
to occur	*sich ereignen*
to occur to	*einfallen*
off track	*auf dem Holzweg*
on its own	*für sich*
the One	*das Eine*
one who dies	*der Sterbende*
one's proper realm	*das Eigentum*
opacity	*die Undurchsichtigkeit*
the open	*das Offene*
to open up	*eröffnen*
open-region	*die Gegnet*
opposing	*das Sich-Widersetzen*
opposition	*die Gegnerschaft*
origin	*der Ursprung*
originary	*ursprünglich*
to ornament	*zieren*
ornament	*die Zier*
ornamentation	*die Verzierung*
the other side	*Jenseits*

outward look	*das Aussehen*
outward view	*die Aussicht*
to over-astound	*überstaunen*
to overlook	*übersehen*
overseeable	*übersehbar*
overtaking	*das Überholen*
own	*eigen*
own free swinging	*die Eigenschwingung*
pacesetter	*der Schrittmacher*
pain	*der Schmerz*
pass beyond	*überholen*
to pass over	*übergehen*
passageway	*der Übergang*
passing beyond	*das Überholen*
passing over	*das Übergehen*
path	*der Weg*
patience	*die Geduld*
to pay attention	*achten*
to pay attention to	*beachten*
pensiveness	*die Nachdenklichkeit*
people	*das Volk*
to perceive	*vernehmen*
perishing	*das Untergehen*
perplexed	*ratlos*
perplexity	*die Ratlosigkeit*
pertaining to the will	*willensmäßig*
phenomenon	*die Erscheinung*
physical (adjectival form of "physics")	*physikalisch*
place	*der Ort; die Stelle; die Stellung*
poetizing	*das Dichten*
to point (out, toward)	*weisen*
to ponder	*nachsinnen*
position	*die Stelle; die Stellung*
power (in the mathematical sense)	*die Potenz*
power to act	*die Tatkraft*
powers of nature	*die Naturgewalten*
the precious	*das Kostbare*
to presage	*ahnen*
to presence	*anwesen, gegenwärtigen*
presence	*die Gegenwart*
presencing	*das Anwesen*

present	*die Gegenwart*
present as waiting-toward	*die Gegenwart*
present-at-hand	*vorhanden*
presentiment	*die Ahnung*
present-waiting-toward	*die Gegenwart*
to preserve	*aufbewahren, bewahren*
presumably	*vermutlich*
to prevail	*walten*
preview	*der Vorblick*
primal origins	*die Ursprünge*
primordial	*uralt*
procedure	*das Vorgehen*
process	*der Vorgang*
process of cognition	*der Erkenntnisvorgang*
to produce	*herstellen*
pro-ducing	*das Her-stellen*
projection	*der Entwurf*
proper	*eigen, eigentlich*
proper aptitude	*die Eignung*
to protect	*beschützen*
provenance	*die Herkunft*
pseudo-essence	*das Scheinwesen*
pure	*lauter, rein*
to purify	*läutern*
to pursue	*betreiben, nachgehen*
purview	*der Gesichtskreis*
to question	*fragen*
question	*die Frage*
rage	*der Ingrimm*
raising to the next power	*die Potenzierung*
rarity	*die Seltenheit*
rash	*voreilig*
to reach beyond	*hinausgreifen*
realization	*die Verwirklichung*
realms of humanity	*die Menschentümer*
reason	*der Grund*
rebellious	*aufständisch*
rebellious uprising	*der Aufstand*
receding depth of vision	*die Gesichtsflucht*
to reckon	*rechnen*
to recognize	*erkennen*
to reflect (on)	*nachsinnen, nachdenken*

reflection	*das Nachdenken; die Überlegung*
to refrain	*absehen, verzichten*
refusal	*die Absage; das Versagen*
refusing	*das Sich-Weigern*
regard	*der Hinblick; die Hinsicht*
to region	*gegnen*
region	*die Gegend*
regioning	*das Gegnen*
related as a sibling	*verschwistert*
related	*verwandt*
relation	*die Beziehung; der Bezug*
relationship	*das Verhältnis*
to release	*lassen*
to release oneself over to	*sich überlassen*
releasement	*die Gelassenheit*
releasing oneself from	*Sichloslassen aus*
relinquishment	*der Verzicht*
to renounce	*absagen*
renouncing	*das Absagen*
to reply	*entgegnen*
repose	*die Ruhe*
reposing	*das Ruhen*
to represent	*vorstellen*
representation	*das Vorstellen; die Vorstellung*
representational setting-before	*das Vor-stellen*
to representationally set before oneself	*sich vorstellen*
representationally-set-out-before-ness	*die Vor-gestelltheit*
representing	*das Vorstellen*
to require	*brauchen*
to research	*forschen*
researcher	*der Forscher*
re-sheltering	*das Zurückbergen*
to reside	*sich aufhalten*
resoluteness, resolute openness	*die Entschlossenheit*
resonance	*der Hall*
to resound	*widerklingen*
resounding	*der Widerhall*
resounding-forth	*der Anklang*
to rest	*ruhen*
to rest (in)	*beruhen (in)*
rest	*die Ruhe*
restful	*ruhig*

restful repose	*die Ruhe*
resting	*das Beruhen*
resting state	*die Ruhelage*
restlessness	*die Ruhelosigkeit*
restraint	*die Verhaltenheit*
retrieval	*das Nachholen*
to retrieve (later)	*nachholen*
to return	*zurückkehren*
return	*die Rückkehr*
re-turn	*die Rück-kehr*
return path	*der Rückweg*
to reveal	*entbergen*
revealing	*das Entbergen; die Entbergung*
to reverse	*umkehren*
to rise up	*aufstehen*
to roam around	*umherschweifen*
rule (over)	*beherrschen*
ruling	*das Herrschen*
to rush (past)	*übereilen*
to safeguard	*hüten*
saying capacity	*die Sagekraft*
scholar	*der Gelehrte*
scholarly	*gelehrt*
the sciences	*die Wissenschaften*
scientific research	*die Forschung*
scientist	*der Forscher*
secret	*das Geheimnis*
securing	*die Sicherung*
security	*die Sicherheit*
to seduce	*verleiten*
to seek, to search	*suchen*
seeker	*Suchender*
seeking	*das Suchen*
self-oblivion	*die Selbstvergessenheit*
self-opening	*das Sichöffnen*
self-righteousness	*die Selbstgerechtigkeit*
the selfsame	*das Selbe*
selfsameness	*die Selbigkeit*
self-will	*der Eigenwille*
to set before	*vorstellen*
to set forth	*herstellen*
to set toward oneself	*auf sich zustellen*
setting-forth	*das Her-stellen*

setting-toward	*das Zu-stellen*
to shake	*erschüttern*
to shape	*gestalten*
shape	*die Gestalt*
to shelter	*bergen*
shelter	*die Geborgenheit*
sheltering	*das Bergen*
to show	*weisen, zeigen*
to shrink back	*zurückweichen*
shrouding	*die Verschleierung*
side paths	*die Seitenwege*
sight	*der Anblick; der Blick*
sign	*das Zeichen*
significance	*die Deutung*
signification	*die Bedeutung*
to signify	*bedeuten*
the similar	*das Gleiche*
similar	*gleich*
similarity	*die Gleichheit*
the simple	*das Einfache*
simplicity	*die Einfachheit*
single	*einzeln*
singular	*einzig*
to sojourn	*sich aufhalten*
sojourn	*der Aufenthalt*
sojourn-in-the-with-hold	*der Auf-ent-Halt*
solution	*die Lösung*
something densely composed	*etwas Gedichtetes*
something effectuated	*Erwirktes*
something healing	*etwas Heilsames*
something indeterminable	*das Unbestimmbare*
something ineffable	*etwas Unsagbares*
something which has drawn near	*ein Genahtes*
to soothe	*beruhigen*
soul	*die Seele*
soundness	*die Gediegenheit*
space	*der Raum*
to speak to	*zuprechen*
to speak together	*mitsprechen*
speaking with one another	*das Miteinandersprechen*
specially	*eigens*
specifically	*eigens*
sphere of meaning	*der Bedeutungsumkreis*
spiritual	*seelisch*

splendid	*schön*
stairs	*die Stiege*
to stand fast	*feststehen*
standing-in-itself	*das In-sich-stehen*
standing-reserve	*der Bestand*
state of affairs	*der Sachverhalt*
state of rest	*die Ruhelage*
stated position	*die Stellungnahme*
to stay	*sich aufhalten*
story	*die Sage*
the strange	*das Seltsame*
strange	*seltsam*
to stray	*abirren*
to stride beyond	*überstreiten*
striving	*das Streben*
sturdy	*gediegen*
subject	*das Subjekt*
subjectivity	*die Subjektivität*
to subsist	*bestehen*
subsistence	*das Bestehen*
to substantiate	*begründen*
substantiating	*das Begründen*
to surmise	*vermuten*
surmise	*das Vermuten; die Vermutung*
to surpass	*übertreffen*
surrounding circle	*der Umkreis*
to survey	*überblicken*
to take hold of	*fassen*
to take into consideration	*beachten*
tale	*die Sage*
to talk	*reden*
tangle	*das Gewirr*
technological	*technisch*
technology	*die Technik*
telling	*das Sagen*
to tempt	*verführen*
tending to	*das Hüten*
to test	*prüfen*
that which is a necessity	*das Notwendige*
theme	*das Thema*
thing-essence	*das Dingwesen*
thingness	*die Dingheit*

to think about	*bedenken*
to think ahead	*vorausdenken, vordenken*
to think along with	*mitdenken*
thinking in physics	*physikalisches Denken*
those who wait	*die Wartenden*
to thoughtfully pursue	*nachdenken*
thoughtfulness	*die Bedachtsamkeit*
thoughtlessly	*unbedacht*
time-period	*das Zeitalter*
topic	*das Thema*
total human condition	*menschlicher Gesamtzustand*
to tower	*sich ragen*
tower	*der Turm*
tower room	*die Turmstube*
tower stairway	*der Turmaufgang*
tower warden	*der Türmer*
traits	*die Züge*
to transcend	*übersteigen*
transcendence	*die Transzendenz*
the transcendent	*das Transzendente*
transcendental	*das Transzendentale*
transcending	*das Übersteigen*
to transform	*verwandeln, wandeln*
transformation	*der Wandel*
transition	*der Übergang*
transitive naming	*die Benennung*
to transplant	*versetzen*
treeness	*das Baumhafte*
the true	*das Wahre*
truly	*wahrhaft, eigentlich*
truth	*die Wahrheit*
tumultuous confusion	*das Wirrsal*
turmoil	*die Wirrnis*
to turn	*kehren*
to turn back	*zurückkehren*
to turn oneself mindfully toward	*sich kehren an*
to turn to enter	*einkehren*
turning	*die Wendung*
turning back	*die Rückkehr*
turning to enter	*die Einkehr*
turning-back	*die Rück-kehr*
unadorned	*schmucklos*
unambiguous	*eindeutig*

the unapparent	*das Unscheinbare*
unapparent	*unscheinbar*
unavoidable	*unumgänglich*
unawares	*unversehens*
uncanny	*unheimlich*
unconcealment	*die Unverborgenheit*
understanding	*das Verstehen*
to understand	*verstehen*
undetermined	*unbestimmt*
the undoubtable	*das Unbezweifelbare*
the ungraspable	*das Unfaßliche*
unhomely	*unheimisch*
unique	*einzigartig*
uniqueness	*Einzigartiges*
the unique one	*das Einzige*
unity	*die Einheit*
unleash	*entfesseln*
the unnecessary	*das Unnötige*
the unprethinkable	*das Unvordenkliche*
unrest	*die Unruhe*
unrestrained	*ungehemmt*
unsayable	*unsagbar*
to unsettle	*beunruhigen*
the unspoken	*das Ungesprochene*
the unsurmised	*das Unvermutete*
to unveil	*enthüllen*
unwholesome	*heillos*
uprising	*der Aufstand*
to use up	*verbrauchen*
usual	*gewöhnlich*
to utilize	*vernutzen*
to vanish	*verschwinden*
variant	*das Abgewandelte*
variation	*die Abwandlung*
varied	*abgewandelt*
variety	*die Verschiedenheit*
to veil	*verhüllen*
to venture	*wagen*
vicinity	*der Bezirk*
view	*die Ansicht; der Ausblick; die Aussicht; der Anblick; der Blick; der Hinblick*
viewing-direction	*die Blickrichtung*
viewpoint	*der Gesichtspunkt*

viewpoints	*die Hinsichten*
violent force	*die Gewalt*
vista	*der Ausblick*
volitional side	*die Willensseite*
to wait	*warten*
waitful	*wartend*
walking course, walking	*der Gang*
to wander about	*umherirren*
to want	*wollen*
wasteland	*die Öde*
watchful	*vorsichtig*
way	*der Weg; die Weise*
welfare	*die Wohlfahrt*
what comes to encounter	*das Entgegenkommende*
what essentially occurs	*das Wesende*
what has the character of a horizon	*das Horizonthafte*
what heals, that which heals	*das Heilende*
what holds in reserve	*das Aufbehaltende*
what-is	*das Seiende*
what is a matter of will	*das Willenshafte*
what is actual	*das Wirkliche*
what is essential	*das Wesenhafte*
what is healing	*das Heilsame*
what is held in reserve	*das Aufbehaltene*
what is in back	*das Rückwärtige*
what is inexhaustible	*das Unerschöpfliche*
what is insurgent	*das Aufrührerische*
what is naturally given	*Naturgegebenes*
what is necessary	*das Nötige*
what is objective	*das Gegenständliche*
what is objectless	*der Gegenstandlose*
what is poetical	*das Dichterische*
what is present	*das Anwesende*
what is thematic	*das Thematische*
what poetically condenses	*das Dichtende*
what presences	*das Anwesende*
what properly characterizes	*das Eigentümliche*
what regions	*das Gegnende*
what settles by bringing to rest	*das Beruhigende*
what steadily endures	*das Beständige*
whole gathering of the drink	*das Getränk*
the will	*der Wille*

to will	*wollen*
will of aversion	*der Widerwille*
the will to have an effect	*das Wirkenwollen*
will-to-hear	*das Hörenwollen*
the will to power	*der Wille zur Macht*
will-essence	*das Willenswesen*
willful	*willentlich*
willful individualism	*die Eigenwilligkeit*
willing	*das Wollen*
willing-to-know	*das Wissenwollen*
will-to-fathom	*das Ergründenwollen*
will-to-represent	*das Vorstellen-Wollen*
with a matter-of-fact attitude	*sachlich*
with regard to intellectual history	*geistgeschichtlich*
withdrawal	*der Entzug*
withheld	*vorenthalten*
the with-hold	*der Enthalt*
without a horizon	*horizontlos*
without a sense of direction	*richtungslos*
wonderful	*wunderbar*
wondering	*die Verwunderung*
the wondrous	*das Wundersame*
workshop	*die Werkstatt*
to world	*welten*
world	*die Welt*
the world's general public	*die Weltöffentlichkeit*
world-order	*die Weltordnung*
world-picture	*das Weltbild*
worldviews	*die Weltanschauungen*
wound	*die Wunde*

German-English Glossary

Abendland, das	Occident
Abgrenzung, die	delimitation
abirren	to stray
ablassen	to cease, to let go
Absage, die	refusal
absagen	to renounce
Absagen, das	renouncing
absehen	to disregard, to refrain
Abstand, der	distance (cf. *Entfernung*)
Abwandlung, die	variation, varying

Abwegige, das	(sense of) having gone astray
achten	to pay attention, to be mindful
Achten, das	mindfulness
Achtsamkeit, die	attentiveness
Adel, der	nobility
adeln	to ennoble
ahnen	to presage, to sense, to have a presentiment
Ahnung, die	presentiment, inkling, sense
Aktivität, die	activity
Anblick, der	sight, view
anblicken	to look at
Andenken, das	commemorating
andeuten	to intimate, to imply, to suggest
aneignen	to appropriate
Anfang, der	inception
anfangen	to begin, to initiate
anfänglich	inceptual, from the beginning
anfertigen	to manufacture
angesichts	in sight of
anhalten	to halt
Anklang, der	resounding-forth
Annäherung, die	approaching, approximation
Ansicht, die	view
Anspruch, der	claim
Anwesen, das	presencing
Anwesende, das	what presences, what is present
Aufbehaltende, das	what holds in reserve
Aufbehaltene, das	what is held in reserve
auf einen Abweg geraten	get off track
aufbehalten	to hold open, held in reserve
aufbewahren	to preserve
Aufenthalt, der	sojourn
Auf-ent-Halt, der	sojourn-in-the-with-hold
aufhalten (sich)	to stay, to sojourn, to reside
Aufrührerische, das	insurgency
Aufstand, der	uprising, rebellious uprising
Augenblick, der	moment, moment of vision
Ausblick, der	outlook, vista
Ausdauer, die	endurance
auskennen (sich)	to know one's way around
Aussehen, das	outward look, look
Aussicht, die	view, outward view

Baumartige, das	the nature of trees
Baumhafte, das	treeness
beachten	to pay attention to, to notice, to take into consideration
Bedacht (mit)	deliberately
bedächtiger	with more careful consideration
Bedachtsamkeit, die	thoughtfulness
bedenken	to consider, to think about
Bedenken, das	reservation, thoughts
bedeuten	to signify, to mean
Bedeutung, die	signification, meaning
Bedeutungsumkreis, der	sphere of meaning
bedingen	to condition, to bething
Bedingen, das	conditioning, bethinging
Bedingnis, die	conditioning, bethinging
be-freien	to free
Befreiende, das	what frees
begegnen	to encounter
beginnen	to begin
begründen	to substantiate
behalten	to keep, to maintain
behaupten	to assert, to claim
Behausung, die	habitat, habitation
beherrschen	to dominate, to rule, to rule over
Behutsamkeit, die	careful attentiveness
bekannt	familiar
benennen	to name
Benennung, die	transitive naming (cf. *Nennung*)
berechnen	to calculate
Bereich, der	domain
bergen	to shelter
beruhen (in)	to rest (in)
beruhigen	to soothe
Beruhigende, das	what settles by bringing to rest
Beruhigung, die	bringing to rest
beschützen	to protect
besinnen (sich)	to meditate
Besinnung, die	meditation, meditating
Bestand, der	standing-reserve
Beständige, das	what steadily endures
bestehen	to consist, to subsist, to withstand, to exist
bestimmen	to determine, to define, to destine

Bestimmung, die	definition, determination, destined assignment
Betrachtung, die	examination, observation, view
betreiben	to pursue, to drive forth, to conduct
beunruhigen	to unsettle
bewahren	to keep, to preserve
Bewandtnis, die	circumstances
beweglich	mobile
Bewegung, die	movement
Be-wegung, die	movement on a way
bewirken	to effect
bezeichnen	to designate
Beziehung, die	relation
Bezug, der	relation
bilden	to form, to construct
Blick, der	look, view, sight
blicken	to look
Blickfeld, das	field of view
Blickrichtung, die	viewing-direction
Boden, der	basis
bösartig	malicious
Bösartige, das	malice
Böse, das	evil, what is evil
brauchen	to require
Denktätigkeit, die	cognitive activity
deuten	to indicate, to clarify, to interpret
Deutlichkeit, die	clarity
Deutung, die	significance
Dialog, der	dialogue
Dichten, das	poetizing
Dichtende, das	what poetically condenses
Ding, das	thing
Dingheit, die	thingness
Dingwesen, das	thing-essence
edel	noble
Edelmut, der	noble-mindedness
eigen	own, proper
eigenmächtig	on one's own authority
eigens	specifically, specially
Eigenschwingung, die	own free swinging

eigentlich	proper, properly, authentic, authentically, truly, really
Eigentum, das	one's proper realm
Eigentümliche, das	what properly characterizes
Eigenwille, der	self-will
Eigenwilligkeit, die	willful individualism
Eignung, die	proper aptitude
Einblick, der	insight
eindeutig	unambiguous
Eine, das	the One
Einerlei, das	homogeneity
Einfache, das	the simple
Einfall, der	idea, idea that has come to one, idea that occurs to one
einfallen	to occur to, to come to
eingelassen	engaged, let into
einhalten	to keep
Einheit, die	unity
Einkehr, die	turning to enter
einkehren	to turn to enter
Einlaß, der	inlet
Eins, die	the numerical one
einweisen	to accomodate
einzeln	individual, single
einzigartig	unique
Einzige, das	the unique one
entbergen	to reveal
Entbergen, das	revealing, de-concealing
Entbergung, die	revealing
entdecken	to discover
entfernen	to distance, to recede
Entfernung, die	distancing
entgegenkommen	to come to encounter
Entgegenkommende, das	what comes to encounter
entgegnen	to reply
Enthalt, der	the with-hold
enthalten	to contain
Enthalten, das	containing as with-holding, the containing with-hold
enthüllen	to unveil
entsagen	to forgo
Entschlossenheit, die	resoluteness, resolute openness
entstehen	to arise

entwöhnen	to disaccustom
Entwurf, der	projection
Entzug, der	withdrawal
erblicken	to catch sight of
ereignen (sich)	to occur
ereignen	to appropriate
Ereignis, das	event of appropriation
Ereignung, die	appropriating
erfahren	to experience, to find out, to receive
erforschen	to investigate
erfragen	to inquire into
Ergrimmen	becoming infuriated
ergründen	to fathom
Ergründenwollen, das	will-to-fathom
erkennen	to recognize
Erkennen, das	cognition
erkennend	cognitive
Erkenntnis, die	cognition, knowledge
Erkenntnisvorgang, der	process of cognition
erklären	to explain
erklingen	to be heard resounding, to begin to resound
erkunden	to inquire into
erläutern	to explain, to elucidate
erörtern	to discuss, to emplace through discussion
Erörterung, die	discussion, emplacing discussion
Erscheinung, die	manifestation, appearance, phenomenon
Erschütterung, die	shaking
erstaunen	to astonish
erstaunlich	astonishing
erwarten	to await, to expect
Erwarten, das	awaiting, expecting
erwirken	to effectuate
etwas Unsagbares	something ineffable
fassen	to take hold of, to grasp, to contain, to hold
Feier, die	celebration
Ferne, das	the far
Ferne, die	farness
fernen	to further

Fernen, die	distances
Fest, das	festival
festhalten	to get a grip on, to hold fast
Festliche, das	the festive, what is festive
festsetzen	to institute
feststehen	to stand fast
feststellen	to ascertain
Feststellung, die	ascertainment
forschen	to research, to investigate
Forschen, das	scientific researching
Forscher, der	scientist, researcher
Forschung, die	scientific research
Fortgang, der	advancement
fortgehen	to go forward
fortschreiten	to advance
Frage, die	question, inquiry
fragen	to question, to ask, to inquire
Fragestellung, die	questioning, mode of inquiry, inquiry
Freie, das	free-dimension, the open
fügen (sich)	to comply
Fügsamkeit, die	compliance
Fühlen, das	feeling
Fülle, die	abundance
Fund, der	find
für sich	by itself, on its own
Gang, der	course, walking course, walking
Gebiet, das	field
gebieten	to have dominion over
Gebild, das	construct
Gebirge, das	mountain range
Geborgenheit, die	shelter
Gedichtetes, etwas	something densely composed
gediegen	sturdy
Gediegenheit, die	soundness
Geduld, die	patience
geeignet	appropriated (to)
ge-eignet	a-propriated
Gefäß, das	container
Gefüge, das	configuration
gefügt	fitting
Gegend, die	region
Gegenstand, der	object, thematic object

Gegenständliche, das	what is objective
Gegenständlichkeit, die	objectiveness (cf. *Objektivität*)
Gegenstandlose, der	what is objectless
Gegenwart, die	present, presence, present as wait-ing-toward, present-waiting-toward
gegenwärtigen	to presence
Gegenwehr, die	defense
Gegenwort, das	counter-word
gegnen	to region
Gegnen, das	regioning
Gegnende, das	what regions
Gegnerschaft, die	opposition
Gegnet, die	open-region
Geheimnis, das	mystery, secret
geheimnisvoll	mysterious
Geist, der	mind
Geisteswissenschaften, die	humanities
geistgeschichtlich	with regard to intellectual history
geistig	mental
Gelassenheit, die	releasement
gelehrt	scholarly
Gelehrte, der	scholar
Geleit, das	escort
geleiten	to escort
gemäß	fitting, fittingly, befitting, in accordance with
Genahtes, ein	a something which has drawn near
Genügsamkeit, die	humble contentment
Genuß, der	enjoyment
Gepräge, das	the mold of its character
Geräumige, das	the capacious
Geringe, das	humble deed
Geschehnis, das	event
Geschichte, die	history
Geschichtliche, das	the historical
Geschichtszeit, die	historical time
Geschick, das	destiny
Geschmückte, das	what is adorned
Geselligkeit, die	conviviality
Gesichtsflucht, die	receding depth of vision
Gesichtskreis, der	circle-of-vision, purview
Gesichtspunkt, der	viewpoint

Gesinnung, die	frame of mind
Gespräch, das	conversation
Gestalt, die	shape, configuration
gestalten	to shape
Getränk, das	the whole gathering involved in the event of drinking, the whole gathering of the drink (cf. *Trank* and *Trunk*)
Gewalt, die	violent force
Gewirr, das	tangle
gewöhnlich	customary, usual
gewöhnliche Verstand, der	commonsense understanding
gewohnt	accustomed
Gewöhnung, die	habituation
gleich	identical, similar
Gleiche, das	the identical, the similar, what is identical or similar
Gleichheit, die	identicalness, similarity
Götter, die	gods
Göttliche, das	the divine
Grenze, die	limit
grenzenlos	limitless
Griechentum, das	the Greek world
Grimm, der	fury
Grimmige, das	furiousness
Großmut, die	magnanimity
Grund, der	basis, ground, reason
gründen	to base, to ground
Grundlage, die	foundation
Grundlegung, die	that which lays the foundation
Grundzug, der	basic trait
halten	to hold
Haltung, die	attitude
Heilende, das	what heals, the healing
heillos	unwholesome
Heilsame, das	what is healing
Heilsames, etwas	something healing
Heimat, die	homeland
Heitere, das	cheerful serenity
herangehen	to go up to
Herangehen, das	going-up-to
Herkunft, die	provenance
Herrschaft, die	dominance

Herrschaftsbereich, der	dominion
herrschen	to hold sway, to reign
herstellen	to produce, to set forth
Her-stellen, das	pro-ducing, setting-forth
Hinausblicken, das	looking out beyond
hinausgehen (über)	to go out beyond
hinausgreifen	to reach beyond
hinausliegen	to lie out beyond
hinaussteigen	to climb out beyond
Hinblick, der	regard, view
hineinblicken	to look into
Hineinhören, das	listening-into
Hingabe, die	dedication
hingeben	to dedicate
Hinsicht, die	regard
Hinsichten, die	viewpoints
hinwegblicken	to look away from
Hinweis, der	suggestion, indication, reference, comment
Historie, die	historiology
Historiker, der	historian
historisch	historiological
Holzweg, auf dem	off track
Hörenwollen, das	will-to-hear
Horizont, der	horizon
horizontal	horizontal, horizonal, horizonally
Horizontale, das	horizonality, the horizonal
horizonthaft	horizonal
Horizonthafte, das	what has the character of a horizon, horizonal character
horizontlos	without a horizon
Horizontwesen, das	horizon-essence
hüten	to heed, to guard, to safeguard
Hüten, das	tending to, safeguarding
Ich, das	ego
Ichheit, die	egoity
In-die-Nähe-gehen	going-into-nearness
In-die-Nähe-hinein-sich-einlassen	letting-oneself-into-nearness
In-die-Nähe-kommen	coming-into-nearness
Ingrimm, der	rage
In-sich-stehen, das	standing-in-itself
Inständige, der	indweller
Inständigkeit, die	indwelling

irreführend	misleading
Irreführung, die	leading astray
Irrgang, der	blind alley
Jenseits	beyond, the other side
kehren (sich an)	to concern oneself with, to mind-fully turn oneself toward, to pay heed to
kehren	to turn
kennen	to know, to be acquainted with
Kennerschaft, die	expertise
Kenntnis, die	knowledge
Kommen, das	the coming
Kommenlassen, das	letting come
Kostbare, das	the precious
Kunde, die	message
kundgeben (sich)	to be apparent, to announce itself, to give itself to be known
Kundschaft, die	acquaintanceship
Langmut, die	forbearance
langweilig	boring
lassen	to let, to release, to leave, to let be
Lassenkönnen, das	being-able-to-let
Lebewesen, das	living being
Leere, die	emptiness
Leistung, die	achievement, achieving
Leistungscharakter, der	achievement character
lichten (sich)	to clear, to open up (itself)
lösen	to free, to remove
Losgelassenheit, die	being-let-loose
Los-Gelassensein, das	being-let-loose
loslassen	let loose
Lösung, die	solution
Machenschaft, die	machination
Mensch, der	the human
Menschenheit, die	humanity
Menschentum, das	humankind
Menschentümer, die	realms of humanity
Menschenverstand, der	common sense
Menschenwesen, das	human being, human essence
menschlicher Gesamtzustand	total human condition

mit-beachten	to be co-attentive to
mitbestimmen	to co-determine
mitdenken	to think along with
Miteinandersprechen, das	speaking with one another
mitsprechen	to speak together
Moral, die	morality
moralisch	moral, morally
nachdenken	to reflect on, to thoughtfully pursue
Nachdenken, das	reflection, reflections
Nachdenklichkeit, die	pensiveness
nachgehen	to pursue
nachholen	to retrieve later, to retrieve
Nachholen, das	later retrieval, retrieval
nachjagen	to chase after
Nachrichtenwesen, das	information industry
nachsinnen	to ponder, to meditate, to reflect
Nahe, das	the near
Nähe, die	nearness
nahen	to draw near
Näherin, die	seamstress
nähern	to near, to bring near
Namenlose, der	the nameless
Nation, die	nation
Nationalität, die	nationality
Nationale, das	what is national, the national
Natur, die	nature
Naturforschung, die	investigation of nature
Naturgegebenes	what is naturally given
Naturgewalten, die	powers of nature
Naturkräften, die	natural forces
Naturwissenschaft, die	natural science
Negative, das	the negative
Nein, das	the no
nennen	to name, to call, to indicate
Nennung, die	intransitive naming (cf. *Benennung*)
Nicht, das	the not/non
Nichten, das	nihilating
nichtig	senseless, null
Nichtigkeit, die	nullity
Nichts, das	the nothing
Nicht-weg-gehen, das	not-going-away

Nicht-Wollen, das	non-willing
Not, die	need
Nötige, das	the necessary, what is necessary
Nötiges	necessary matter
Notwendige, das	that which is a necessity
Notwendigkeit, die	necessity
Obhut, die	guardianship
Objekt, das	object
Objektivität, die	objectivity (cf. *Gegenständlichkeit*)
Öde, die	wasteland
offenbaren (sich)	to manifest (itself)
Offenbarung, die	manifestation
Offene, das	the open
Ort, der	place, focal-place
Ortschaft, die	locale
physikalisch	physical (adjectival form of "physics")
physikalisches Denken	thinking in physics
Potenz, die	power (in the mathematical sense)
Potenzierung, die	raising to the next power
Prägung, die	molding
prüfen	to test, to examine
ragen (sich)	to tower
raten	to advise
ratlos	perplexed, helplessly perplexed
Ratlosigkeit, die	perplexity
Rätsel, das	enigma
rätselhaft	enigmatic
Raum, der	space
rechnen	to calculate, to reckon
Rechnen, das	reckoning
Rechnungen, die	calculations
reden	to talk
richtungslos	without a sense of direction
Rückkehr, die	return, turning back
Rückwärtige, das	what is in back
Rückweg, der	return path
Ruhe, die	rest, repose, restful repose
Ruhelage, die	state of rest, resting state
Ruhelosigkeit, die	restlessness
ruhen	to rest

Ruhen, das	reposing
ruhig	restful, restfully, calmly
Sache, die	matter, matter at issue
sachlich	with a matter-of-fact attitude
Sachlichkeit, die	matter-of-factness
Sachverhalt, der	state of affairs
Sage, die	story, tale
Sagekraft, die	saying capacity
sagen	to say, to tell
Sammlung, die	gathering
Scheinen, das	appearing
Scheinwesen, das	pseudo-essence
schicken (sich)	to adapt (oneself)
schicklich	aptly
Schicksal, das	fate
Schmerz, der	pain
Schmuck, der	adornment
schmücken	to adorn
schmucklos	unadorned
schön	beautiful, splendid
Schöne, das	the beautiful
Schrittmacher, der	pacesetter
Schuld, die	guilt
Schwärmen, das	enthusing
Seele, die	soul
seelisch	spiritual
Seiende, das	beings, what-is
Seiendes	beings
Sein, das	being
Seinsvergessenheit, die	forgottenness of being
Seinsverlassenheit, die	abandonment of being
Seitenpfad, der	bypath
Seitenwege, die	side paths
Selbe, das	the selfsame
Selbigkeit, die	selfsameness
Selbstvergessenheit, die	self-oblivion
Seltenheit, die	rarity
seltsam	strange
Seltsame, das	the strange
Seyn, das	beyng
Sichauskennen, das	knowing one's way around
sicheinlassen auf	to engage in, to let oneself engage in, to let oneself be involved in
Sicherheit, die	security

German	English
Sicherung, die	securing
Sichloslassen aus	releasing oneself from
Sichöffnen, das	self-opening
Sich-Weigern, das	refusing
Sich-Widersetzen, das	opposing
Sittenlehre, die	ethical doctrine
Sittliche, das	morality
Sprachgebrauch, der	linguistic usage
Staunen, das	astonishment
Steg, der	footbridge, landing, step
Stege, die	steps
steglos	bridgeless
Stelle, die	place, point, position
Stellung, die	place, position
Stellungnahme, die	stated position
sterben	to die
Sterbende, der	one who dies
Sterbliche, der	the mortal
Sterblichkeit, die	mortality
Stiege, die	stairs
Streben, das	striving
Subjektivität, die	subjectivity
suchen	to seek, to search
Sucht, die	obsession
Taten, die	deeds
tatenlos	idle
Tätigkeit, die	activity
Tatkraft, die	power to act
tatsachennah	near to the facts
Tatsachensinn, der	factual sense of reality
Technik, die	technology
technisch	technological, technologically
Thema, das	topic, theme
Thematische, das	what is thematic
tragen	to bear
Tragkraft, die	carrying capacity
Trank, der	drink offered
Transzendentale, das	transcendental
Transzendente, das	the transcendent
Transzendenz, die	transcendence
Trunk, der	drink received
Turm, der	tower
Turmaufgang, der	tower stairway
Türmer, der	tower warden

Turmstube, die	tower room
Turmwesen, das	essence of the tower
überblicken	to survey
übereignen	to appropriate over to
übereilen	to rush, to hasten by, to rush past
Übereilung, die	haste, hastiness
Übergang, der	transition, crossing-over, passageway
übergehen	to pass over
Übergehen, das	passing over
überholen	to pass beyond
Überholen, das	overtaking, passing beyond
überlassen (sich)	to release oneself over to
überlassen, etwas sich selbst	to leave something to itself, to leave alone
Überlegung, die	consideration, deliberation, reflection
übersehbar	overseeable
übersehen	to overlook, to assess
überstaunen	to over-astound
übersteigen	to transcend, to climb over
Übersteigen, das	transcending, climbing-over
Überstieg, der	climbing over
überstreiten	to stride beyond
übertreffen	to surpass
Übertreffen, das	surpassing
umgreifen	to encompass
umgrenzen	to delimit
Umgrenzung, die	delimitation
umherirren	to wander about
umherjagen	to chase around
umherschweifen	to roam around
umkehren	to reverse
Umkehren, das	reversing
Umkreis, der	surrounding circle
unausdenklich	cannot be preconceived
unbedacht	thoughtlessly
Unbestimmbare, das	something indeterminable
unbestimmt	undetermined, indeterminate
Unbestimmte, das	the indeterminate, the undetermined
Unbezweifelbare, das	the undoubtable
Undurchsichtigkeit, die	opacity
unerschöpflich	inexhaustible

Unerschöpfliche, das	what is inexhaustible
Unerschöpflichkeit, die	inexhaustibility
Unfaßliche, das	the ungraspable
Ungeduld, die	impatience
ungehemmt	unrestrained
Ungesprochene, das	the unspoken, what is unspoken
Ungewisse, das	what is uncertain
Unheil, das	disaster
unheimisch	unhomely
unheimlich	uncanny
Unnötige, das	the unnecessary
Unruhe, die	unrest
unsagbar	ineffable, unsayable
unscheinbar	unapparent
Unscheinbare, das	the unapparent
Unsterblichen, die	immortals
Untätigkeit, die	inactivity
unterbringen	accommodate
Untergehen, das	perishing
unterscheiden	to distinguish
Unterschied, der	difference, distinction
Unterschiedlose, das	the indistinct
Untersuchung, die	examination
unumgänglich	unavoidable, inevitable
Unverborgenheit, die	unconcealment
Unverborgenseinlassen, das	letting-be-unconcealed
unvermutet	unsurmised
Unvermutete, das	the unsurmised
Unvordenkliche, das	the unprethinkable
Unwesen, das	the disruptively inessential
Unwirklichkeit, die	ineffective unreality
uralt	primordial
Ursprung, der	origin
Ursprünge, die	primalorigins
ursprünglich	originary, originarily
veranlassen	to occasion, to be an occasion for
Veranlassung, die	occasioning which allows
verantworten	to answer to
verbergen	to conceal
Verbergung, die	concealment
verbrauchen	to use up
verdecken	to cover up
vereignen	to *a*-propriate

verfertigen	to manufacture
verfügen	to decree
Vergegenständlichung, die	objectification
vergegnen	to enregion
Vergegnis, die	enregioning
Vergessenheit, die	forgottenness
Verhalten, das	comportment, behavior, conduct
Verhaltenheit, die	restraint
Verhaltensweisen, die	manners of comportment
Verhältnis, das	relationship
verheimlichen	to keep secret
verhüllen	to veil
verkehren (sich)	to be turned around
verkennen	to fail to recognize
verlassen	to abandon, deserted, abandoned
Verlassenheit, die	abandonment
Verlegenheit, die	awkward predicament
Vermögen, das	enabling-capacity, capability, faculty
vermuten	to surmise
vermutlich	presumably
Vermutung, die	surmise
vernehmen	to perceive, to behold
Verneinung, die	denial, negation
vernichten	to annihilate
Vernichtung, die	annihilation
vernutzen	to utilize
Verödung, die	desolation
verraten	to divulge
Versagen, das	refusal, failure
versammeln	to gather
Versammlung, die	gathering (cf. *Sammlung*)
Verschiedene, das	the different
Verschiedenheit, die	variety
Verschleierung, die	shrouding
Verschlossene, das	what is closed shut
verschwistert	related as a sibling, kindred
versetzen	to transplant
verstehen	to understand
Verstrichung, die	entanglement
Versuchung, die	temptation
vertraut	intimate, familiar
verwahren	to harbor

Verwahrlosung, die	disregard
verwandeln	to transform
verwandt	interrelated, related, akin
Verwandte	kindred ones
Verwehrung, die	barring
verweilen	to abide, to bring to abide, to linger
Verweilen, das	abiding, lingering
verweisen	to direct, to refer
verwendbar	deployable
Verwenden, das	deployment
Verwerfliche, das	what is reprehensible
verwirklichen	to actualize
Verwirklichung, die	actualization, realization
Verworrenste, das	the most confusingly entangled
verwunderlich	amazing
Verwunderung, die	wondering
ver-wüsten	desert-ify
Verwüstung, die	devastation
Verzicht, der	relinquishment
verzichten	to abstain, to refrain
Verzierung, die	ornamentation
Verzögerung, die	delay
Volk, das	people
Vollendung, die	completion
vollziehen	to carry out
vorausblicken	to look ahead
vorausdenken	to think ahead
vorausgreifend	far-reaching
Vorblick, der	preview
voreilig	rash
Vorgang, der	process
Vorgehen, das	procedure
Vor-gestelltheit, die	representationally-set-out-before-ness
vorhanden	present-at-hand
vorsichtig	watchful
vorstellen (sich)	to conceive of, to representationally set before oneself
vorstellen	to represent, to set before
Vorstellen, das	representing, representation
Vor-stellen, das	representational setting-before
Vorstellen-Wollen, das	the will-to-represent

Vorstellung, die	representation, idea
wagen	to venture
Wahre, das	the true
wahren	to keep safe
Wahrheit, die	truth
Wald, der	forest
walten	to prevail
Walten, das	prevailing, reign
Wandel, der	transformation
wandeln	to transform
warten	to wait
wartend	waitful
Wartenden, die	those who wait
wartender	more waitful
Wechsel, der	change
wechseln	to change
Weg, der	path, way
wehren (sich)	to resist
Weile, die	abiding-while
weilen	to abide
Weise, der	guide
Weise, die	manner, way
weisen	to show, to point, to point out, to point toward, to indicate
Weisung, die	indication
weit	far, far-extending
Weitblick, der	far-reaching vision
Weite, die	expanse
Welt, die	world
Weltanschauungen, die	worldviews
Weltbild, das	world-picture
welten	to world
Weltöffentlichkeit, die	the world's general public
Weltordnung, die	world-order
Wendung, die	turning
Werkstatt, die	workshop
wesen	to essentially occur, to essentially prevail
Wesen, das	essence, essential occurrence
Wesen, ein	a being
Wesende, das	what essentially occurs, essential occurrence
Wesensauslegung, die	interpretation of essence
Wesensbau, der	essential structure

Wesensbereich, der	essential domain
Wesensherkunft, die	essential provenance
Wesenskennzeichnung, die	characterization of essence
Wesenssphäre, die	essential sphere
Wesung, die	essential occurring
Widerhall, der	resounding
widerklingen	to resound
Widerwille, der	the contrary will of an aversion, will of aversion
Wille, der	the will
Willenshafte, das	what is a matter of will
willensmäßig	pertaining to the will
Willensseite, die	volitional side
Willenswesen, das	will-essence
willentlich	willful
Willkür, die	arbitrary act, arbitrariness
Wink, der	hint
wirken	to effect, to be effective
Wirkenwollen, das	the will to have an effect
wirklich	actual
Wirkliche, das	what is actual
Wirklichkeit, die	actuality
Wirkung, die	effect
Wirrnis, die	turmoil
Wirrsal, das	tumultuous confusion
wissen	to know
Wissen, das	knowledge (cf. *Erkenntnis, Kenntnis*)
Wissenschaften, die	the sciences
Wissensseite, die	epistemic side
Wissenwollen, das	willing-to-know
wohnen	to dwell
wollen	to will, to want
Wollen, das	willing
Wortbedeutung, die	dictionary definition
Wunde, die	wound
wunderbar	wonderful
Wundersame, das	the wondrous
wüst	desolate
Wüste, die	desert
wütend	angry
Zauber, der	enchantment
Zeichen, das	sign
zeigen	to show

Zeitalter, das	time-period, age
Zerstörung, die	destruction
Zier, die	ornament
zieren	to ornament
Zufall, der	coincidence, coincidental occurrence
Zu-fall, der	the occurrence of a coincidence
zuinnerst	most intimately
zulassen	to allow, to allow for
zum voraus	in advance
Zumutung, die	demand, audacious demand
zuordnen	to assign
zuprechen	to address, to speak to, to award
Zurückbergen, das	re-sheltering
zurückkehren	to return, to turn back
zurückweichen	to shrink back
zusammenfallen	to collapse
zusammenfügen	to join together
Zusammengehören, das	belonging-together
Zusammengehörigkeit, die	belonging-togetherness
Zusammenhang, die	connection, coherence
zustellen, auf sich	to set toward oneself
Zu-stellen, das	setting-toward
zuvorkommend	with anticipatory courtesy
zuweisen	to assign
Zweideutigkeit, die	ambiguity
Zweifel, der	doubt
zwiespältig	ambivalent
Zwischenfrage, die	interim question

Printed and bound by CPI Group (UK) Ltd, Croydon, CR0 4YY

09/06/2025

14685935-0003